Hawaii

A GUIDE TO ALL THE ISLANDS

By the Editors
of Sunset Books
and
Sunset Magazine

Lane Publishing Co. • Menlo Park, California

CONTENTS

Bamboo forest, Akaka Falls State Park

Editor:
David E. Clark

Supervising Editor:
Barbara J. Braasch

Design:
JoAnn Masaoka

Special Consultants,
Sunset Magazine:
Nancy Bannick
Jeff Phillips

Contributing Editors:
Joan Erickson
Dean Eyre
Marianne Lipanovich
Cynthia Spoor

Two–color Maps:
**John Parsons, Eureka
Cartography**

Full–color Illustrations:
H. Tom Kamifuji

Cover:
One of the most photographed beaches in the islands,
Lumahai on Kauai's north
shore provides the setting
for many movies.
Photographed by Jeff Gnass.

Mahalo…

The editors of Sunset are deeply
appreciative of the help provided
by the many people and organizations of Hawaii. In addition to
the invaluable assistance we received from the Hawaii Visitors
Bureau, we also gratefully ac-
knowledge the help provided by
the Department of Research and
Development of the County of
Hawaii, Maui County Visitors
Association, and Stryker Weiner
Associates, Inc.

And for her way with words, a
special note of appreciation to
copy editor Barbara Mathieson.

Special Features

Fourth printing (Updated)
June 1988

Hours, admission fees, prices, telephone numbers, and highway designations in this book are accurate as of the time this edition went to press.

Nene, the state bird

Kauai

Niihau

Oahu

Honolulu

The

Flying across the Pacific from the mainland, you strain your eyes to see the first of the eight major islands that compose the state of Hawaii. Seven of these islands are inhabited; the eighth, Kahoolawe, is used by the navy for bombing and gunnery practice.

Hawaii—the largest island—is usually referred to as the "Big Island." With an area of 4,034 square miles, Hawaii is almost twice as large as all the other islands combined. It boasts two mountain peaks that rise more than 13,000 feet from sea level, two active volcanoes, and a national park.

Maui is the second largest island. It contains some of the state's most magnificent beaches, a variety of resort areas, a refurbished whaling port, and the vast, colorful crater of dormant Haleakala.

West and northwest of Maui, the islands of Lanai and Molokai are quiet and still comparatively undeveloped. Much of Lanai is planted to pineapple; Molokai is largely ranch land.

Oahu, third in size, is first in number of people. Honolulu, the state capital, is located here, as are such famous landmarks as Diamond Head, Waikiki, and Pearl Harbor.

Westernmost of the main islands are Kauai and Niihau. Kauai is a mixture of sugarcane fields, resort areas, homes, and ranches. Lush vegetation blankets its mountains. Tiny Niihau is privately owned and can be visited only by invitation.

Stretching beyond Niihau lie a series of tiny islets and atolls officially named the Northwestern Hawaiian Islands. Military installations on Midway and Kure and small wildlife facilities are the only marks of habitation.

Aloha Spirit

Molokai

Maui

Lanai

Kahoolawe

Hawaii

You'll stand on volcanoes ...

Devastation Trail, a volcanic reminder

E verywhere you travel in Hawaii you're atop a volcano. The volcanic activity that formed the Hawaiian Islands began at the northwest end of a chain commonly called the Leeward Islands. These islands are estimated to be 5 to 10 million years old, the main Hawaiian Islands 1 to 5 million. On the Big Island, volcanic activity still continues; it's said that Pele, the goddess of fire, traveled from island to island looking for a home before settling down in Hawaii.

To view Madam Pele's latest handiwork, visit Hawaii Volcanoes National Park. Here Kilauea, the nation's "drive-in volcano" (so named for its accessibility) still smokes and intermittently belches fire and rock. Mauna Loa, though quieter, erupted in early 1984, sending streams of molten lava down her slopes. By comparison, Maui's mighty Haleakala last erupted some 200 years ago.

Haleakala, Maui's "House of the Sun"

Steaming Kilauea caldera

...splash in the sea

A windsurfing capital

S wimming, surfing, snorkeling, scuba diving, boating, windsurfing—these are all part of Hawaii's water world. Even if you're not a sports enthusiast, sometime during your stay you'll toast on a beach or test the ocean's temperature with your toes.

The Recreation Guide for each island provides specific information on the activity for which the area is noted. On page 53 we provide a guide to "The Perfect Wave"; on page 92 we caution against the ocean's vagaries.

From the early-morning splashing of the surf against the shore until the late-evening painting of the sun on the waves, you'll notice the sea. It blends with the land to create the vacation destination that is Hawaii.

Sailboats in Waikiki

Surfing off Maui coast

...meet the people

The people of Hawaii are a fascinating mixture of races and cultures. Each succeeding wave of migration added a dash to the melting pot of the island society—Polynesian, Oriental, and Caucasian.

Today, the pure Hawaiian is only a small percentage of the total population, but there is an increasing number of part-Hawaiians. And a new cultural awareness preserves the language and customs of the past.

At the Polynesian Cultural Center on Oahu, you'll catch glimpses of the South Seas cultures represented in the islands; tours of Japanese shrines, Chinese markets, and Filipino restaurants add a second dimension; and a visit to Kauai's Grove Farm Homestead offers a peek into the sugar plantation era.

Lei-bedecked dancer

Shinto priest

Aspiring hula enthusiast

A beautiful kama'aina

...smell the flowers

Creamy plumeria

Showy blossoms, pervasive perfume, and riotous hues characterize Hawaii's exotic floral display. Hibiscus and *hau*, a cousin of the state flower, and bougainvillea sprays decorate roadsides. Orchids, anthuriums, plumeria, and ginger are only a few of the other tropical blooms that delight the eye.

Showy torch ginger

Bird of paradise

Vanda tricolor orchid

...enjoy the music and dance

Melody of the islands

First used as a religious ritual or war dance and performed only by men, the hula still conveys a story by means of movements and gestures.

Accompanying chants and songs performed by drum, ukulele, and guitar linger in a visitor's memory even after the return to the mainland.

Exhorting the gods in dance

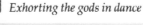

...savor the food

Coconut milk shake

Dining in Hawaii can become an adventure in food. Most menus include island specialties like teriyaki steak and mahimahi. You'll find coconut, pineapple, and macadamia nut waffles, pancakes, and ice creams; guava and *liliko'i* (passion fruit) sherbets; curries; and Kona coffee. Among the array of fresh fruits are papayas, mangoes, pineapples, and bananas.

Try the various kinds of Chinese noodles and *dim sum* (stuffed pastries). Sample *sashimi* (raw fish) and different kinds of Japanese *sushi* (stuffed rice). *Saimin*, a filling noodle soup, is unique to the islands.

Most visitors want to join in at least one luau, complete with roast pig, raw fish, *lomi lomi* salmon, poi, *lau laus* (taro tops or spinach, chicken, and fish steamed in ti leaves), *haupia* (coconut pudding), and fresh fruits. By all means sample "crack seed," the Chinese dried and preserved whole fruits, and the fruit-flavored "shave ice" (snow cones) that children love.

Food from the sea

14 THE ALOHA SPIRIT

...admire the pageantry

Hula—Tahitian style

Portrait of ali'i

Costuming, history, and ritual combine to create the colorful performances enjoyed by vacationers to the islands.

Hawaiians love to celebrate on every possible occasion, and there's usually an occasion someplace on the islands. Many events are local festivals, others are all-island activities.

Everything from the opening of the Hawaii State Legislature in January (music, hula, flowers, prayers), narcissus and cherry blossom fetes, pageants honoring King Kalakaua (Merry Monarch in April) and King Kamehameha (June 11), to Aloha Week (October) includes parades, performances, music, and flowers.

For a partial listing of year-round events, see pages 20–21. For information on exact dates and times, check the local Hawaii Visitors Bureau office or newspapers.

A fire performance

Statue of Father Damien *stands beside his church on Molokai's Kalaupapa peninsula where he served leprosy victims, before succumbing himself.*

W hen you first approach the Hawaiian Islands you may wonder how explorers centuries ago ever found these bits of land. Actually, they discovered them not by chance, but through impressive feats of navigation.

The Early Polynesians

Polynesians from the Marquesas as early as A.D. 500 and from Tahiti about 500 years later crossed the uncharted ocean in large sailing canoes and landed in Hawaii with their families, plants, animals, and personal belongings. For hundreds of years, they knew only a Stone Age life, making *tapa* cloth, grass houses, outrigger canoes, and carvings. They subsisted on fish, poi, and other fruit of the land.

A United Hawaii

When British navigator Captain James Cook discovered the islands in 1778 (he named them the Sandwich Islands for the Earl of Sandwich) during the third and last of his famous South Pacific voyages, he found each a separate kingdom organized in a feudal manner with chiefs, priests, and commoners. By 1810 the king of Hawaii island, Kamehameha, had brought all of the islands under his domain. He and his descendants reigned until 1872. They were followed by rulers from another ancient family of chiefs that included Queen Liliuokalani, who was ruler in 1893 when the monarchy was overturned. A provisional government was set up at that time.

An Immigrant Society

The waves of immigrants who came to Hawaii during the 19th century rearranged Hawaiian society. Traders landed from Captain Cook's time on. In the middle years, whalers beached, seeking provisions and entertainment. Companies of missionaries arrived starting in 1820. These stern, dedicated New Englanders braved the hazardous journey to the mid-Pacific to convert natives to Christianity and to introduce plantation agriculture, commerce, and democratic government. Many of their descendants are still prominent in the islands.

In the last half of the century came Chinese, then Portuguese and Japanese, and later on Filipinos to work the sugarcane and pineapple plantations started by early New Englanders.

The 50th State

On July 4, 1894, the Republic of Hawaii came into existence with Sanford B. Dole (another missionary descendant) as president. The islands were annexed by the United States in 1898 and made a territory in 1900. Dole was appointed governor of the territory and Prince Kuhio (a nephew of Queen Liliuokalani) became one of the first delegates to Congress. A tireless fighter for the rights of the native Hawaiians, Prince Kuhio also introduced the first Hawaiian statehood bill in 1919.

During the time between Hawaii's annexation and World War II, the sugar and pineapple industries continued to prosper and the number of immigrants brought in to work the vast holdings increased. And the military became interested in the islands. In 1908, a gigantic naval base at Pearl Harbor was approved by Congress—the scene of the bombing on December 7, 1941, that drew the U.S. into war.

Though Hawaii was still seen by some as too far away, statehood was assured when Alaska joined the Union in January of 1959. On March 12, 1959, Congress passed the bill that made Hawaii the 50th state, ending a statehood campaign waged for nearly half a century.

Today, the state's resident population is more than a million. Visitors increase the figure by some 100,000.

PLANNING YOUR TRIP

Information on getting to and around each of Hawaii's major islands can be found in "The Essentials" section for that island. You'll also discover information on accommodations, sightseeing trips, restaurants, and shops. Details on camping and picnicking, swimming, surfing, diving, snorkeling, beachcombing, boating, bicycling, golf, tennis, hiking, horseback riding, and fishing are contained in the "Recreation Guide" for each island. See pages 20–21 for a roundup of festivals and special events.

Getting to the Islands

Hawaii lies about 2,400 miles/3,840 km southwest of California. By air, the trip takes approximately 5 hours from West Coast cities, 9 hours from Chicago, and 11 hours from New York. Honolulu is a port of call on some round-the-world and Pacific cruises, and there is some cargo-liner service. By sea, the trip takes about 4½ days from West Coast cities.

Mainland-to-Hawaii air service. You'll have your choice of airlines to Hawaii. Most have been flying to the islands for many years. Among the largest and best known are American, Continental, Delta, Hawaiian, Northwest, Pan American, Trans World, and United. All of them fly to Honolulu. United also serves Kona on Hawaii and the islands of Maui and Kauai from the mainland, Delta serves directly, and American offers service to Maui through Honolulu.

Honolulu is also a stopover point for several foreign airlines on flights between Los Angeles and San Francisco and foreign destinations: Air New Zealand, China Airlines, Garuda Indonesia, Japan Air Lines, Korean Air, Philippine Airlines, Qantas, and Singapore Airlines. Canadian and Wardair fly between Honolulu and Canadian cities.

Passengers booked on foreign airlines cannot fly solely between two U.S. cities (San Francisco and Honolulu, for example), but they are permitted a stopover in Hawaii en route to or from a foreign destination.

Interisland air travel. Frequent interisland flights connect all major island airports and serve most smaller ones at least once a day. At one time, if you purchased a round-trip ticket between Hawaii and a U.S. or Canadian mainland city on a U.S. or Canadian flight, you could island-hop for a nominal charge per stop. This "Common Fare Plan" no longer exists. Today, you'll have to pay regular, though competitive, fares to travel beyond your direct-flight terminus.

Four scheduled carriers service the islands. Some offer frequent service to major airports; others fly to more out-of-the-way destinations. Aloha Airlines and Hawaiian Air serve the islands of Oahu, Kauai, Maui, and Molokai. Princeville Airways serves Oahu, Kauai (Princeville), Maui (Kahului, Hana, and Kapalua-West Maui), Hawaii (Waimea-Kohala), Molokai, and Lanai. Air Molokai-Tropic Airlines serves Oahu, Maui (Kahului), Molokai, and Lanai.

For interisland charter service and plane rentals, see the "Recreation Guide" section for each island as well as the Yellow Pages of the phone book.

Steamship service. In 1980, American Hawaii Cruises began week-long, interisland cruises from Honolulu (see page 18). Two ships, the S.S. *Independence* and S.S. *Constitution*, offer ports of call on Kauai, Maui, and Hawaii as well as a passing look at Molokai, Lanai, and Kahoolawe islands.

Joining American Hawaii Cruises on the interisland cruise circuit is Aloha Pacific Cruises's S.S. *Monterey*, also sailing from Honolulu on seven-day cruises to Kauai, Maui, and Hawaii.

Honolulu is also a port of call on round-the-world cruises and South Seas and circle-Pacific cruises. Cruise lines calling at Hawaii include Cunard Line, Holland America Cruises, Princess Cruises, and Royal Viking Line. You cannot travel on a foreign ship only between Honolulu and the U.S. mainland; your trip must begin or end in a foreign port.

Special tour packages. Tour companies, airlines, and hotels offer many combinations for travel to and between the islands, ranging from all-expense tours with an escort to packages that cover only your hotels in the islands. Interisland tours range from one-day trips from Honolulu to one other island to trips of a week or longer covering four Neighbor Islands.

Where to Stay

A wide range of accommodations is available on all the major islands. Resorts, major hotel chains, smaller hotels, and condominiums are discussed in each of the island's chapters.

For detailed information on rates and room availability, consult your local travel agent.

Getting Around the Islands

Before you rent a vehicle in Hawaii, check the various rates and special packages that are offered. There are many from which to choose—flat rates with no mileage charge, weekly specials covering cars on several islands, fly-drive combinations, and others. By checking the possibilities in advance, you can select the plan best suited to the type of driving you intend to do. There is sometimes a shortage of cars during big conventions, school vacation periods, holiday weekends, or when a major event (such as a golf tournament) is scheduled. For this reason, it is a good idea to make car reservations in advance.

It is impossible to list in our limited space every car rental agency in the islands; you'll find all the nationwide companies (Alamo, Avis, Budget, Dollar, Hertz, National, and Thrifty). The following agencies also rent cars

...Planning Your Trip

on all of the major islands: Robert's, Travelers, Tropical, and United. If you shop around after you arrive in the islands, you'll find other rental agencies at the airports, in resort areas, and in the larger towns. For complete listings, check the Yellow Pages of the telephone directories for the various islands.

Check with your travel agent for rental of campers and 4-wheel-drive vehicles at the time you book your trip. The supply is limited.

How's the Weather?

The islands are in the tropics, but fresh trade winds from the east and northeast prevail most of the year, keeping the air pleasantly balmy. In lowland areas, such as Waikiki, temperatures range from an average low of 65° to an average high of 80° in winter, and from 73° to 88° in summer. Atop the highest mountains, the temperature occasionally drops into the 20s, and in many upland sections the range is from the low 50s to low 70s.

Sometimes the trades break down and a spell of *kona* (a leeward wind) weather sets in, with southwesterly breezes and high humidity. In summer and early fall, a kona wind is synonymous with sticky weather; in winter it brings a few storms (gales and torrential rain) but also some of the islands' clearest days.

Winter trades can get blustery and drop frequent showers even on dry areas such as Waikiki, which receives only 20 to 25 inches of rain a year. In spring and summer, showers are few and come mostly at night, drifting down from the mountain peaks. The surprise of island weather is that a year's rain may amount to more than 100 inches of rain in one place and less than 20 in another just a few miles away.

What to Wear

Lightweight clothing is the rule throughout the year. Around resorts and for touring, women wear casual attire (short *mu'umu'us*, shorts, or pants); men wear sport shirts with shorts or slacks. Women may want a scarf or other covering to protect hairdos from island breezes. Informal clothes are also suitable in the evening; a few restaurants do require men to wear a coat and tie. In business offices, the dress is the same as in any mainland city in the summertime.

A sweater or lightweight jacket is sometimes welcome on a cool evening or in an air-conditioned restau-

CRUISING THE HAWAIIAN WAY

Fragrant leis swirl over shoulders, pink parasols bob in exotic drinks, and red, white, and blue streamers sail overhead as the ship slips into the night—you've embarked on an exploratory cruise of the Hawaiian islands.

Whether it's your first trip to Hawaii or a repeat performance, you may decide that cruising provides the maximum in island-hopping entertainment with the minimum of inconvenience in packing and unpacking. And there's no better way to receive unparalleled island views than from a sea perspective.

On a seven-day cruise from Honolulu, your ship itinerary includes four ports of call on three islands—Kauai, Maui, and Hilo and Kona on the Big Island. You'll also spend a leisurely day sailing past the shores of Molokai, Lanai, and Kahoolawe, off the coast of Maui.

Your daytime options might include shore excursions to major island attractions, golf or tennis on seaside courses and courts, snorkeling sallies, volcano tours, or browsing and shopping. You can arrange to charter a boat in Kona to seek the world-record fish that inhabit those waters. To learn about the Hawaiian culture, attend a luau or join a ship's class on lei making, ukulele playing, or hula dancing. Some people prefer to simply soak up the sun around the deck's pool.

While the ship travels from port to port at night, a variety of entertainment and activity keeps passengers occupied: Broadway revues, films, and dancing are just a few of the choices.

All meals, shipboard activities, entertainment, and services are included in the cost of the cruise package. Land tours, beverages, and tips are an added expense.

Three ships cruise among the islands. American Hawaii Cruises' two ships—the S.S. *Independence* and S.S. *Constitution*—both carry 750 passengers. Originally built for trans-Atlantic and Mediterranean travel, the ships' designs reflect a period when cruising was a first-class luxury. The 600-passenger Aloha Pacific Cruises' S.S. *Monterey* returned to Hawaiian waters after a long hiatus and a multimillion-dollar renovation. In years past, the ship sailed between California and Hawaii.

You can combine a cruise with a hotel package on Oahu, or one of the outlying islands. For information on cruises, add-on packages, and special air fares, contact your travel agent or American Hawaii Cruises, 550 Kearny Street, San Francisco, CA 94108, and Aloha Pacific Cruises, 510 King Street, Alexandria, VA 22314. It's wise to make reservations well in advance.

rant. A fold-up umbrella is useful during occasional rainy periods (a raincoat is usually too warm); take lightweight rain gear, though, if you plan to do much hiking or camping.

Shopping—A Potpourri from Many Lands

Shopping centers and resort shop complexes on all the islands carry a tremendous selection of clothes, handicrafts, jewelry, food, flowers, homewares, and decorative items. You'll find much repetition; the more you browse, the more selective you will probably become. Prices are similar to mainland prices, but Hawaii offers a wider selection of merchandise from the Pacific islands and Asia. You'll find unusual items in Japanese department stores (Hawaii has several), Honolulu's Chinatown, and country stores on all the islands. Here are some buying suggestions:

Clothes and fabrics. Stores are full of shirts, gowns, and sportswear turned out by more than 100 Hawaii garment manufacturers. Many island-design prints are also sold on yard goods counters and racks, along with interesting fabrics from Asia. Most plentiful are easy-care cotton and synthetic prints, ranging from bright modern florals to traditional Pacific motifs. Well worth searching out are the small fabric shops that feature such imported fabrics as batiks, Japanese printed *yukata* cotton, and silks. Even though these places offer smaller selections, fabric pieces are frequently one-of-a-kind.

Handicrafts. Locally made handicrafts are featured in gift and specialty shops in the big, new shopping complexes that are springing up everywhere in the islands, in gift sections of department stores, and in isolated small shops and factories. At many places you can watch crafts-people at work on their products. Look for bowls and trays of monkeypod, koa, and some rare native woods; *lauhala* handbags, hats, and mats; jewelry of pink and black coral, seeds and shells, obsidian, olivines, wood, and hand-wrought silver; lava curios; ceramics; ukuleles; hula accessories and Hawaiian dolls in all sizes, shapes, and materials.

Oriental and South Pacific imports. Almost every store has imports; many shops are exclusively devoted to the products of one country. Consulates and ethnic chambers of commerce can tell you where to buy the wares of the countries they represent. Look for ivory, jade, and pearl jewelry; basketry and other woven articles; oriental tableware and cookware; china, pottery, lacquer, bronze and brass ware; rattan and wicker furniture; masks; bamboo fishing poles, nets, floats, and reef-walking *tabi;* and costly *objets d'art.*

Foods, flowers, plants. Many Hawaiian foods come giftboxed, separately or in combinations. Favorites to bring or mail home are pineapples, jams, jellies, syrups, maca-

He sells shells *at a stall near Kauai's blowhole, Spouting Horn.*

damia and coconut confections, and Kona coffee. Avocados and papayas must be treated before shipment; bananas and litchis can't be shipped. (For more information contact the Agricultural Quarantine office of the U.S. Department of Agriculture in Honolulu.)

At street stands, in flower shops, and at the airport, you can buy leis of plumeria, *pikake*, orchids, carnations, tuberoses, crown flowers, and ginger. Cut flowers include anthuriums and bird of paradise. Dried arrangements of coconut sheaths, woodroses, papyrus, and koa pods are popular.

All baggage of air travelers going from Hawaii to the U.S. mainland is subject to inspection at the airport by the U.S. Department of Agriculture. Not permitted to enter the mainland are fruits other than pineapples and treated papayas and avocados; mauna loa, gardenia, and jade vine; coffee berries; other berries and pulpy seeds; cactus plants; sugarcane; and plants in soil. You can take plants potted in a fiber medium and bare-root plants, properly packed and inspected by the State Department of Agriculture. Many flower shops and nurseries carry preinspected potted plants.

Aloha Week float

Cowboys and canoes, festivals and feasts, pageants and parades all combine in the kaleidoscope of special events that Hawaii offers its visitors. Flower and craft shows, rodeos, athletic competitions, and religious ceremonies abound. Holiday periods, such as Christmas and the Fourth of July, are packed with a variety of activities. The Hawaii Visitors Bureau offices on the major islands, and hotel activities desks provide information on events of interest during your stay.

January

Hula Bowl. Honolulu, Oahu. Football classic features college senior stars from around the country.

Ka Molokai Makahiki. Kaunakakai, Molokai. A fun-filled weekend, featuring traditional, Hawaiian games.

NFL Pro Bowl. Honolulu, Oahu. NFL all-star game held in Aloha Stadium.

Opening of the State Legislature. Honolulu, Oahu. The legislature begins its session with a colorful ceremony, Hawaiian music and dancing, and the presentation of leis.

Narcissus Festival. Honolulu, Oahu. Five weeks of festivities coinciding with Chinese New Year.

Volcano Marathon and Rim Runs. Hawaii Volcanoes National Park, Hawaii. A 26-mile race that crosses the Ka'u Desert and a 10-mile run around Kilauea Caldera.

February

The Hawaiian Open International Golf Tournament. Honolulu, Oahu. Top professional golfers compete.

Carol Kai Bed Race. Lihue, Kauai; Lahaina, Maui. The highlight of this annual parade is a race down a main street, featuring decorated beds. Also held in March in Honolulu and July in Hilo.

Cherry Blossom Festival. Honolulu, Oahu. A series of events presented by the Japanese community continues through March.

Captain Cook Festival. Waimea, Kauai. A two-day party in the port where Cook first landed in Hawaii.

Great Waikoloa Horse Races and Rodeo. Waikoloa, Hawaii. A combination of rodeo events and horse races.

March

Prince Kuhio Day. All islands. A state holiday honoring Prince Kuhio, a delegate to Congress from 1902 to 1922. Kauai's week-long celebration of its native son includes songs, dances, canoe races, and a royal ball.

Kona Stampede. Honaunau, Hawaii. This two-day rodeo is a favorite among local paniolos.

Women's Kemper Open Golf Tournament. Princeville, Kauai. Stars of the LPGA Tour compete.

Mauna Kea Ski Meet. Mauna Kea, Hawaii. Two international cup races and one cross-country race on the volcano snow. Other meets in April and June.

April

Easter Sunrise Service. Honolulu, Hawaii. Service is held at Punchbowl National Memorial Cemetery.

Buddha Day. All islands. The birth of Guatama Buddha is commemorated.

Merrie Monarch Festival. Hilo, Hawaii. A competition among the best hula schools from all islands highlights this tribute to Kalakaua, Hawaii's fun-loving last king.

May

Lei Day. All islands. Islanders don leis to greet spring during this annual celebration; statewide lei competitions and exhibits are the highlights.

Memorial Day. Honolulu, Oahu. The many thousands of markers at Punchbowl Crater are heaped with flower leis strung by school children on all the islands. A memorial service is held in the morning.

50th State Fair. Honolulu, Oahu. The fair continues into June. A special highlight is Hawaiian crafts.

June

King Kamehameha Day. All islands. A state holiday with parades and pageantry honoring King Kamehameha I, who founded the all-islands kingdom.

Hilo Orchid Society Show. Hilo, Hawaii. Hundreds of varieties are displayed.

Hawaii State Farm Fair. Honolulu, Oahu. Hawaii's largest agricultural show, with produce, flowers, livestock, and poultry competitions and exhibits—and a carnival. Continues into July.

July

Bon Odori Festival. All islands. The Buddhist festival of souls, with colorful *bon* dances Friday and Saturday nights at each temple ground, in turn. A few temples have nighttime floating lantern ceremonies.

Little Transpac. Oahu-Kauai. A biennial race that follows the Transpacific Yacht Race (see below).

Makawao Statewide Rodeo. Makawao, Maui. One of the top old-time rodeos, this is the biggest and oldest.

Prince Lot Hula Festival. Honolulu, Oahu. An ancient hula festival.

Puuhonua O Honaunau Cultural Festival. Kona Coast, Hawaii. A three-day festival where visitors can try *lauhala* weaving, lei making, and poi pounding under the watchful eyes of the feather-bedecked royal court.

Run to the Sea. Kahului, Maui. A 37.5-mile run from sea level to the 10,000-foot summit of Haleakala.

Transpacific Yacht Races. Oahu; Maui. In odd-numbered years the boats leave San Pedro, CA, for Diamond Head. In even-numbered years they sail from Victoria, B.C., to Lahaina, Maui, while multihulls race the San Pedro-Diamond Head course.

Ukulele Festival. Honolulu, Oahu. Hundreds of ukulele artists perform in this toe-tapping event.

Parker Ranch Rodeo and Horseraces. Waimea, Hawaii. Paniolos from the largest singly-owned ranch in the U.S.

Honomu Village Fair. Honomu, Hawaii. A 46-mile relay race from Volcano to Honomu, with 25 competing teams, is a highlight of the fair.

August

Establishment Day. Puukohala Heiau, Hawaii. Festival emphasizing Hawaiian traditions, with ancient hulas, an artifact show, and workshops in lei making, Hawaiian language, and ancient schools.

Hawaiian Canoe Racing State Championship Regatta. Site varies. Koa canoe championships, with top crews from each island. Individual island championships are held in July.

Hawaiian International Billfish Tournament. Kailua-Kona, Hawaii. The leading international marlin-fishing tournament.

Macadamia Nut Harvest Festival. Honokaa, Hawaii. Harvest celebration with a run, golf tournament, recipe contest, and other activities.

Pacific Rim International Volleyball Championship. Hilo, Hawaii. A major junior volleyball event drawing participants from Pacific Rim countries.

September

Aloha Week Festivals. All islands. Hawaiian pageantry, street entertainment, luaus, balls, parades, and canoe races are just some of the highlights of this week-long celebration of the aloha spirit. Each island has its own week of festivities; some are held in October.

Molokai to Oahu Women's Canoe Race. Molokai-Oahu. Endurance classic in the rough water between the two islands.

Waikiki Roughwater Swim. Honolulu, Oahu. Two-mile swim from Sans Souci Beach to Duke Kahanamoku Beach.

Annual Great Molokai Mule Drag. Kaunakakai, Molokai. Features a mule race down "main street," other contests, and food booths.

October

Bishop Museum Festival. Honolulu, Oahu. The museum's big fund-raiser, with shows by popular entertainers, special shows, and behind-the-scenes tours.

Ironman Triathlon World Championships. Kailua-Kona, Hawaii. The original triathlon, with a 2.4-mile rough-water swim, 112-mile bicycle race, and a 26.2-mile marathon.

Makahiki Festival. Waimea Falls Park, Oahu. Ancient Hawaiian games, crafts, chants, dances, and a luau.

Maui County Fair. Kahului, Maui. The oldest county fair in Hawaii.

Molokai to Oahu Men's Canoe Race. Molokai-Oahu. This endurance race with Hawaiian canoes crosses the rough channel between Molokai and Oahu.

November

Hawaiian Rodeo Association Championship Rodeo. Hawaii. Two days of competition featuring top paniolos.

Na Mele O Maui. Lahaina and Kaanapali Beach, Maui. Two-day festival of Hawaiian arts, crafts, and music.

Kapalua International Championship of Golf. Kapalua, Maui. Some of the world's finest professionals compete.

Kona Coffee Festival. Kailua, Hawaii. A celebration of the harvest of America's only commercially grown coffee.

December

A Christmas Tradition. Hilo, Hawaii. The Lyman House Museum's annual New England Christmas observance.

Hawaiian Pro-Surfing Championships. Oahu. Usually three big meets with dates and places determined by wave action; Men's Masters always at Banzai Pipeline.

Christmas in the Country. Volcano Art Center, Hawaii. Arts, crafts, Christmas music, and hot apple cider every day until Christmas up at 4,000 feet where the hearth fire is welcome.

Start of Parker Ranch rodeo

Honolulu's light show—Waikiki to Diamond Head

OAHU

• A MIX OF CITY AND COUNTRY •

Diamond Head, the Pali, Pearl Harbor, the long stretch of Waikiki Beach—you may see some of Oahu's famous sights as your plane circles the island's edge before landing at Honolulu International Airport.

Though Oahu ranks only third in size among the islands, it contains more than three-fourths of Hawaii's people, almost half of whom live in Honolulu. Appropriately named "The Gathering Place," this capital island of approximately 600 square miles/1,560 square km (40 miles/64 km long and 26 miles/42 km wide) lies between Kauai and Molokai.

The Koolau Range that runs from northwest to southeast and the Waianae Mountains along the west coast are the remains of two volcanic domes which formed the island. Lava flows and erosion joined the two ranges, creating the fertile Schofield (or Leilehua) plateau where much of Oahu's sugar and its pineapple are grown today.

Monarchy to Statehood

Evidence of human culture—bits of volcanic glass dated to A.D. 500—has been unearthed at Bellows Field Beach at Waimanalo, the earliest site of habitation yet discovered in these islands. Waikiki, with its coconut groves, fishponds, and walled taro patches, became a favorite seaside resort of early monarchs. Oahu was added to the all-island kingdom in 1795 when King Kamehameha and his warriors from Hawaii island landed at Maunalua Bay and Waikiki and took the Oahu king's forces in a famous battle; they supposedly pushed some of the Oahu men all the way up to the Nuuanu Pali, forcing them to leap from the precipice to their deaths.

With its fine harbors, the island gradually developed into the state's political, economic, military, educational, and cultural center. Honolulu Harbor, first investigated by an English sea captain in 1792, became a key Pacific port of call for whalers and sandalwood and fur traders. The sailing vessels used a mere reef-protected slip at the mouth of Nuuanu Stream; since then, men have dredged and widened it, carved two inlets, and added fill to make shelter and berths for the world's largest liners and freighters. Pearl Harbor came into importance decades later when ships exchanged sails for engines and nations set about building strategic bases.

In the mid-19th century the court moved permanently to Honolulu, which has been the seat of the islands' governments—monarchy, republic, territory, state—ever since. Until the governor and legislature moved into the monumental State Capitol in 1969, Hawaii's capitol was Iolani Palace; the first one stood from 1845 to 1879 and served five kings. The present palace, used for decades as the executive building after the monarchy was overthrown in 1893, has been restored to the grandeur it first enjoyed as the home of King Kalakaua and later his sister, Queen Liliuokalani. It's now a museum.

An Economic Center

Though other economic activities have long surpassed Oahu's agriculture, this island has more land planted with pineapple than any other; its sugar plantations produce more than 16 percent of the state's crop; its truck farms and orchards yield 15 to 20 percent of Hawaii's fruits and vegetables.

Most of the state's servicemen and their families live on Oahu, the site of all the large military bases. Including service personnel, the island's population is about 800,000.

Oahu hosts the majority of visitors—now about 5 million—who come to the islands each year, making tourism the largest source of revenue in its economy. Manufacturing—everything from petroleum to surfboards and Hawaiian apparel—is also important business; aquaculture and high technology are infant industries. And though construction has tapered off since the 1960s and 1970s, the bulldozer, pile driver, crane, and jackhammer are always at work somewhere—in Waikiki, along the waterfront, downtown, or out in former cane fields.

Most flights across the central Pacific stop at Honolulu International Airport; except for a few trips directly to other islands, Honolulu is the terminus of all mainland-to-Hawaii flights. Interisland flights generally are routed through the Oahu terminal. See page 17 for more on how to reach the islands.

Getting Around

Your airline or hotel can help arrange bus transportation or a taxi for your first trip—the 9 miles/14 km between Honolulu International Airport and Waikiki. If you prefer to drive, car rental terminals are located in both places;

the biggest agencies also have desks in several hotels. See page 17 for the names of agencies that operate on all major islands. The Oahu Yellow Pages list smaller firms, some with lower rates.

For later excursions, rental agencies will supply maps and help you plot a route. To rent 4-wheel-drive vehicles, campers, motorcycles, mopeds, or bicycles, check the Yellow Pages.

Municipal buses reach all parts of the island (see feature on page 25). In addition, shuttle buses travel several times a day between the Hilton Hawaiian Village and Turtle Bay Hilton and the Sheraton Waikiki and Sheraton Makaha, and hourly from 8 A.M. to 11 P.M. between

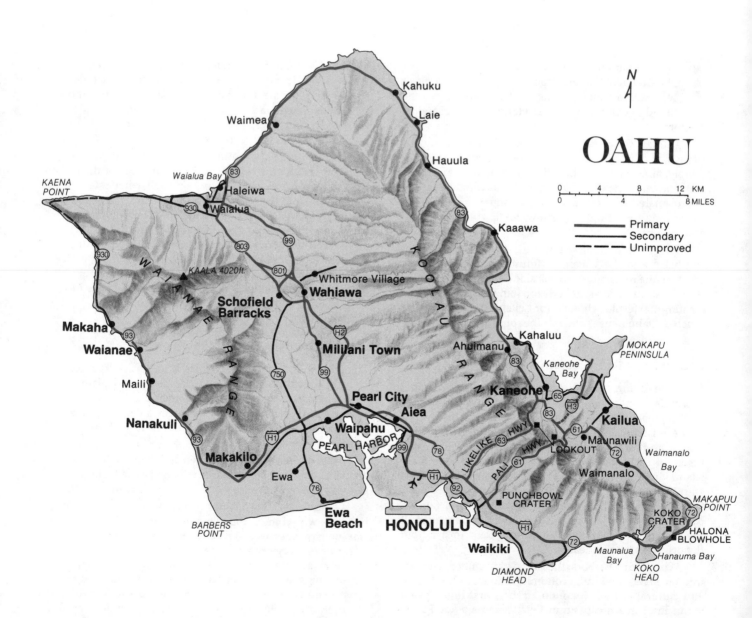

the Kahala Hilton and Waikiki. The North Shore Shuttle Bus leaves each morning from the Diamond Head side of the Moana Hotel for the Polynesian Cultural Center and returns after the night show. This company also runs morning shuttles to Hanauma Bay with afternoon returns. Call Benjamin Kekona (677-9600) for reservations.

You can best explore Oahu by dividing your sightseeing into three separate trips: a circuit of the greatest part of the island, crossing the Koolaus on the Pali or Likelike Highway, going around the north end, and returning to Honolulu by way of Wahiawa and Pearl Harbor (about 90 miles/144 km); a loop around the east end of the island past Koko Head, through Waimanalo and then the Pali tunnels (about 40 miles/64 km); and a drive through Leeward Oahu and along the Waianae Coast to Makua and back (about 85 miles/136 km). You can also include some city sights on each trip.

Where to Stay

Waikiki, Honolulu's resort district, has about 32,000 rooms in its thicket of hotels and condominiums. Of the more than 20 hotels strung along the waterfront, only a handful are in the luxury class. Most accommodations are in highrises, but a few low-profile clusters still remain. Apartments usually offer weekly and monthly rates.

On page 32 you'll find the names and locations of major Waikiki hotels. Look for descriptions of the foremost hotels in the Waikiki section of this chapter and in the sections where the following resorts are located: Kahala Hilton on the beach at the end of Kahala Avenue; Turtle Bay Hilton & Country Club at Kahuku, Oahu's north tip; and Sheraton Makaha Resort & Country Club in Makaha Valley on the Waianae Coast.

Makaha and Kahuku also have condominiums; the Windward Coast offers apartments in Pat's at Punaluu and hotel rooms in Laniloa Lodge at Laie; the North Shore's Mokuleia Beach Colony has condominium apartments. Near Ala Moana Center are the Ala Moana Americana and Pagoda hotels and, close to the airport, Holiday Inn-Airport, Pacific Marina Inn and the Plaza Hotel-Airport. Many apartment rentals are handled by condominium agencies, well known to travel agents.

Bed and breakfast accommodations are available at the John Guild Inn in Manoa Valley, a restored Victorian mansion, and in homes all about the island.

Sightseeing Tours

Honolulu tour agencies will usher you in buses, minibuses, vans, limousines, or sedans on sightseeing trips of the city and the Koko Head-Waimanalo-Pali loop (each a half day) and the greater Oahu circuit (all day). Their packages include various combinations of trips for a comprehensive look at such attractions as Sea Life Park, the Polynesian Cultural Center, Waimea Falls Park, and the Arizona Memorial. Tour agencies or travel agents can also arrange custom tours.

Air tours. For an overview of the island from a helicopter, check the tours of Hawaii Pacific Helicopters, Kenai Helicopters, and Royal Helicopters; the Yellow Pages may list other tour operators and air charter services (see also page 67). Glider rides are offered daily from 10 A.M. until late afternoon from Dillingham Field at Mokuleia; no reservations are required.

Boat tours. You'll notice a fleet of cruise boats and catamarans plying the waters off the city every evening. They are out on sunset and moonlight cruises that include dinner and Hawaiian entertainment, departing from Kewalo Basin, Honolulu Harbor, or Waikiki. In the daytime, some of the small craft you see are catamarans giving a fast sail to Waikiki beach-goers or large cats and motor vessels on three-hour cruises morning and afternoon to Pearl Harbor.

First Pearl Harbor Cruise (morning cruises) and Hawaiian Cruises (afternoon cruises) depart Fisherman's Wharf at Kewalo Basin on 3-hour tours of Pearl Harbor. The *Ani Ani* (Glass Bottom Boats Hawaii) sails the waters off Waikiki on 1-hour glass-bottom boat trips four times daily, and Leahi Catamaran departs Waikiki Beach 5 times daily on 1-hour sightseeing sails. All Hawaii Cruises' glass-bottom catamaran will take you on a trip along the Windward Coast and Windward Expeditions' Zodiacs travel to the small islands off the Windward Coast.

FOR CITY SIGHTSEEING

Bold black and white letters identify "TheBus," part of Honolulu's transportation system throughout Oahu. The white and yellow buses are so popular with visitors that bookstands sell guides, visitor publications cover bus travel to main attractions, and the transportation company maintains a telephone staff to answer questions about routes and fares; call 531-1611.

From the information booth at Ala Moana Center (*mauka* side, street level), you can board a bus serving any island destination. Bus numbers 2, 4, 8, 20, and 58 connect Waikiki with downtown Honolulu, the Bishop Museum, Ala Moana Center, Ward Warehouse, airport, Arizona Memorial at Pearl Harbor, University of Hawaii, Nuuanu Valley and Pali, Kahala Mall, Sea Life Park, and Kailua. Or you can board No. 14 on Paki Avenue or Kapahulu Avenue to go to Kahala, Maunalani Heights, and St. Louis Heights. On weekends and holidays, the Beach Bus leaves Waikiki Shell on Monsarrat Avenue for Hanauma Bay and Sandy and Makapuu beaches (no surfboards or boogie boards).

Buses run from 6 A.M. to 10:30 P.M. You'll need exact change. Avoid rush hours, and remember the driver is not a tour guide.

...The Essentials

Special Interest Tours and Activities

Nothing can more effectively enhance your knowledge and appreciation of Oahu's unique attractions than the guided tour—on foot or by vehicle. In addition to tours offered by some museums, theme parks, and public gardens (details are included with their individual descriptions in this chapter), guides will take you walking through the Capital District (page 37) and Chinatown (page 45). You can take a self-guided tour of the University of Hawaii's Manoa Campus (page 51). Pick up a free map and map-guide to the fine trees and plants on the campus from the Office of University Relations in Hawaii Hall.

Unusual industries. You can visit several factories for Hawaiian apparel, tee shirts, and chocolate-covered macadamia nuts located near downtown on a tour that includes free bus transportation to and from Waikiki and a stop at Dole Pineapple Cannery to see a film and drink fresh pineapple juice; when the cannery is operating you can tour it for a small charge.

Honolulu has any number of small factories that turn out unusual products—Chinese and Japanese noodles and *saimin*, Japanese fish cake, Portuguese sausage, ukuleles, monkeypod bowls and other wood articles, to name a few. Many places will let visitors watch their operation—but do call ahead. Look in the Yellow Pages under product and ethnic names and note factories mentioned in this chapter's area sections.

Fish auction. United Fishing Agency's lively fish auction is held Monday through Saturday from 6 to about 9 A.M. at 117 Ahui Street fronting Kewalo Basin. Much of the competitive bidding of wholesalers and retailers is in pidgin English—language as colorful as the sights. Longline sampans and other vessels unload their catches of *ahi* (yellowfin and big-eye tuna), mahimahi, marlin, red snapper, and mackerel at Kewalo and at Piers 15, 17, and 18 starting about 4 A.M. Picturesque, high-prowed *aku* (skipjack tuna) boats unload at Kewalo in late afternoon or early evening as well as the wee hours, with some of their catch going to the basin's Hawaiian Tuna Packers cannery, producers of Bumble Bee and Coral brands.

Handicrafts. Free demonstrations of Hawaiian crafts at hotels and shopping centers are Waikiki institutions along with free hula lessons; in the Waikiki section we point out the spots with the most active programs. The Bishop Museum and Polynesian Cultural Center also sponsor regular shows and demonstrations. At Lanakila Crafts, a rehabilitation center at 1809 Bachelot Street, workers turn out many of the handicrafts you see in tourist gift shops. The center's gift shop is open weekdays from 8 A.M. to 3:30 P.M., and tours of the workshop are given Tuesday and Thursday at 1 P.M.

The Entertainment Scene

Complimentary programs of Hawaiian music and dance are presented by many hotels and shopping centers (see the Waikiki section and look for listings in the many visitor giveaway publications). Most famous is the Kodak Hula Show (Tuesday, Wednesday, and Thursday, 10 A.M.), staged especially for photographers next to the Waikiki Shell lawn. A tradition for more than 50 years, the hula show is great fun, its costumed performers mostly old-timers.

On the beach in front of the Reef Hotel, visitors and local people gather with ukuleles, guitars, and beach mats for an informal Hawaiian jam session each Sunday at 8 P.M.

Big Polynesian revues are offered with either dinner or just cocktails. Luaus, however, are a food-and-entertainment package. Two of the commercial parties are held at the edge of Waikiki Beach, at the Royal Hawaiian Hotel Sunday night and at the Outrigger Waikiki Hotel Sunday, Tuesday, and Friday nights. The Germaine's and Paradise Cove luaus are held almost every night on beaches at Ewa; the packages include transportation from Waikiki. Look, too, for benefit luaus being offered by a church or club; they're inexpensive and feature food and a show to please islanders.

Music. The Honolulu Symphony, one of the country's major orchestras, performs both a classics and pops series of concerts from early fall to spring in Blaisdell Concert Hall and a Starlight pops series at Waikiki Shell in late summer (it also gives free community concerts around the island). Hawaii Opera Theatre presents three different operas in midwinter at Blaisdell Concert Hall. A half dozen or more chamber music ensembles perform

---

WHICH WAY SHALL I GO?

Islanders have a simple way of giving directions. On every island, you either go toward the sea (*makai*) or toward the mountains (*mauka*). Since the mountains always form the center of each island and the sea always surrounds it, the directions are easy to follow.

Each island and each part of an island has its own terms for directions around the island's perimeter, based on local landmarks. In Honolulu, you might go *Waikiki* or *Diamond Head*. You'll hear someone say, "Go two blocks *Diamond Head* on Kalakaua, then *mauka* on Kaiulani." Beyond Diamond Head, the term will change to *Koko Head*. If you are going in the opposite direction from Waikiki in Honolulu, you are going *Ewa* (toward Ewa, beyond Pearl Harbor).

---

throughout the year, mostly at Orvis Auditorium, the Academy Theatre, Mamiya Theatre, and churches. The Royal Hawaiian Band (see page 34) plays some Hawaiian numbers along with good band music at its regular concerts. The Honolulu Boy Choir gives periodic shows that are always a delight. About 200 boys, aged 7 to 13 and of all ethnic strains, are trained to sing heartily and with expressive faces; the repertoire includes Hawaiian songs and hulas.

Dance. Ballet Hawaii and Hawaii Ballet Theatre For Youth present occasional concerts. Dances We Dance, Inc. stages modern dance programs periodically at its Jones-Ludin Dance Center, 930 McCully Street upstairs, and also presents monthly programs by local ethnic dance groups or visiting artists; among these may be performances by the best hula *halau* (hula schools), the Pamana or Pearl of the Orient Philippine dance companies, or perhaps Onoe Kikunobu Kai in Japanese classical dances. Be on the lookout for music and dance programs by every one of Hawaii's ethnic groups—Honolulu is a city hard to equal for its variety of cultural offerings.

Theater. Any month you can expect to find a production staged by at least one of these companies: Honolulu Community Theatre (at Ruger Theatre) and Windward Theatre Guild (at a school auditorium) perform popular plays and musicals; Hawaii Performing Arts Company (Manoa Valley Theatre) and University Theatre (Kennedy Theatre) present classical and contemporary works, some experimental; the University-sponsored Kumu Kahua (Kennedy) produces original plays with an island theme; and the Honolulu Theatre for Youth (school auditoriums) has won national acclaim for its plays for youngsters—that also delight their parents.

Art. Honolulu's prolific community of artists exhibits in office buildings, shopping centers, and at fairs in parks as well as in conventional galleries. Their associations range from the Hawaii Artists League, the most selective for artists in all media, to Hale Naua III, for artists of Hawaiian ancestry, to groups of artists who specialize in watercolors, prints, stained glass, weaving, pottery, various handicrafts, or stitchery and fiber arts; all present at least one exhibition each year. You'll find mention of good places to see and buy local art throughout this chapter.

By all means visit the Honolulu Academy of Arts for its elegant building as well as carefully selected oriental and local art and, at least for its setting (the quality of work is mixed), the Art Mart held along Honolulu Zoo's Monsarrat Avenue fence. Fifty different local artists display and sell on Saturday and Sunday (10 A.M. to 4 P.M.), and some turn out Wednesday mornings as well (9 A.M. to noon or later).

The Sporting Guide

On Oahu you'll find the sporting events you'd expect of a major urban and college center. This island is the home of

Airport lei stands *supply traditional island greeting, farewell to mainland-bound vacationers.*

the Hawaii Islanders of the Pacific Coast League (a Class AAA baseball league). The University of Hawaii at Manoa, a member of the Western Athletic Conference, has teams in most sports and, recently, outstanding baseball and women's volleyball teams. This island's four small private colleges and the University of Hawaii at Hilo are all members of the National Association of Intercollegiate Athletics (NAIA) and enter teams in several sports. Basketball is most popular; Chaminade's teams have earned that university a national reputation.

Look also for good swimming meets, road races, triathlons (swimming, bicycling, running), rodeos and horse shows, golf and tennis tournaments, periodic boxing and wrestling matches (professional sumo once in a while), and regular auto racing at Hawaii Raceway Park.

Because of its cultural diversity, Oahu provides a rare opportunity to observe sports that are unusual to many visitors. Amateur competition in the Oriental martial arts such as karate, judo, and kung fu continues all year. Check the Yellow Pages for lists of schools; the City-County Department of Parks and Recreation also sponsors classes. There's amateur sumo wrestling every Sunday from 2 to 5 P.M. at Aala Park and occasionally a tournament featuring amateurs from Japan. Cricket—especially popular with Samoans—is played in Kapiolani and Keehi Lagoon parks, rugby in several places including Kapiolani Park; check with the Department of Parks and Recreation. Outrigger canoe races—regattas or distance races—go on most of the year.

The islands' international, professional, big wave surfing meets are held on Oahu's west and north shore beaches in late fall and winter. Good amateur contests are scheduled in spring and summer in or near Waikiki, where waves are of average size. See "Annual Events" (pages 20-21) for details on the biggest crowd-pullers in all sports.

HONOLULU: A CAPITAL CITY

Sunlovers line sands *in front of Royal Hawaiian Hotel, city's venerable "Pink Palace."*

Honolulu sprawls over 25 miles/40 km of Oahu's south shore, from Hickam Air Force Base to Makapuu Point. Its residential sections burrow into the jungled valleys of the Koolaus and climb the steep ridges toward the city limits—the tops of the green-clad peaks. At night, lights of houses on the ridges, or heights, create a patchwork backdrop to the vast central plain, occupied largely by business, industry, apartments, and the resort community of Waikiki. Residential districts also extend from Diamond Head all the way to Koko Head.

A melange of Polynesia, the Orient, and the contemporary mainland, Honolulu is a city shaped by people of a dozen different ethnic strains, whose heritage and cus-

toms assert themselves in many ways upon the urban scene. You'll find both English and foreign-language newspapers, films, and programs on radio and TV; lunch wagons and "mom and pop" stores (often with a "shave ice" machine); and open-front markets full of strange foods popular in the Orient.

Because of its beautiful setting in the lee of the mountains and its large, protected harbor, Honolulu has burgeoned in recent years. Though the city is crowded (population 370,000), possesses thickets of concrete towers, and matches freeway congestion with any other major city, growth has also brought sophisticated modern squares studded with handsome sculpture, high-fashion stores, galleries with quality antiques and fine art, museums, concerts, theaters, and restaurants for almost every cuisine.

The land-scarce community retains old buildings in styles that bespeak its history, quaint box houses with "chop suey" gardens huddled together along narrow lanes, and elegant homes with expansive grounds. Forest trails with waterfalls and swimming holes, tree-lined boulevards, fine beaches, boat harbors, and generous city parks are used intensively for sports, family outings, group picnics, concerts, fairs, and festivals.

Still, Honolulu retains a friendly, small town atmosphere. People wear sports or "aloha" attire everywhere, with *zori* (go-aheads) on their feet, and navigate their autos over streets with seldom a honking of the horn.

Greater Waikiki

Officially, Waikiki is a peninsula about ½ mile/1 km wide by 2 miles/3 km long, bounded by the ocean, Ala Wai Canal, and Kapahulu Avenue. But Waikiki Beach extends almost to Diamond Head and thus so does Greater Waikiki, taking in the world of Kapiolani Park.

Most visitors spend at least part of their stay in this resort region. Though it's fashionable to malign the tumble of buildings, tacky tourist shops, clogged streets, and crowded sands, remember that the area became overgrown because it combines the best climate and friendliest ocean swimming of any island seashore. Informal and full of camaraderie, Waikiki is a great place for strolling. And with a grand city park at each end of the district (Ala Moana and Kapiolani), it offers a wide variety of experiences.

Waikiki is not only a tourist enclave; you can still mingle with people who aren't other mainlanders. An average day in the district finds about 60,000 visitors—many from foreign lands, especially Japan—rubbing shoulders with the 22,200 people who live there and some 30,000 local people who work in the area. You'll meet islanders on the streets, in stores, dining, swimming, surfing, and enjoying the parks.

Along with new hotels, apartments, and shopping centers has come an explosion of pools, fountains, gardens, and art works. Most shops are open well into the evening, when the balmy air invites you out for a stroll. You might catch a street-side Polynesian show or listen to music emanating from an open-air dining spot. Your choices for dinner or cocktails range from outdoor terraces to vantage points in the sky and, for food, everything from hamburgers to a nine-course Chinese feast. During the day, you can also sun, swim, surf, take a hula lesson, and visit the reef fish at the aquarium or rare tropical birds at the zoo.

Waikiki is plagued with typical resort-center problems. You'll want to watch your wallet and purse, and it's not wise to walk alone on the streets at night. Shops and sidewalk stands may seem repetitious, but competitive pricing is their redeeming feature.

Some of the bustle is wacky and fun. If it becomes overpowering, you'll find the beaches deserted early or late in the day. At night, the sands are enhanced by the moon and stars, the drift of lights, and music from neighboring hotels.

Waikiki Beach is not one continuous crescent of sand but a series of beaches, some natural, some manmade, each with its own flavor and habitués. The whole strip is public and accessible by right-of-ways; you can walk on sand and connecting sea walls from Duke Kahanamoku Beach to Kuhio Beach Park or on to Sans Souci Beach. And even when the ocean is rough, you can swim anywhere without fear of dangerous currents.

Several beaches are territories for outrigger canoes, catamarans, surfboards, and beachboys who give surfing lessons or take you on boat rides. Most of the action takes place a half-mile offshore where the waves break, beyond most swimmers but within view of beach-sitters.

Ala Wai Canal was dredged in the 1920s to drain surrounding swamps and duck ponds and carry runoff from the streams that occasionally flooded Waikiki. Apartments strung along Ala Wai Boulevard look across the waterway to Ala Wai Golf Course and Field (the open lands that let the trade winds into Waikiki) and to the developed heights and wild green peaks beyond.

Early morning or late in the day, residents jog or just walk along the canal's promenade; in the afternoon, outrigger canoes skim the water as muscular paddlers train for forthcoming races. At any time of day, anglers sit comfortably on banks overhung with Chinese banyans between the Kalakaua and Ala Moana bridges, plucking *akule, papio,* mullet, and even crabs from the silty water.

Ala Wai Yacht Harbor shelters more than 1,000 private boats (no commercial craft). Broad piers make it easy to visit them. The State of Hawaii has 780 berths filled with 20 to 100-foot sailboats, including more than 100 "liveaboards." Waikiki Yacht Club on Ala Moana Park Drive has 185 slips and Hawaii Yacht Club at the end of Mole A, about 25 spaces for boats of up to 60 feet. Both clubs and the harbor have long waiting lists.

Exploring Waikiki's attractions takes you through several neighborhoods, each trying to make its major

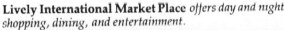

Lively International Market Place *offers day and night shopping, dining, and entertainment.*

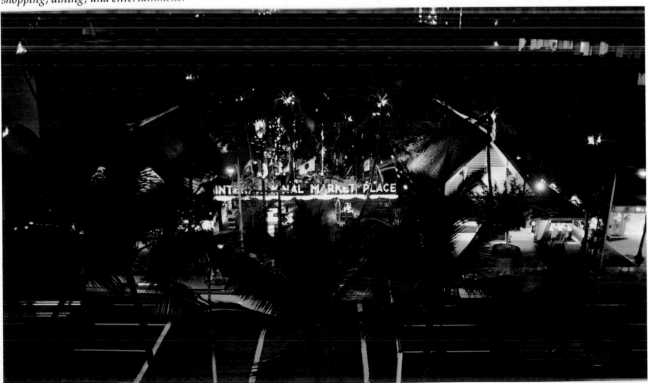

hotels and shopping centers stand out from the others. The area's center includes the blocks along and off Kalakaua and Kuhio Avenues from Waikiki Gateway Park to Kaiulani Avenue. Its beach and swimming area—from the Royal Hawaiian to Kuhio Beach Park—is the most spacious but also accommodates Waikiki's largest concentration of surfers, outrigger canoes, and catamarans.

Our tour of the highlights starts in the Ala Moana district and proceeds *Diamond Head*.

If you travel on foot, you won't have to master the one-way street system. You can use TheBus (see page 25) to span longer distances; buses travel on Kalakaua and Kuhio avenues, Saratoga and Kalia roads, and Ala Moana. Or you can hire one of the popular pedicabs.

Discovery Bay Shopping Center, 1778 Ala Moana, has shops and restaurants beneath twin apartment towers. Among them are an elegant McDonald's with koa paneling and Bon Appetit, offering a superb French dinner.

Eaton Square, 444 Hobron Lane, captures a touch of Europe with brick paving, lights made from London gas lamps, and imported iron gates and roof tiles—but has rubbish containers that respond in ''pidgin'' when you feed them. Its several levels contain oriental restaurants and antique shops, an art gallery, Meheula Flowers with authentic Hawaiian Leis and arrangements, the popular 24-hour King's Bakery and Coffee Shop, and Chez Michel with renowned Continental and French fare.

The Ilikai Hotel, 1777 Ala Moana, with 800 large units, has 6 garagetop tennis courts and a broad terrace with colored fountains, the scene of a torch-lighting ceremony. A glass elevator lifts you 30 stories to dinner at Top of the I where you'll have a view of yachts in the harbor below at sunset, and then city lights.

Waikikian Hotel, 1811 Ala Moana, one of the few remaining 1950s Polynesian style hotels, has frame bungalows set in a lush garden. Its lobby is a hyperbolic paraboloid patterned after a South Seas spirit house. The Tahitian Lanai restaurant has tables in thatched huts or under parasols overlooking Duke Kahanamoku Lagoon.

Duke Kahanamoku Beach, named for Hawaii's famous Olympic swimming champion, encloses a lagoon (also known as Hilton Lagoon) with constantly circulating ocean water.

Hilton Hawaiian Village, 2005 Kalia Road, begun in the 1950s by the late industrialist Henry J. Kaiser, is Hawaii's largest resort complex with 2,522 hotel rooms, 279 residential apartments, shops, restaurants, and pools. Hawaiian crafts are demonstrated on the grounds daily.

Both land and sea ends of the Rainbow Tower have 30-story murals by Millard Sheets, made in 17 colors of ceramic tile and lighted after dark. The first Buckminster Fuller geodesic dome ever built of aluminum (by Henry Kaiser) is the scene of such entertainment as the Don Ho Polynesian Revue.

Casual attire *and indoor-outdoor settings make island dining an informal delight.*

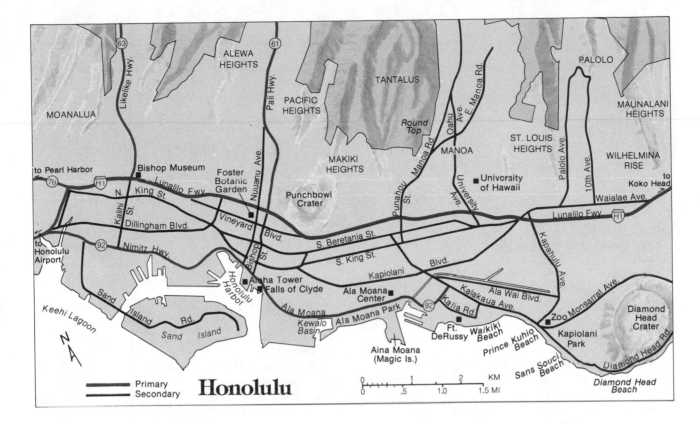

Primary
Secondary

Honolulu

0   1   2   KM
0 .5 1.0 1.5 MI

At the Rainbow Bazaar, you view Hawaiian and Pacific wares in three areas: Imperial Japan, with a 400-year-old farmhouse imported and rebuilt without nails for Benihana of Tokyo (where a chef teppan-broils your entrée with great flourish); Hong Kong Alley, arranged around a court with moon gate; and the South Pacific, with buildings missionaries might have erected.

Fort DeRussy, built on filled fish and duck ponds as part of Oahu's coastal defense system, is now primarily a recreation base for military personnel—and an inviting greensward in Waikiki. The public is welcome on DeRussy's long, wide beach of hard sand, but its hotel, Hale Koa, and other facilities are reserved for members of the armed forces and their families.

In the U.S. Army Museum (Tuesday through Sunday 10 A.M. to 4:30 P.M.; free), you can tour a labyrinth of corridors and concussion chambers in Battery Randolph and walk along its 22-foot-thick top. Displays cover the history of the Army in the Pacific and aspects of Hawaii military history. In the superstructure, the Corps of Engineers presents a film on its Pacific Basin projects.

Urasenke Foundation of Hawaii Tea Room, 245 Saratoga Road (Wednesday and Friday 10 A.M. to noon; free) makes a good spot to stop. Kimono-clad Japanese perform the tea ceremony, serving sweets and green tea (donation welcome). The authentic *tatami*-mat tea room is in the rear of the Breakers Hotel.

Gray's Beach borrowed its name from Grays-by-the-Sea, an early boarding house. Good swimmers head for "the rock," a remnant of an old mooring in the sandy channel part-way out to the reef.

Halekulani, 2199 Kalia Road and on Gray's Beach, reopened in 1983 with 456 deluxe rooms in hip-roofed buildings varying from 2 to 16 stories and clustered around the old Halekulani's "Main Building," architect C. W. Dickey's handsome 1931 structure. The pitched-roof and open-walled building has been remodeled into two dining rooms, a big living room with fireplace, and a barroom, Kimballs Lounge, named for the old hotel's founder.

Another tie with the past is the popular lunch and cocktails-with-entertainment area, the Sunset Terrace with its century-old *kiawe* tree, and a new, second House Without a Key, the open-walled bar made famous in a Charlie Chan mystery.

Waikiki Parc, 2233 Helumoa Road, lies adjacent to the Halekulani, its sister hotel. The 298-room, 22-story hotel includes restaurants and an 8th-floor pool deck.

Canlis, a well-known restaurant at 2100 Kalakaua Avenue, has been attracting attention since 1954 with its lava rock walls, steep copper roof and skylights, and tropical gardens outside and in.

The Kuhio District, most of Kuhio Avenue's *makai* 2100 block, attracts a variety of people to its novel but modestly priced restaurants and shops. The banyan-shaded courtyard of Hula's Bar & Lei Stand is open afternoons and evenings for drinks, *pupu* (hors d'oeuvres), and disco-dancing. In the late afternoon on the last Sunday of the month you'll hear live "backyard" Hawaiian music. Restaurants have such intriguing names as Hamburger

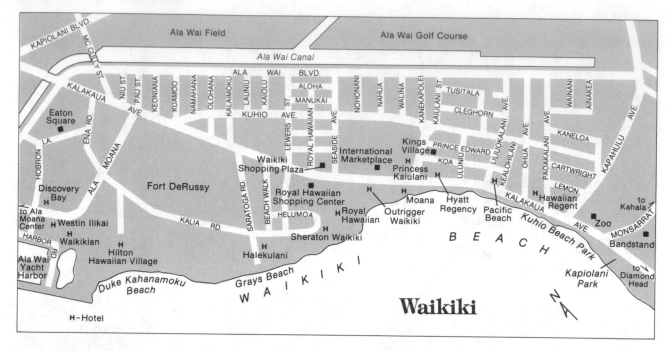

Waikiki

H – Hotel

Mary's Organic Grill, The Stuffed Potato, Hernando's Hideaway & Cantina, and Rada's Piroscki. Shops include Apparels of Pauline (branch of a Lahaina, Maui, store selling handmade wear featuring handpainted fabrics).

Cherry Blossom, 2184 Kalakaua Avenue, now Waikiki's only dry-goods store, has occupied the same spot since 1950. Started in Chinatown before World War II, the family-owned shop carries tapa and *pareu* prints, Hawaiian patterns, muumuus, and aloha shirts.

Gump Building, 2200 Kalakaua Avenue, a landmark masonry building with perforated grilles, flared roof of blue tile, and teak woodwork, was designed by architect Hart Wood in 1929 for a S. and G. Gump store, a store of quality oriental imports. The building now has a sidewalk McDonald's, Crazy Shirts (the best of printed tees), and a Hawaiian Holiday Macadamia Nut Factory with 200 nut products at discount prices to mail home or sample (other stores are located at 2430 and 2098 Kalakaua—the latter, The MacNuttery, with an ice cream parlor and small factory.

Woolworth's, 2224 Kalakaua Avenue, is the best-known occupant of the unusual tower with the concrete arches. It offers an unusual selection of goods including Hawaiian wear, curios, and take-out ethnic foods.

Waikiki Shopping Plaza, 2250 Kalakaua Avenue, has escalators, open-front shops, and restaurants rising around a 75-foot lighted fountain of acrylic bowls. Fast-food eateries on the lower level are topped by three floors of shops and two of specialty restaurants. The fourth-floor showroom is the location of "Waikiki Calls," a free hula show (Monday through Saturday, 6:30 and 8 P.M.).

Waikiki Business Plaza, 2270 Kalakaua Avenue, houses the Hawaii Visitors Bureau offices and information center on the eighth floor. A revolving restaurant, The Top of Waikiki, is 21 stories up.

Waikiki Trade Center Shopping Mall, Seaside and Kuhio, an arcade of a 22-story sculptured tower with lots of black glass and portholes, houses several haute couture shops and specialty restaurants.

Meitengai, Seaside and Kuhio, inspired by a Tokyo back street, contains shops and specialty restaurants in remodeled two-story buildings, most with blue tile roofs.

Royal Hawaiian Shopping Center, along Kalakaua from Lewers to the Outrigger Waikiki Hotel, is composed of three 4-story buildings connected by bridges. Vines and gardens hang from lava rock and coral-textured walls and decorate atriums and interior promenades. Several restaurants open to the Royal Hawaiian Hotel garden, including a McDonald's that displays contemporary Hawaiian art inspired by ancient legends. In the Building B atrium grows one of Hawaii's three *akee* trees, the *Blighia sapida* named for Captain Bligh of *Mutiny on the Bounty.*

The center has department stores, two Hawaiian handicraft shops, and a China Friendship Store featuring handmade wares from the People's Republic of China. Specialty dining spots range from expensive Japanese to inexpensive Mexican. In the waterfall courtyard facing Kalakaua, free entertainment takes place several times a week. Daily (except Sunday) demonstrations by Hawaiian artisans are offered. In Building A's third-floor Bridge Room, view a film recounting the Tahitian voyage of the *Hukule'a,* a replica of an ancient double-hulled canoe (see page 41).

Sheraton Waikiki, 2255 Kalakaua Avenue, Sheraton's largest hotel in Hawaii, has 1,900 rooms and a vast curved facade. A glass elevator shoots up 30 stories to the Hanohano Room where the view is spectacular at cocktail, dinner, or Sunday brunch time. Photographs of old Waikiki are displayed in the Historical Room on the convention floor.

Royal Hawaiian Hotel, 2259 Kalakaua Avenue, is familiarly known as the "Pink Palace." Now under the Sheraton banner, the Spanish Mission style hotel was opened in 1927; the tower wing was added in the 1960s. Though the gardens have been reduced, they still include palms growing in 1870 when King Kamehameha V had a beach cottage on the site. Lovely shops off the lobbies and arcades offer oriental antiques and local artists' works. A stunning, mirror-backed floral arrangement, spotlighted for photographers, is at the end of the gallery to the Monarch Room, scene of good cocktail and dinner shows Tuesday through Saturday and a tea dance late Monday afternoon (except in summer). The Royal's Surf Room and Mai Tai Bar back up to the beach and are popular for food, drinks, and music.

Moana Hotel, 2365 Kalakaua Avenue, also part of the Sheraton complex, was Waikiki's first large tourist hotel. It opened in 1901 with 75 rooms in the old-fashioned central frame structure; the concrete wings were added in 1918. The hotel's Ocean Lanai wing was the original Surfrider Hotel, built in 1952. The Moana's recent multi-million dollar renovation has returned the hotel to its former glory.

The Moana's Banyan Court is named for a Honolulu "exceptional tree" (see feature). More than a century old, it once provided shade and inspiration for writer Robert Louis Stevenson.

Princess Kaiulani Hotel, 120 Kaiulani Avenue, is named for the lovely heir to the throne who was only 23 when she died in 1899. Her estate, Ainahau, would today be a park had the government accepted the gift of her father, Archibald Cleghorn, a governor of Oahu who landscaped Honolulu's first parks. Hotel banquet rooms are named for the estate, Cleghorn, his wife (Princess Likelike), and author Stevenson, a family friend. The handsome Japanese-roofed shops that line Kalakaua are among the original parts of this Sheraton hotel built by Matson Navigation Company in 1955.

International Market Place, 2330 Kalakaua Avenue, is a two-level bazaar in wood and thatch beneath spreading banyan trees. It's unbelievably crammed with open-front restaurants, shops, kiosks, and carts; you'll find apparel, jewelry, baskets, and handicrafts from Hawaii, other Pacific islands, and Asia—everything from schlock to good folk art.

Duke's Lane, along the *Ewa* side of the bazaar, is lined with still more souvenir stands; adjoining Kuhio Mall has more shops and restaurants.

Hyatt Regency Waikiki, 2424 Kalakaua Avenue, features a block-long promenade through the hotel that opens to three balcony levels of shops, restaurants, and lounges (Bagwells 2424, Spats, Colony, and Trappers all popular). The Great Hall, an atrium between the two 40-story octagonal towers, contains hanging sculpture, waterfalls, bridges, a marble staircase, and Harry's Bar, a "sidewalk cafe" (drinks, coffee, light breakfasts and lunches) for watching the parade of people.

In the late afternoon and evenings, the Great Hall fills with music. A Friday afternoon show at 5 P.M. features Hawaiian music and dance. On the second floor, an Hawaiiana expert displays artifacts and museum-quality Hawaiian art work, and shows you how they are made.

King's Village, 131 Kaiulani Avenue, features a cobblestoned Monarch's Walk that winds up three levels past shops and restaurants in buildings resembling those of Honolulu a century ago. At night the buildings are outlined with lights. Plaques commemorate Hawaii's *alii* (royalty). You can watch a Changing of the Guard ceremony, performed by guardsmen dressed like King Kalakaua's Royal Guard, at the entrance evenings at 6:15 P.M., and a children's hula show in Bishop Court Sunday at 1 P.M.

Pacific Beach Hotel, 2490 Kalakaua Avenue, has a 280,000-gallon oceanarium of tropical marine life that rises three stories from the lobby. A diver feeds the fish five or six times a day; you can watch from the lobby or from the first or second-floor restaurants. Diners in the Japanese restaurant, Shogun, on the third floor view the waterfall that fills the tank with sea water.

EXCEPTIONAL TREES

Oahu contains nearly a hundred "exceptional trees," magnificent aged specimens or groves of trees that are on an official register and can't be trimmed or removed without city approval. A 1975 state law required each county to pass a tree preservation statute and appoint an arborist advisory committee to designate its worthy trees. New nominations are made each year. The majority stand in parks and botanical gardens and along streets; some are mentioned throughout this chapter.

Hawaii's famous volunteer organization, The Outdoor Circle, actively supported the ordinances. To celebrate its 70th anniversary in 1982, the group published *Majesty: The Exceptional Trees of Hawaii*, available in island bookstores. It contains a list—and locations—of the 114 trees then registered on Oahu and Kauai, handsome color photographs and descriptions of 47 of them, and a history of The Outdoor Circle, to which Hawaii owes its absence of billboards. The organization, now with branches on several islands and in rural Oahu, has also planted countless trees over the years and worked to preserve open space, acquire and improve parks, and control litter.

A current list of Oahu's exceptional trees is available from the city clerk's office in Honolulu Hale (City Hall). You can obtain lists for other islands at their county buildings: for Kauai, from the county clerk's office in Lihue; Hawaii, from the planning department in Hilo; and for Maui, Molokai, and Lanai, the Maui County Department of Parks and Recreation in Wailuku.

St. Augustine's Church, 130 Ohua Avenue, holds weekend masses featuring native songs by a choir of Hawaiians or Tongans. The Damien Museum, located behind the church, houses historical photographs and the personal possessions of Father Damien (see page 124).

Hawaiian Regent Hotel, 2552 Kalakaua Avenue, has a handsome open-to-the-sky court in its Kalakaua Tower with a dramatic stairway to The Library (a piano bar), and on to The Third Floor, a popular restaurant. Hawaiian music emanates nightly from the Kuhio Tower lobby.

Kuhio Beach Park stretches from the Moana Hotel to Kapiolani Park and is bordered by a broad promenade with trees, benches, and steps down to the sand. In the pavilions, chess, checkers, and card players gather day and night. Four legendary "wizard stones" stand on the sand beside the Moana, supposedly endowed with healing powers by four Tahitian *kahuna* (priests). The walkway jutting into the sea at the end of Kapahulu Avenue, takes you into the midst of local board and body surfers.

Kapiolani Park sprawls over some 170 acres between Kapahulu Avenue and Diamond Head. A gift to the people from King Kalakaua in 1877, the park was named for his queen. It has a zoo, aquarium, beaches, tennis courts, archery and golf-driving ranges, and an encircling jogging path. On the grass lawns people play softball, soccer, volleyball, cricket, and rugby; fly kites; feed the birds; exercise their dogs; and picnic under enormous shade trees.

Most park concerts and programs take place at the Waikiki Shell, an outdoor amphitheater, and the Kapiolani Bandstand, site of a 2 P.M. Sunday concert and a 7:30 A.M. Sunday marathon clinic. The old-fashioned green and gold pavilion nearby was a 1900s trolley station.

Monkeypods, weeping banyans, and ironwoods line the drives. Near the Louise Dillingham Memorial Fountain on Kalakaua Avenue are yellow and pink rainbow shower trees that bloom in spring and summer. In Queen Kapiolani Garden, stunning pink butterfly hibiscus trees border the *lokelani* roses.

Honolulu Zoo, 151 Kapahulu Avenue (daily 8:30 A.M. to 4:30 P.M.; admission fee), is a 42-acre tropical garden home for some 900 species of mammals, amphibians, fish, reptiles, and birds. Here children meet Mari, an Indian elephant, climb a spiral stair to get eye to eye with the giraffes, and venture into the African savanna exhibit. Picnicking is popular around the snack bar. In borders outside the zoo's Kapahulu and Paki fences, local people tend crops in a community recreational garden; outside the Monsarrat Avenue fence you'll find the colorful Art Mart.

Waikiki Aquarium, 2777 Kalakaua Avenue (daily 9 A.M. to 5 P.M., free, but adult donation requested), contains Hawaii's greatest variety of tropical Pacific marine life. In addition to giant clams, cuttlefish, and Hawaiian monk seals (an endangered species), there's an oceanfront "Edge of the Reef" tidepool exhibit with living coral and fish common to Hawaii's shallow reefs and tidepools.

The park waterfront starts with Queen's Surf Beach, popular with residents. Broad Sans Souci Beach (shallow, placid water ideal for children or novice swimmers) takes its name from the resort lodge built on this site in the 1880s. The sandy channel running out to the reef contains remnants of the first Honolulu–to–San Francisco oceanic

THE ROYAL HAWAIIAN BAND...MUSIC SINCE MONARCHY

Stroll by the bandstand at Iolani Palace on a Friday at noon and you'll find yourself part of a 100-year-old tradition as the Royal Hawaiian Band serenades listeners with selections ranging from Hawaiian tunes to European classics to Broadway showstoppers.

King Kamehameha III formed the band in 1836, and it has continued to play throughout Hawaii's transition from monarchy to statehood. Band membership has grown from 10 to 39; in 1909, after a number of changes, the group was officially named the Royal Hawaiian Band.

What saved the band from fading into obscurity was the arrival in 1872 of Henry Berger, sent from Prussia on a four-year loan. Four years stretched into 57, and Berger remained in the islands as a naturalized citizen until his death in 1929. During his 43 years as bandmaster, Berger welded the group into a harmonic unit that played over 32,000 concerts (as many as five a day).

Berger was more than just the bandmaster. A composer whose credits include Hawaii's state song, "Hawaii Ponoi," Berger taught at the local school for orphans and wayward youth, inviting promising musicians to join the band. It was Berger who began the tradition of playing during the festivities at Aloha Tower celebrating ship arrivals and departures. It was also Berger who pushed the band to the forefront of Hawaiian society. Berger is still honored in a yearly concert.

Today the Royal Hawaiian Band is the only full-time municipal band in the United States. Membership is a highly coveted prize and auditions for the occasional openings are rigorous.

Currently under the direction of Aaron Mahi, the band has toured the mainland and Europe. Back home, it continues to perform the Friday noon concerts as well as Sunday afternoon in Kapiolani Park and monthly at Bishop Square. The band can also be found marching in parades, giving benefit concerts, and participating in cultural events—performing the music that is a part of Hawaii's history.

ON THE PALACE GROUNDS

A palm-lined drive off King Street leads through iron-fenced lawns to picturesque Iolani Palace (guided tours Wednesday through Saturday 9 A.M. to 2:15 P.M.; admission fee; reservation required), restored to look as it did a century ago when Hawaii's last king and queen lived in it.

Built by King Kalakaua and inspired by his European travels, the palace was completed in 1882. After his death it became the official residence of his sister, Queen Liliuokalani, until the monarchy ended in 1893. It later served as Hawaii's capitol for 75 years.

The turreted structure of cement faced brick has double lanais on all sides, unusual upper-floor corner tower rooms, and delicate cast-iron columns and balustrades. The throne room, dining room, and the king's library upstairs are furnished. Royal portraits and niches with vases and statuary line the walls of the splendid main hallway with its curved staircase of koa.

Replacing the furniture sold at auction when the kingdom was toppled may take years, but there is still plenty to see on the hour-long tour: sculptured plaster, etched glass doors, carved woodwork, mirror-polished floor, and crystal and bronze light fixtures.

The palace shop and ticket office are in Iolani Barracks, the rebuilt 1871 headquarters of the kingdom's household guards. The fortresslike building has coral block walls, slate roof, crenelated parapets, and towers with decorative loopholes. It will become a military museum when the visitor center is moved to the Kanaina Building in the late 1980s.

This 1906 Classical Style structure on the other side of the palace was the first building in the country designed as a public archives; it now houses state offices. In front are legendary sacred boulders and Oahu's only memorial to Captain Cook. Across the lawn, a fenced, planted mound marks the site of the tomb where the bodies of Kamehameha II and Queen Kamamalu were buried from 1825 until 1865, when they were transferred to the Royal Mausoleum.

The present State Archives, built in 1954, has a wealth of research material, historical photographs, and drawings from which prints can be ordered. The building is separated from the palace by an enormous banyan (originally two trees) that Kalakaua's queen, Kapiolani, planted in the 1880s.

Iolani Palace Bandstand, an octagonal pavilion, was built by Kalakaua in front of the palace for his belated coronation in 1883. It soon became a bandstand and was moved to its present site on the *Ewa-makai* lawn.

On special occasions, the restored or reproduced gates to the palace grounds are manned by ceremonial guardsmen dressed in uniforms like those of Kalakaua's guard.

Conch shells signal start of festivities

Kamehameha the Great *presides from atop pedestal in front of the Judiciary Building.*

Diamond Head

The craggy profile of this crater, formed some 150,000 years ago in a series of underwater volcanic explosions, is as familiar as the Rock of Gibraltar. Diamond Head was once a coast defense fort, bristling with guns poked through its high walls. Now gardens of fine homes built upon the lower slopes create a greenbelt. Diamond Head won its name when some 19th century British sailors discovered calcite crystals on its slopes and mistook them for diamonds. The federal government bought Diamond Head in 1904, fortified and used it through World War II, and then gave it to the state in 1950. It's now a state park and monument and national natural landmark.

To circle the crater you take Diamond Head Road from Kapiolani Park, drive under the spreading trees of fine oceanfront estates, then climb the *kiawe*-covered Kuilei Cliffs to the lighthouse and turnouts. The panorama of residential Honolulu spreads below you, from Black Point to Koko Head and Koko Crater. Notice tobacco heiress Doris Duke's white-columned, Persian style "Shangri-La" at Black Point. One lookout has a monument to famous aviatrix Amelia Earhart.

Diamond Head Lighthouse, rising 55 feet from its cliffside perch, has an automatic light visible 17 miles out to sea. Beneath the cliffs, two unimproved beach parks make up an unbroken strip of sand fringing a sea floor grown with coral. Diamond Head Beach Park, on the *Ewa* side and reached by Beach Road, attracts reef-explorers and sunbathers. Surfers populate Kuilei Cliffs Beach Park *Koko Head* of the light, hauling their boards down paths from the lookouts above. You can walk the shore on sand or lava to Black Point and swim at Kaalawai Beach, where sandy pockets and channels stretch out to surfing grounds, or at breakwater-protected Duke's harbor.

From its highest point above the sea, Diamond Head Road descends between cliffside houses to a junction with Kahala Avenue, then climbs the crater's east side through Fort Ruger, the Army's first garrisoned coastal artillery fort in Hawaii.

Monsarrat Avenue takes you down the crater's western slope, past Fort Ruger's Cannon Club.

Drive into Diamond Head through a tunnel off Diamond Head Road near 18th Avenue (open 6 A.M. to 6 P.M.). The vast, desolate interior is open space except for the Hawaii National Guard Armory and the Federal Aviation Administration's Air Route Traffic Control Center, which directs aircraft over 10 million square miles.

A trail to the 761-foot seaward rim of the crater leads up a gently graded path, traversing the *kiawe* and koa-covered slopes to a fine lookout facing Koko Head and Koko Crater. From here, a series of steps, stairways, and a tunnel lead to the summit; your reward is a spectacular view over much of the island.

Island Outdoor Tours offers a daily morning crater hike. The price of the package includes transportation to and from your hotel.

cable, completed in 1903. Sans Souci is also site of the New Otani Kaimana Beach Hotel, 2863 Kalakaua Avenue; an aged *hau* tree shelters the main dining spot.

The Outrigger Canoe Club Beach and swimming channel, also serving the Colony Surf and Colony East hotels (2895 Kalakaua) and the Elks Club (2933 Kalakaua), were manmade in the early 1960s. The clubs offer informal indoor-outdoor oceanfront dining. The hotel and condo complex houses Michel's, an elegant French restaurant with open windows and beach views, and Bobby McGee's Conglomeration, where salads are arrayed in a Victorian bathtub and waiters and waitresses appear as Attila the Hun, Wee Willie Winkie, and other characters.

The Outrigger Canoe Club (2909 Kalakaua) was on the site of the Outrigger Waikiki Hotel for 55 years. Its Hau Terrace, a dining institution, was reestablished in this handsome home.

Greater Downtown

The downtown area extends inland about 6 blocks from Honolulu Harbor. Each of its three districts (Capital, Downtown Center, and Chinatown) are just the right size to explore on foot; good walkers can cover the whole area, from South Street to Nuuanu Stream, in one visit. (Office buildings are open weekdays, generally from 7:30 or 8 A.M. to 4:30 or 5 P.M.; most stores are open until 5 P.M. and on Saturday.)

Hawaii Capital District

The Capital District, from South to Richards streets, contains architectural treasures arrayed in a gardenlike setting—structures of missionaries and monarchs and later bureaucrats span more than a century and a half. This is the center of Hawaii's state government. Guides take you through the museums—Iolani Palace (see page 35) and Mission Houses Museum (see page 38); the latter museum offers a guided walk through the district (weekday mornings by reservation) with tours inside Kawaiahao and St. Andrew's churches and the Capitol; or, for just the admission price to its historic structures, you'll receive a self-guiding tour booklet describing the area. When the legislature is in session the first months of the year, you can tag along with school classes touring the Capitol.

Hawaii State Capitol, between Beretania Street and Hotel Street Mall. Designed by architects John Carl Warnecke and Associates and Belt, Lemmon, and Lo, the Capitol rises out of its reflecting pool like the islands from the sea. The open-ended central court, flanked by conical legislative chambers, is topped by a volcano-shaped crown open to the sky. Concrete columns supporting the balconied office stories suggest royal palms. From spectator galleries in the House and Senate chambers, you can view Otto Piene's light spheres symbolizing the sun and moon and Ruthadell Anderson's Hawaiian-motif tapestries.

The court is always open and elevators are unlocked. On the court floor, note Tadashi Sato's circular mosaic, *Aquarius*. From the fifth floor you can look down upon the court, up to the sky, and out over the city; the reception rooms of the governor and lieutenant governor display works by local artists and make extensive use of Big Island koa in paneling and furniture.

A huge copper state seal, derived from the monarchy's coat of arms, hangs over both Capitol entrances. On the Beretania side is Marisol's striking bronze of Father Damien; on the grass mall between the Capitol and the palace grounds (see page 35) stands Marianna Pineda's melancholy figure of Queen Liliuokalani, her outstretched hand often bearing a flower lei.

Hawaii State Library, 478 South King Street (Monday through Saturday 9 A.M. to 5 P.M.; Tuesday and Thursday until 8 P.M.). On a monkeypod-shaded lawn stands the columned and tile-roofed library, built in 1913 with side wings added in 1929. Its open-air central court and surrounding loggias provide inviting spots for reading.

Honolulu Hale (City Hall), King and Punchbowl streets. This Spanish Colonial style building houses the offices of the mayor and city council around a tiled court open to the sky. Built in 1929 and expanded in 1952, the Hale has a grand staircase off the courtyard, a speaker's balcony, fine cast stone carving, coffered ceiling with frescoes, and bronze chandeliers and entrance doors. The court is the scene of frequent art shows and a free concert each month (tickets are available in advance from the building's information office).

On the expanse of green around City Hall you'll notice *Sky Gate*, a 24-foot-high black steel abstract sculpture by Isamu Noguchi.

Mission Memorial Buildings, 530–558 South King Street. The three Georgian style buildings of red brick and white trim beside City Hall were built for the association of Congregational churches in memory of their founders, the missionaries who reached the islands between 1820 and 1848. The large two-story building and attached auditorium were finished in 1916; the small Christian Education Building alongside was added in 1930. All three were converted to city and county offices after World War II.

Honolulu Municipal Building, 650 South King Street. Designed to accent the Capital District's Waikiki boundary without stealing any thunder from its decorative old-

A lively pedestrian way, *attractive Fort Street Mall extends from Nimitz Highway to Beretania Street.*

timers, this plain but well-articulated tower has housed most city departments since 1975. Broad entrance walks slope up through banks of tropical gardens to the open-walled lobby.

Kalanimoku Building, 1151 Punchbowl Street. The contemporary state office building features four stained glass murals by Erica Karawina, conceptions of the islands at different times of day using the four chief gods of old Hawaii. Though lighted for night viewing, the murals show off best against the sun from fourth-floor offices.

Board of Water Supply Headquarters, 630 South Beretania Street. Three distinct structures comprise the eclectic complex: the 1957 Public Service Building, its facade of vertical aluminum sun-control grilles inspired by Peking's Imperial Palace; the 1938 Engineering Building with bas-reliefs around its entrance; and the 1926 Beretania Pumping Station with tiled hip roof, arches, and a steam stack used until 1971, still the hub of Oahu's water-pumping network.

Mission Houses Museum, 553 South King Street (daily 9 A.M. to 4 P.M.; admission fee includes guided tours).

Falls of Clyde, *world's last full-rigged four-master, receives visitors in new role as floating maritime museum.*

Three houses, restored and furnished, depict the history of the early Protestant missionaries from New England: Hawaii's oldest frame house, prefabricated in Boston and shipped around the Horn in 1821; the 1841 coral stone printing house, outfitted with a working replica of the original Ramage press brought to Hawaii by the first missionaries aboard the brig *Thaddeus*; and a two-story, coral block home and storehouse built in 1831 by Levi Chamberlain, the mission's business agent. The Chamberlain house has changing exhibits and a fine shop.

Mission Historical Library, 560 Kawaiahao Street (Monday through Friday 10 A.M. to 4 P.M.). Built in 1950, the library houses the collections of books, pamphlets, and original manuscripts of the Hawaiian Mission Children's Society (missionary descendants and operators of Mission Houses Museum) and the Hawaiian Historical Society.

Kawaiahao Church, 957 Punchbowl Street (open daily 8 A.M. to 4 P.M.). Oahu's oldest remaining church was built in 1842 of coral and timber by Hawaiian converts led by King Kamehameha III. Named for "the waters of Ha'o," a nearby sacred spring, the church stands on the site of Hawaii's first mission (1820) and was preceded by four thatched structures. In the last century Kawaiahao was the setting for royal inaugurations, weddings, christenings, and funerals; it still knows pageantry when Hawaiian societies march in regalia to honor royal forebears, commemorated inside by pews, plaques, and paintings. The Sunday service (10:30 A.M.) in Hawaiian and English is highlighted by Hawaiian hymns and a talk afterwards on the church's history. The grounds contain congregation and mission cemeteries as well as King Lunalilo's tomb, completed in 1875.

Adobe School House, 872 Mission Lane. Kawaiahao's preschool now uses the restored school house, built by missionaries in 1835 of sun-dried bricks. Honolulu's only remaining adobe building has walls 30 inches thick, originally whitewashed dirt and lime but later plastered.

Old Brewery, 549 Queen Street. A picturesque derelict that awaits a restorer, this four-story brick brewery with decorative towerlike facade turned out beer from 1900 until it closed in 1960 (except during Prohibition).

Old Kakaako Fire Station, 620 South Street. Another old-timer awaiting a new use, this tile-roofed station (built in 1929) has served as a storehouse and a ballet studio since being replaced in 1974. Notice the tall hose-drying tower, now obsolete.

Old Kakaako Pumping Station, 653 Ala Moana. On this fanciful landmark of local cut basaltic bluestone, tiled hip and gable roofs, arches, and cornices decorate all sections—even its 80-foot chimney. It was built in 1900 for the steam-powered pumps of Honolulu's first sewage disposal system.

United States Immigration and Naturalization Service, 595 Ala Moana. Dominating the cluster of graceful 1934 stuccoed structures with variegated tile roofs is the administration building with dramatic entrance lanai set far back on a sweeping lawn. The station is the third on this site, the Pacific "Ellis Island" started by King Kalakaua.

Prince Jonah Kuhio Kalanianaole Federal Building, 300 Ala Moana. The enormous complex, marked by massive "silos" for stairways and restrooms, has contained the U.S. Courthouse and federal offices since its completion in 1976.

It is graced with large metal abstracts and courtyard fountain with waterfall gushing from a wall of Hawaiian-motif masonry sculptures.

Kaahumanu Hale, 777 Punchbowl Street. Completed in 1983, the seat of the state's First Circuit Court was designed to complement the Federal Building and form a *makai* gateway into the Capital District. The lobby, an open atrium, rises four stories to Erica Karawina's 24-by-45-foot skylight—a faceted glass mosaic with tapa motif. Glass parapets on the surrounding balconies and the dramatic double-winged stair often playfully mirror the ceiling.

Keelikolani Hale, 830 Punchbowl Street. An arcade circles the ground floor of this enlarged state office building; benches set between textured piers sometimes attract weary sightseers. Inside, landscaped courts rise four floors to the sky. Still under construction, this square block will eventually have just two buildings and a park.

Hale Auhau, 425 Queen Street. An expanse of grass and tall palms sets off the other large building on the block, the State Tax Office (1939). In the Spanish style, it features two-story-high windows, cast concrete grilles with a Hawaiian motif, and a balconied entrance with coral columns.

Kapuaiwa Building, 426 Queen Street. Though planned for Kamehameha V's Civic Center, this building was not put up until 1884 by King Kalakaua; it was to house government records, but has always been used for government offices. In Renaissance style like its older neighbor Aliiolani Hale, it features walls of massive concrete blocks with molded edges and tooled joints. The Waikiki wing was added in 1930.

Kekuanaoa Building, 465 King Street. Built by the federal government in 1926 for its Hawaii administration offices, this six-story state office structure still bears the inscription "Territorial Office Building." It was recently painted to emphasize the Neoclassical features—tall columns and pilasters, decorative pediments, parapets, and a double-landing entrance stair. The first floor rotunda culminates in a dome of cut glass with the Hawaiian coat of arms encircled by American flags.

World War II Memorial, King and Punchbowl streets. Though erected as a temporary memorial in 1944, this 18-foot shaft has become a permanent treasure. The names of many of Hawaii's World War II casualties are hand-painted on its base.

Aliiolani Hale (Judiciary Building), 417 South King Street. It looks like a palace because that's what Kamehameha V had in mind. But since the government needed an office building, plans were modified and the building was finished in 1874 to house the Supreme Court, legislature, and some ministries. King Kalakaua also used it at night for balls and receptions. Aliiolani has served as the Judi-

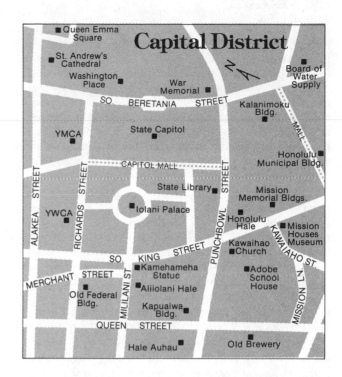

ciary Building ever since other departments moved to Iolani Palace in 1893, after the monarchy's overthrow.

This restored, Renaissance style treasure has walls of precast concrete blocks, arched doors and windows, lanais with Ionic columns, balustrades, and a marvelous entrance tower that rises four levels from arched portals to a clock with four faces. Inside, the rotunda (1911) features an octagonal stained glass skylight, curved stairs, and a balcony topped with cast-iron pineapples. The first floor exhibits tell the history of Hawaii's courts.

Statue of Kamehameha the Great. In front of Aliiolani Hale stands a bronze figure with gilded clothing, a duplicate of the original in Kohala on the Big Island (see page 164). The figure was to commemorate the centennial of Captain Cook's discovery of Hawaii but was lost off the Falkland Islands en route from American sculptor Thomas Gould's workshop in Italy. The original was recovered, only after insurance money had paid for another casting. The statue was unveiled for Kalakaua's belated coronation ceremony in 1883; the original went to Kohala, the land of Kamehameha's birth.

Old Federal Building, 335 Merchant Street. Meandering over a whole city block along Palace Square are the arcades, courtyard, towers, and red tile roofs of the Spanish Colonial style Old Federal Building. Built in 1922, it housed the United States Post Office, Custom House, Courthouse, and federal offices. (Customs and Post Office now share the building with state agencies.)

In 1927 the same New York architects designed the companion Hawaiian Electric Company Building standing at the end of Palace Square. Its arched entrance and Merchant–to–King Street arcade have vaulted ceilings (the first hand-painted).

Richards Street YWCA, 1040 Richards Street. A beautiful 1927 Spanish Colonial style building, the work of pioneer woman architect Julia Morgan of San Francisco, faces the palace grounds; two-story wings arranged around dining and swimming pool courts are separated by loggias. The columns and whimsical pool-court wall decorations are among the late Mario Valdastri's earliest ornamental cast stone work in the islands. The patio dining room is open to the public. The Y offers inexpensive courses (a few short term) in such subjects as hula, ukulele, oriental cooking and flower arranging, and lei making.

Armed Services YMCA, 250 South Hotel Street (always open). The large, U-shaped building with red tile roof opposite the Capitol lawn was constructed in 1928 on the site of the first (1872) Royal Hawaiian Hotel. Contributing to this structure's Mediterranean character are its elaborate frontispiece with Moorish columns and loggia, painted designs under the eaves, and central court with swimming pool. The building contains a restaurant, fitness center, and locker room; more than 200 rooms are available for short-term rental to the public.

St. Andrew's Cathedral, Queen Emma Square (open 6 A.M. to 6 P.M.). The cathedral of Hawaii's Episcopal Diocese took almost a century to complete. A year after King Kamehameha IV introduced the English Anglican Church, he died unexpectedly (in 1863) on the feast day of St. Andrew—inspiring the name of the Gothic Revival cathedral begun in 1867 by his queen and his brother, Kamehameha V. Queen Emma went to England for drawings and funds and shipped much of its stone around Cape Horn as ballast (local cut sandstone was used for later parts). Construction was intermittent throughout the next century: though the first services were held in 1886 and the church was consecrated in 1902 with only two bays complete, the present structure with square carillon tower and grand front stained glass window wall was not finished until 1958.

The columns of the nave arcades are ornamented with classical and Hawaiian floral designs. Most aisle windows have fine 19th century English stained glass. Gracing the plaza is a fountain with bronze sculptures of St. Andrew, the fisherman apostle, and his fish.

Queen Emma Square, 1275 Queen Emma Street. The lawn separating St. Andrew's Cathedral and Priory School was Honolulu's second park (after Thomas Square), set aside by Kamehameha IV in 1858 to honor his queen. Only a spreading Moreton Bay fig (an "exceptional tree," see page 33) remains from the early landscaping. Midway in this century the square gained a garden pool and seats and a terra cotta bust of Queen Emma.

St. Andrew's Priory School, 224 Queen Emma Square (open weekdays 7 A.M. to 4 P.M.). Queen Emma founded the Episcopal college-preparatory day school in 1867 to prepare Hawaiian girls for careers as nurses, teachers, and Christian homemakers. The original wooden buildings have all been replaced by concrete, most with Gothic features; the main Kennedy Hall is a recently enlarged and remodeled 1909 structure.

St. Peter's Episcopal Church, 1317 Queen Emma Street (office open weekdays 8 A.M. to 3:30 P.M.). This charming Gothic church with crenelated parapets was built in 1914 by a Chinese rector for a Chinese congregation. One Sunday service is still conducted in Cantonese. Fine koa trusses and pews and a Chinese baptismal font decorate the interior.

Washington Place, 320 South Beretania Street. The governor's home and the oldest continuously occupied house in Hawaii, the Greek Revival style mansion was built in 1846 of cement-faced coral stone and wood. The original owner, Captain John Dominis, disappeared at sea just after moving in; his widow rented rooms to the American commissioner, who named the mansion—his legation—in honor of George Washington. In 1862 the captain's son, John Owen Dominis, married Lydia Kapaakea, the future Queen Liliuokalani. The queen inherited the home and lived here after she was deposed in 1893 until her death in 1917.

The government acquired the estate and opened it as the executive mansion in 1922. Several downstairs rooms, on view only for receptions and special tours, display the queen's possessions, including the koa piano on which she played her compositions such as the famous "Aloha Oe."

Capitol Mall, across Beretania from the Capitol. In a promenade flanked by royal palms stands the *Eternal Flame*, Bumpei Akaji's abstract copper and bronze sculpture dedicated to all islanders who have died serving in the U.S. Armed Forces.

Queen's Medical Center, 1301 Punchbowl Street. King Kamehameha IV and Queen Emma opened the hospital in 1860 to treat the large numbers of Hawaiians dying of smallpox and measles. The current buildings were constructed piecemeal from the 1890s to the present. The grounds still have exceptional trees planted by the first medical director, Dr. William Hillebrand, whose own estate became Foster Botanic Garden. The Center's Historical Room (weekdays 10 A.M. to 4 P.M.) displays early photographs, letters, and medical records; Queen Emma Gallery (daily 9 A.M. to 4 P.M.) presents monthly exhibitions by local artists. Administrative offices are now in the 1932 Harkness Nurses' Home designed by pioneer architect C. W. Dickey, handsome indeed with sloping tile roofs, broad overhangs, an arcade, and balconies. Adjacent to Harkness are the contemporary brick Hawaii Medical Library with graceful concrete columns and the 1941 Mabel L. Smyth Memorial Auditorium, its windows trimmed with *ape* leaves wrought in concrete.

Downtown's Center

Downtown's Center, from Richards Street to Nuuanu Avenue, contains Hawaii's major financial institutions and business firms. Mixed in with the high-rises are structures that date from the mid-19th century; most have face-lifts and new roles. You tour Downtown's Center on your own.

The Waterfront. A good place to start a walk is at the waterfront near Aloha Tower. Here, around the piers, you'll discover a busy world of ship repair, fishing sampans, tugboats, tour boats, and cruise liners. Pole fishermen still inhabit the main piers, seemingly oblivious to the action around them, while downtown workers enjoy lunchtime picnics at Irwin Park and the grassy shoreline fringe between Piers 5 and 6.

The new Aloha Tower Plaza, scheduled for completion in the late 1980s, will include new terminals, hotel, restaurants, promenades, and an expanded park and Hawaii Maritime Center which now includes the tower's museum, the *Falls of Clyde*, and the *Hokule'a*.

Aloha Tower, Pier 9 at the foot of Fort Street (tenth-floor observatory, daily 8 A.M. to 9 P.M., free; ninth-floor museum, Monday to Friday 8:30 A.M. to 4 P.M., Saturday 10 A.M. to 4 P.M., free). Downtown's landmark since 1926, the 184-foot white tower greets everyone who arrives or departs the harbor with a friendly "Aloha" inscribed on all four sides which also each show a face of the tower's huge bronze clock. Above its green dormered roof rises a mast with cross arm for displaying signals to ships—the tower controls harbor traffic.

Tenth floor decks offer a grand view of the city and harbor. Museum exhibits trace the history of the harbor and its ships from 1792.

Irwin Memorial Park, in front of Piers 8 and 9. This pretty park is part parking lot under an oasis of monkeypod trees and part terrace with fountain and an escalator to the passenger terminal above and the approach to the Aloha Tower elevator. Redevelopment plans call for removing the terminal, its driveway ramp, and portions of several piers. Once again it will be possible to view the tower from its base.

Falls of Clyde, Pier 7 (daily 9:30 A.M. to 4 P.M.; admission fee). The world's only four-masted, full-rigged sailing ship afloat is now a museum ship that's still being restored. Built in Glasgow in 1878 and named for a Scottish waterfall, the iron-hulled vessel's exterior reflects the ship's first 20 years as a tramp freighter. On board is evidence of the ship's other careers: a Matson passenger-freighter, oil tanker, and floating oil depot in Alaska. About to be sunk for a breakwater in the early 1960s, the hulk was rescued by Hawaii residents and towed to Honolulu. Attractions include the teak steering wheel and wheel box, brass binnacles, the saloon and its etched glass dome, and the narrow galley.

Hokule'a, Pier 7 (daily 9:30 A.M. to 4 P.M.; admission fee). It was in double-hulled, voyaging canoes similar to this 60-foot replica that, anthropologists believe, the ancient Polynesians sailed the ocean between island groups. Built in 1974 with modern materials, the canoe reflects traditional design—from crab-claw sails to large steering paddles. Though it's too small for visitor-boarding, a pier pavilion contains fascinating exhibits; some detail history-making *Hokule'a* sailings by contemporary islanders to Tahiti in 1976, 1980, and 1985. Navigating only by stars, wave patterns, and native lore, they proved that their

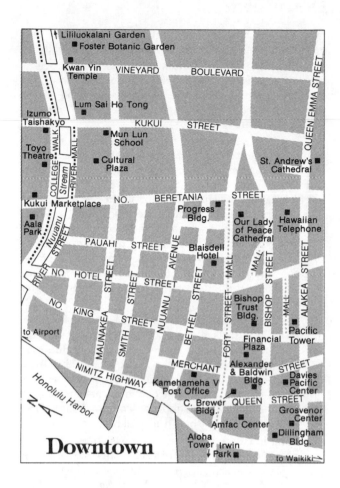

ancestors discovered and settled various Pacific islands because of knowledge and skill, not accidents.

Bishop and Alakea Streets. Central downtown's main thoroughfares, Bishop and Alakea streets, are lined with office structures. Four are island homes of the famous "Big Five"—Amfac, Alexander & Baldwin, Castle & Cooke, Theo. H. Davies, and C. Brewer and Company—sugar factors that once controlled Hawaii business. (All five have now branched into other fields and spread around the world.)

Amfac, Hawaii's largest corporation, is headquartered in one of the twin marble-and-glass towers of Amfac Center. The center's garage has a public, rooftop garden with trees, picnic pergolas, great views, and a jogging track. Amfac Plaza Exhibition Room (Monday through Friday 8:30 A.M. to 5 P.M.) hosts shows by major Hawaiian artists each month. Outside is Walker park, a memorial to a former Amfac chief executive; it covers the *makai* block of Fort Street Mall and features an oval pool with four fountains surrounded by sculptural bollards.

At Grosvenor Center, you admire the Italian Renaissance features of the Dillingham Transportation Building. Named for Benjamin F. Dillingham, who founded early railroads on Oahu and the Big Island, the 1929 building has rich ornamentation, arcades, and an elegant lobby.

The plaza of the Davies Pacific Center attracts a lunchtime crowd on the fourth Friday of each month for free beer and entertainment. Attractive anytime are its random-pattern brick paving, palm trees, and volcano-shaped fountain.

The 1929 Alexander & Baldwin Building stunningly combines Oriental and Mediterranean styles in its peaked and overhanging tile roof, terra cotta-faced walls, and Chinese-inspired ornamentation. Three buildings of different heights and shapes comprise the 1968 Financial Plaza of the Pacific, but all share a sculptural quality, volcanic aggregate facade, and tinted bronze windows. (Castle & Cooke has the projecting top floor of the 22-story tower.) The King-Bishop corner plaza has a geometric pool, fountains, and the mirror-polished bronze *Sun Disc*, movable though it stands 11 feet tall and weighs 5 tons.

The block-long, Neo-Classical S. M. Damon Building framed by high-rises is an attractive sight from Tamarind Park on the King-Bishop corner just opposite. Built in 1925 to house both the Bishop Bank and Bishop Trust Company started by Charles Reed Bishop (husband of Princess Bernice Pauahi, last of the Kamehamehas), it remains the home of Bishop Bank's descendant, First Hawaiian. Today, the Bishop Trust Building is catty-corner.

Tamarind Park is an acre of grass, trees, terraces, benches, and ledges. A pretty stream falls into reflecting pools; one has an arresting 11-foot bronze by noted sculptor Henry Moore entitled *Upright Motive No. 9*. This Bishop Square gathering place, created by landscape architect James C. Hubbard, is named for Charles and Bernice Bishop, whose nearby home was shaded by a tamarind tree—the park has two tamarinds. Noontime concerts are performed here on the second and fourth Wednesdays of each month—those on the fourth by the Royal Hawaiian Band (see page 34).

The 30-story, textured concrete Pacific Tower was built in 1972. Its 1983 companion is the stunning, 28-story Pauahi Tower of gleaming black glass with an elegant two-story lobby of Italian marble. Take the polished brass escalator to the mezzanine, scene of changing art exhibits mounted by the Honolulu Academy of Arts.

On Bishop Street *mauka* of Hotel Street, notice the white-columned Hawaiian Telephone Company tower; the Union Mall, an arc between Bishop and Hotel streets; and a mural depicting 19th century Honolulu in the lobby of the building at 1136 Union Mall.

Along Alakea Street are two prominent 1980s buildings. Central Pacific Plaza at the corner of King has *Mana-La* ("sun power"), a 12-foot-tall rectangle of granite topped by three stainless steel blocks; two have solar cells and move. In the bank lobby, a gallery (Monday through Thursday 8:30 A.M. to 3 P.M.; Friday 8:30 A.M. to 6 P.M.) shows the work of promising young local artists. Kauikeaouli Hale, home of the State District Court, is a fortress of coarsely textured concrete, recessed window slits, and

protruding stairwells; from the open-walled entrance plaza, big escalators rise almost to its high glass roof.

Fort Street Mall. Downtown's main shopping street and lively pedestrian way runs six blocks, from Beretania Street to Nimitz Highway, the approximate site of the fort that guarded the harbor from 1817 to 1857. It's lined with stores, eateries, refurbished old buildings, benches, trees, vine trellises, and speakers for music. An underpass beneath King Street has a waterfall and pool and a 70-foot wall of crushed *pahoehoe* lava incised with petroglyphs by contemporary artist Edward Stasack.

At Beretania, Damien Plaza's *padrao*—a tall, carved, masonry column with capital—memorializes Hawaii's first Portuguese immigrants who landed in 1878. Surrounding the plaza, noteworthy buildings include the Central Fire Station in 1930s Moderne style with Art Deco aluminum doors.

Our Lady of Peace Cathedral (open in daytime; masses several times each day) is the oldest remaining downtown building. Begun in 1843 as a coral block rectangle with steeple on the site of Hawaii's first Roman Catholic chapel, it has been enhanced over the years with new towers, columned lanai, tile roof, buttresses, and, inside, a vaulted, hand-painted ceiling, balconies, and choir loft. The tower contains French bells and a Chilean clock from the 1850s; in the courtyard stands the stump of Hawaii's parent *kiawe* tree, started from seed in 1828, and an 1893 statue of Mary, Our Lady of Peace.

Just across the mall is the restored 1898 Model/Progress Building, with dark, sturdy, rusticated walls and fortresslike parapet. A remodeled 1937 store next door houses Hawaii Pacific College, where nearly 4,000 students study for bachelor's degrees in liberal arts and business while working. All the rooms in the 1912 Blaisdell Hotel across Chaplain Lane have been converted to office suites, but they're served by a 1915 wrought-iron cage elevator (now enclosed in glass).

Walk over to the Bethel-Pauahi corner to see the Hawaii Theatre, built in 1922 for movies and stage shows and now awaiting restoration. Its Beaux Arts styling and Art Deco ornamentation are mostly intact; periodic concerts are given on its console organ.

Near the foot of the mall stands the haciendalike C. Brewer and Company Building, headquarters for the oldest of the "Big Five" (founded in 1826). The tiled, double-pitched hip roof, overhanging eaves, lanais, and garden courts make it a superb example of Hawaiian architecture. Built in 1930 of concrete and cut stone, its railings and grilles represent waving sugar cane; lights are shaped like sugar cubes.

Historic Merchant Street. Walk Merchant Street from the Capital District to Chinatown and, with a few jogs, you'll see the city's oldest remaining commercial buildings, most put to new uses, with their handsome detailing all restored. Just behind Hawaiian Electric on Palace Square stands an earlier (1901) home of the company at 222 Merchant Street, now The Croissanterie, a coffee house and gallery with exhibits of contemporary paint-

Buddhist and Taoist deities *grace Chinatown's Kwan Yin Temple. You'll usually see people engaged in the rituals of blessing.*

Chinatown's open-air markets *contain many wonders from the sea, are always crowded with neighborhood shoppers.*

ings, prints, or photographs by island artists. The coffee is roasted on the floor below, the plant of historic (1864) Lion Coffee.

Cafe Bon Bon on the Merchant-Alakea corner occupies the Romanesque style bluestone Podmore Building (1902). The turn-of-the-century, six-story Stangenwald Building, 119 Merchant, and the five-floor Judd Block, next door on the corner of Fort Street Mall, have elegant Renaissance terra cotta ornamentation. The Stangenwald set an informal height limit not exceeded by other commercial or residential structures in Honolulu for five decades.

On the *makai* side of Merchant between the mall and Nuuanu, four old-timers await restoration. The old Bishop Estate Building, a Romanesque Revival bluestone, was erected in 1896 by Charles Bishop to administer the estate and Bishop Museum, both established in the name of his late wife, Princess Bernice Pauahi. The building shares a wall with the 1878 second home of Bishop Bank (now First Hawaiian), an Italian Renaissance brick structure later stuccoed. On a Bethel corner stands the oldest of all, the 1854 Melchers Store, its coral stone walls now hidden beneath layers of stucco and paint. The huge Spanish Colonial beauty across Bethel was built in 1931 as the

Self-guided tours *at Foster Botanic Garden invite strolls past tropical plants such as bamboo.*

Honolulu Police Station and later converted to a courthouse. This building and the Melchers are being restored for new uses by the city.

On one Merchant-Bethel *mauka* corner is former Kamehameha V Post Office (1871), Hawaii's first postal station and the first building of precast concrete blocks and iron reinforcing bars built in the United States. In the adjacent park, the tree wells of the royal palms are paved with granite brought from China as ballast in the 19th century. The old Yokohama Specie Bank adorns the fourth Merchant-Bethel corner with its terra cotta brick, frieze, copper window frames, and triumphal arch entrance.

The small, two-story, brick Friend Building next door was erected in 1887 by missionary Samuel C. Damon for his *Friend of Temperance and Seamen*, Hawaii's oldest periodical (started in 1843); his church on the site was destroyed earlier in the 1886 Chinatown fire. The McCandless Building, a restored bluestone on the Bethel-King corner, was built in 1906 by the three McCandless brothers; between 1880 and 1930 they drilled more than 700 artesian wells in Hawaii (note water fountain motif).

Merchant Square. Restaurateurs have taken over several rehabilitated old-timers around the Merchant-Nuuanu intersection, given it an identity as Merchant Square, and participate in *pau hana* (after work) musical entertainment and dancing on a closed-off Merchant Street many Fridays from early evening to midnight. Jameson's occupies the old Waterhouse Warehouse. Royal Hawaiian Tavern, the single-story corner brick building next door, began life in 1890 as the Royal Saloon, popular with the seafaring crowd. Adjacent on Nuuanu is the 1916 home of Wing Wo Tai, an import and retail firm founded in 1877, a building awaiting a new eatery.

O'Toole's, across Nuuanu, occupies the T. R. Foster Building—a treasure now with its brick walls, tall narrow windows, and elaborate facade decoration of masonry and cast iron, but just a run-of-the-mill office structure when built in 1891 by the old Inter-Island Steam Navigation Company and named for its founder.

The 1896 bluestone at 914-928 Nuuanu belonged to the *Hawaii Times* from 1923 until 1982. Now defunct, it was descended from an 1895 Japanese newspaper and had a Japanese name before the Pearl Harbor attack—reasons for the building's nameplate.

The white plaster facade of the One North King Street Building conceals a coral block structure built before 1860 by J. Robinson & Co., owner of the first (1820s) shipyard in the Pacific. The building barely escaped the 1886 Chinatown fire.

Part of King's Court at 12 South King Street also survived the 1886 fire. The brick shell of the popular Merchants' Exchange saloon remained standing and was reused for its successor; it was erected by the same man who did the brick work on Iolani Palace.

The refurbished brick Two South King Street Building next door was originally a corner saloon that went up soon after the famous fire leveled its grocery-store predecessor.

Chinatown and Lower Nuuanu Stream

Early in the 19th century, Chinese traders, shopkeepers, and businessmen began to settle near the outlet of Nuuanu Stream, mostly in the blocks bounded by Nimitz Highway, Nuuanu Avenue, Beretania Street, and Nuuanu Stream that are today's official Chinatown. The area is contiguous to old Merchant Street, and, similarly, on the National Register of Historic Places.

Though relatively few Chinese residents remain, the district is still the financial, commercial, cultural, and social center of Oahu's Chinese community. It has always been a first home in the city for immigrants; its current mix of Filipinos, Vietnamese, and other recent settlers support a concentration of dry-goods stores and ethnic restaurants found nowhere else.

Chinatown has twice burned down; most of its older buildings today sprang up soon after the 1900 fire. Typically, they are harmonious ensembles of two and three-story structures of brick, stone, or concrete with decorative cornices and window trim. Their almost-continuous corrugated iron awnings extend over narrow congested sidewalks often edged with wares bursting out of open-front shops.

Many buildings have been restored; some now have offices of architects, artists, and other professionals in their former upper-story living quarters and landscaped courtyards in back. But you still experience markets with exotic foods and pungent odors, cluttered drygoods and import stores, lei stands, Chinese noodle factories, bakeries, chop suey houses, and herb shops with the making of centuries-old medicines, a Japanese confectionary and some *okazu-ya* (delicatessens), signs in oriental calligraphy, and people chatting in native tongue. Expect, too, bars, night clubs, pool halls, and other miscellany that inhabit an area that has street people and entertains servicemen on the town.

Tours. Inexpensive guided walking tours of Chinatown start at 9:30 A.M. most weekdays. You'll visit markets, import stores, a Chinese bakery, noodle factory, herb pharmacy-acupuncture center, and temples along Nuuanu Stream. Luncheon is extra and optional. The Hawaii Heritage Center Tour (Monday, Wednesday, Friday) leaves from 1128 Smith Street; the Chinese Chamber of Commerce tour (Tuesday) from 42 North King Street.

Nuuanu Avenue. First Interstate Bank of Hawaii on the corner of King has refurbished the 1914 Hocking Building's classical features and given this branch bank an appropriate old-fashioned interior. For more than a quarter of a century this was the Hotel Hocking, a rooming house, though the bank has occupied the first floor since 1916 when it was founded as Chinese American Bank.

Just *mauka* are restored brick buildings, constructed right after the 1886 fire, sporting decorative cornices, segmental-arch windows, and canopies with a jigsaw-carved fringe. Now The Designers Emporium (1028-1044 Nuuanu), they are home to a courtyard restaurant (Separate Tables), and a local artists' gallery.

Punchbowl Crater's Columbia *watches over final resting place of war dead.*

At Hotel Street, the 1889 Encore Saloon Building and the 1888 Perry Block stand on opposite corners. Both the Perry and the restored 1903 McLean Block next door have dentiled cornices and parapets inscribed with their "vital statistics." Next to McLean is the Pantheon Bar, proclaiming itself to be Honolulu's oldest. Begun in another spot in 1883, the original bar with brass rail and mirror was moved to this building in 1911. Just up the street are two art galleries of note: Pollitt Gallerie, 1139 Nuuanu (Monday through Saturday 10 A.M. to 5 P.M.) and the Pesse Hopper Gallery, 1160A Nuuanu (weekdays 11 A.M. to 5 P.M.). The Liberty Theatre at 1179 Nuuanu, the oldest left in Hawaii, was recently closed. It was built in 1912 for stage performances but later converted into a movie house.

Smith Street. Two Mendonca Buildings face each other at the corner of Smith and Hotel. The one with the red-trimmed arched windows went up in 1913. Its block-long partner (1901) contains an array of enterprises including, on the second floor, The Artisan's Workshop, with stalls for artists and craftsmen overlooking the new green courtyard. Just *mauka* of Mendonca is the 1920 Tan Sing Building with ornate cast plaster carving in its upper-story window arches.

Maunakea Street. At the corner of Pauahi, a colorfully painted, three-story building houses Chinese community groups over the street-level noodle factory. Three of the groups are mutual aid societies formed by early immigrants; they have become perpetuators of traditional social and religious customs. Their meeting rooms contain carved altars, shrines, folk images in bronze and gold leaf, and Chinese carved furniture, often antique. Wo Fat on the corner of Hotel Street is a Chinatown landmark; Honolulu's oldest Chinese cafe, it dates back to 1882, though the present tile-roofed structure with unrestrained interior decor was built in 1936. Across Maunakea stands a typical ensemble of octogenarians.

Protected, reef-filled waters *lure throngs of snorkelers to Hanauma Bay. Remnants of nature's volcanic handiwork outline the state's first underwater conservation park.*

Toothy grins *from wahine and false killer whales greet visitors at Sea Life Park's Whaler's Cove. Performing porpoises and sea birds show off in front of scenic Makapuu Point.*

...Downtown

King Street. The Oahu Market (Monday through Saturday 6 A.M. to 5 P.M.; Sunday 6 A.M. to noon) at King and Kekaulike bristles with shoppers drawn from all over the island by its wide selection of fresh fruits and vegetables, fish, and meat. Here you'll find ethnic favorites not available in supermarkets—red sweet pork and crispy duck, wing beans, pumpkin blossoms, taro and ti leaves, fish fresh from the morning's auction, every variety of local banana, lychees, mangoes, soursops, and cherimoyas in season. The stalls are family businesses, some now third generation; the 22 owners recently formed a corporation, bought the open-walled, iron-roofed, 1904 building, and restored it. "Oahu Market Island Recipes & Shopper's Guide," available inside, gives a history of the market and its families and recipes for foods from the stalls.

Markets and shops of the newest immigrant groups—Vietnamese, Laotian, Samoan—have opened in other rehabilitated buildings on King Street. Catty-corner from Oahu Market is the 1909 brick L. Ah Leong Building; its builder came to Hawaii as a cook and made a fortune in the wholesale-retail business. At King and River streets, two structures form an attractive gateway into Chinatown from Nuuanu Stream: the Armstrong Building, a 1905 bluestone, and the 1904 Chang Building, of exposed lava rock and plastered brick painted light blue and trimmed in red.

Nuuanu Stream. This picturesque watercourse offers a view up Nuuanu Valley to the Pali. Fishermen moor small boats under the arched bridges that connect River Street with College Walk—both largely pedestrian malls. Dotting the malls are arbors with tables for chess, checkers, or *mah jong* and abstract sculptures by E. M. Brownlee. At River and Beretania is a statue of Sun Yat-sen, founder of modern China, who lived and was educated in Hawaii before leading the overthrow of the Manchu dynasty in 1911. Across the bridge on College Walk stands a figure of Jose Rizal, Filipino hero who died in 1896 while leading the Philippines' fight for liberation from Spain.

Old Oahu Railway Station, North King and Iwilei streets. Now the Kalihi-Palama Multi-Service Community Center, its handsome, 1925 Spanish Mission-style porte cochere, arcades, patios, balconies, tile roofs, and four-sided clock tower are all restored. From this depot, trains ran around the island to Kahuku until 1948.

Aala Park. The triangle between North King, North Beretania, and Nuuanu Stream is a neighborhood gathering place. Here retired men play cards and "talk story" under the old banyans and monkeypods; young boys show off with acrobatics on wheels in the skateboard arena; and sumo amateurs wrestle in the *dohyo* (sumo ring) on Sunday afternoons (see "The Sporting Guide," page 27). The park also contains a fountain, bandstand—scene of frequent multiethnic festivities—and stream bank covered with the city's oldest bougainvillea, planted half a century ago.

Along College Walk. At the Beretania end of this mall is Town Square, roofed in striking blue tile and filled with specialty shops and restaurants. Toyo Theatre, 1230 College Walk, is a concern of preservationists now that its days as a cinema have ended. Built in 1938 for Japanese films and stage shows, its style recalls a Japanese shrine. In the entrance court, weathered balustrades surround a Japanese garden; entry and exit walks bridge fish ponds.

Izumo Taishakyo Mission, College Walk and Kukui Street (open all day; service the 10th of each month at 7 P.M.). A typical *torii* and hand-washing basin stand at its entrance; the roof ridge ends with protruding gable boards and barrel. The shrine was built without nails by a carpenter from Japan in 1923 and then moved to this site in 1968. The Taishakyo sect of Shinto, the ancient Japanese religion in which gods represent elements of nature, was started in Hawaii in 1906. On New Year's, from midnight on through the day, thousands line up to make offerings, ring the bell as the priest waves a wand over their head, drink sake, and take home packets of blessed rice.

Along River Street Mall. The low contemporary buildings of Chinatown Cultural Plaza fill a square block beside the stream from Beretania to Kukui streets. The plaza contains small shops, oriental restaurants, fish and produce market, exhibit hall and stage for ethnic shows, and four Chinese societies. At the two Chinese language schools—Sun Yat-sen School at Kukui and River, Mun Lun at 1290 Maunakea Street—you can look in on large groups of children learning Chinese, weekdays from 3:30 to 5 P.M. Lum Sai Ho Tong at River and Kukui (open mornings) is a Taoist temple of the Lum clan (including surnames Lam, Lim, and Lin).

Kwan Yin Temple, 170 North Vineyard Boulevard (open all day). Flamboyant with its green tile roof, red trim, and colorful interior, the temple is dominated by a ten-foot statue of Kwan Yin, Chinese Buddhist goddess of mercy. Worshippers come and go, leave offerings of fruit or flowers, consult a fortune teller, light joss sticks at altars, and burn heavenly money and symbolic paper clothing in incinerators on the terrace.

Foster Botanic Garden, 180 North Vineyard Boulevard (daily 9 A.M. to 4 P.M.; admission fee includes self-guided tour pamphlet or guided tour Monday, Tuesday, Wednesday at 1:30 P.M. by reservation). On 20 acres are excellent collections of palms, orchids, bromeliads, gingers, heliconias, and prehistoric plants; more than a score of the city's protected "exceptional trees" (see page 33); and a nursery with thousands of newly introduced plants. The tropical oasis began in 1855 as the home garden of Dr. William Hillebrand (see "Queen's Medical Center," page 40). It was enlarged by the Thomas Fosters and bequeathed to the city by Mrs. Foster when she died in 1930. A gift shop has books, plant and seed packets cleared for mainland entry, and plant-related handicrafts.

The Pacific Club, 1451 Queen Emma Street. The venerable businessmen's club organized in 1851 has deferred to the times and, since 1984, admits women. The handsome contemporary building and lush gardens occupy the former estate of Archibald Cleghorn, father of Princess Kaiulani.

On the *Ewa* side of Nuuanu Stream are the old districts of Palama, Kapalama, and Kalihi, a mix of humble dwellings and small businesses and industries, and above them, residential Alewa Heights, Kapalama Heights, and Kalihi Valley. Farther out are vast new industrial and housing tracts and big military bases. Several routes to the airport, Pearl Harbor, and beyond cross this side of the city and open up some worthwhile sightseeing.

If you want to do a lot of stopping, drive on North King Street or North School Street, or near the sea on Nimitz Highway (92) or Dillingham Boulevard, which becomes Kamehameha Highway and merges with Nimitz at Keehi Lagoon. Highway 92 then travels under H-1 Freeway past Honolulu International Airport to Nimitz Gate at Pearl Harbor Naval Base. Kamehameha Highway continues (as Highway 99) past the entrance to the Arizona Memorial museum and boat dock (see page 62) and around Pearl Harbor.

H-1 Freeway has several off-ramps into the old districts and exits to the airport, Hickam Air Force Base, Nimitz Gate, and Kamehameha Highway where it starts around Pearl Harbor. From where H-1 turns *makai* at Middle Street, you can continue on an inland route on freewaylike Moanalua Road (78) which intersects with H-1 and Kamehameha Highway near Aloha Stadium.

Dole Cannery Square, 650 Iwilei Road. The cannery, topped by a pineapple-shaped water tower, offers continuous factory tours including a multimedia slide show, pineapple juice sampling, and the chance to see pineapple being processed. Pineapple posters and antique labels decorate the square's shopping/dining mall.

Sand Island. Manmade protection for Honolulu Harbor, Sand Island houses busy industrial yards, coast guard bases, and unoccupied oceanfront spots popular for camping and fishing. Sand Island State Recreation Area covers 85 acres on the tip of the island, offering picnic areas, fine views of the city waterfront, and play places in old military structures.

Honolulu International Airport. Lei stands line the approach roads to the terminal, their fresh flower offerings providing the perfect aloha to travelers. The open-air terminal, with eating spots and a variety of shops, overlooks Chinese, Japanese, and Hawaiian gardens; the information centers offer guides to commissioned works of art scattered throughout the main lobbies and central concourse. *Wikiwiki* buses provide free shuttle service between the main and interisland terminals. In the central concourse is the Pacific Aerospace Museum, with aeronautical exhibits and a theater.

Hickam Air Force Base. Adjacent to Honolulu International Airport is the chief military airfield in the Pacific. Its octagonal water tower, a local landmark, rises 171 feet.

Bishop Museum, 1525 Bernice Street (Monday through Saturday and first Sunday of the month; admission fee).

This outstanding museum was founded in 1889 by Charles Bishop in memory of his wife, Princess Bernice Pauahi Bishop, last member of the Kamehameha dynasty. In the three-story Hawaiian Hall, images of ancient gods guard exhibits on Hawaii's peoples and cultures to 1900—everything from feather capes and royal jewels to Chinese ivory carvings and a missionary's diary. Polynesian Hall exhibits concentrate on Pacific Basin cultural history.

Recent additions include the Atherton Halau, where a daily music and dance performance augments the displays and demonstrations of Hawaiian arts and crafts (9 A.M. to 3 P.M.), and Ululani Jabulka Pavilion, the museum entrance, a gift and book shop, and restaurant. Other exhibits are found in the Hall of Hawaiian Natural History, the Hall of Discovery, and the Shell Room. The Planetarium operated by the museum has shows twice daily and on Friday and Saturday evenings.

Kamehameha Schools campus. Occupying 618 acres on Kapalama Heights, these prestigious schools for boys and girls of Hawaiian blood were founded in 1887 as the sole beneficiary of the estate of Princess Bernice Pauahi Bishop. You can pick up a map at the main entrance.

Moanalua Gardens. On Moanalua Road at the Tripler off ramp, this private estate with magnificent monkeypod trees, two streams, carp pond, and taro patch is open to the public for picnics and strolls. Notice two historic buildings moved here from a nearby site: the Victorian gingerbread cottage built as a summer house by Kamehameha V, and Chinese Hall, a party pavilion.

Tripler Army Medical Center. Built by the army in 1948 and used by all the services, Tripler is the world's largest military hospital. Its 560-bed capacity can be expanded to 1,500 during emergencies. The sprawling pink buildings are a mountainside landmark.

Temples and churches. Scattered throughout this district are temples and churches reflecting the diversity of Hawaii's religious organizations. Among them are the Korean Christian Church, 1832 Liliha Street (English-Korean services); Higashi Hongwanji Temple, 1685 Alaneo Street (Buddhist); Kaumakapili Church, 766 North King Street (Hawaiian hymns); and Kotohira Jinsha, 1045 Kama Lane (one of Oahu's four Shinto shrines).

Fascinating food stops. This area is dotted with small businesses and shops. Two of particular interest are located on North King Street.

Nisshodo Candy Store, 425 North King Street (Monday through Saturday 7 A.M. to 4 P.M.; Sunday 7 to 11 A.M.). This 70-year-old family enterprise manufactures Japanese rice and wheat flour confections (*mochi, manju, chi chi dango*) sold throughout Oahu and available here.

Tamashiro Market, 802 North King Street (Monday through Saturday 9 A.M. to 6 P.M.; Sunday 9:15 A.M. to 4 P.M.). Hawaii's largest retail fish market sells all fish and shellfish caught in local waters, many of them still live.

Two boulevards run from the downtown area to Waikiki: Ala Moana near the waterfront and Kapiolani several blocks inland. King and Beretania, two of downtown's parallel one-way streets, connect with Kalakaua Avenue at its *Ewa* end (King traffic moves toward Waikiki, Beretania toward downtown), and King Street and Kapiolani Boulevard meet in the Capital District.

The Kakaako District

From the Capital District to Ala Moana Center and the sea to Kapiolani Boulevard is Kakaako (*Waikiki* of Ward Avenue, strictly speaking, is Kewalo). It's a district of narrow, traffic-clogged streets shaded here and there by an aged mango tree; of auto repair shops, mom and pop groceries, hole-in-the-wall cafes, lunch wagons, fishing supply stores, antique dealers, and all sorts of other small businesses and industries.

There is much to see and visit. The Contemporary Arts Center of Hawaii, News Building, 605 Kapiolani Boulevard, exhibits new work of artists with an island connection. Kamaka Hawaii, 550 South Street (tours by arrangement) is Hawaii's only ukulele factory, in business since 1916. Blair, Ltd., 404A Ward Avenue, manufactures serving pieces, furniture, and decorative articles from local woods. Ala Moana Farmers Market, 1020 Auahi Street, includes about a dozen wholesalers and retailers of fruit and produce, fish, and Hawaiian and oriental food favorites. Eurasian Antiques, a warehouse with a mix of treasures, Indich Collection with oriental rugs, and Jade East, Ltd. with antique jade and Chinese porcelain, are all at 1108 Auahi Street.

Along Ala Moana

In this area you'll find a shopping complex, harbor, and an expansive ocean-front playground.

Ward Warehouse and Ward Centre. Between Ala Moana and Auahi and opposite Kewalo Basin, are low-rise complexes with shops, arts and crafts galleries, and a concentration of specialty restaurants to rival Waikiki's. Ward Warehouse was built of rough-sawn lumber to resemble a wharfside marketplace; Ward Centre has stucco buildings and two tiled interior malls.

Kewalo Basin. You'll find a jam of boats for sport-fishing charter, diving, glass-bottom and Pearl Harbor tours, and dinner cruises. Sampans and other commercial fishing craft unload for the fish auction (see page 26). It is held on the *Ewa* side of the basin, where you'll also find Fisherman's Wharf and John Dominis' seafood restaurants and access to Point Panic surfing grounds (take Ahui Street off Ala Moana).

Ala Moana Park. On the *Diamond Head* side of the harbor is a 76-acre expanse of grass, tree-shaded arbors, ponds, and a long sand beach bordering a swimming lagoon. This ocean-front playground is well used. On a typical weekend, you'll find park-goers participating in picnics, softball, lawn bowling, tennis, jogging, canoe paddling, fishing, or just sun-bathing. McCoy Pavilion includes a Balinese style courtyard with Indian banyans and reflecting pools.

Magic Island. Jutting out near the *Waikiki* end of Ala Moana Park is this landscaped, 32-acre, manmade peninsula completed in 1972 with a beach that continues as a seaward curve from Ala Moana's and a lagoon protected by a rock breakwater used by fishermen and surfing spectators.

Ala Moana Center. This enormous "shopping city," bordered by Ala Moana and Kapiolani boulevards, Piikoi Street, and Atkinson Drive, is a place to browse, shop, eat, and people-watch. Several levels contain a fantastic variety of shops; more than 150 stores and restaurants (with almost 8,000 parking stalls) make it one of the world's largest. Restaurants here feature an intriguing assortment of oriental and occidental foods. Malls display the works of some of the state's most famous artists; colorful carp (*koi*) share ponds with fanciful sculptures.

Between Kapiolani and H-1 Freeway

You'll discover Honolulu cultural centers (symphony and opera, and arts) in this region.

Neal S. Blaisdell Center, along Ward Avenue between Kapiolani Boulevard and South King Street, consists of a 2,158-seat concert hall, exhibition and assembly rooms, and a large sports arena in a park-like setting with coconut palms, lawns, and a large fishpond. The concert hall is the home of Honolulu's symphony and opera (see page 26) and is used by various performing groups.

Thomas Square, outlined by Ward Avenue and South Beretania, Victoria, and South King streets, has a central fountain and four Indian banyans, a bordering hedge, carpet of grass, and other large trees. The park honors British Admiral Richard Thomas who restored Hawaii's independence in 1843 a few months after a lower-ranking officer had unofficially seized the Islands for the Empire from King Kamehameha III.

Honolulu Academy of Arts, 900 South Beretania Street (Tuesday through Saturday, 10 A.M. to 4:30 P.M.; Sunday, 1 to 5 P.M.; free; a walk-in tour is given each day; check for time). A treasure of a building as well as a museum, the Academy has thick textured masonry walls, sloping tile roof with broad eaves, columned lanai and loggias, and many galleries opening to handsome courtyards.

The museum is noted for its Asian art pieces, has a part of the Kress Collection of Italian Renaissance paintings, shows good local work and changing, often traveling, exhibitions. Additions to the 1927 building include the Clare Boothe Luce Wing (with contemporary art)

Colorful Byodo-in Temple *occupies striking setting against backdrop of fluted cliffs in Ahuimanu Valley.*

overlooking a sculpture garden and the Academy Theatre for films, concerts, and lectures (usually admission fee). The Academy has a shop and a popular Garden Cafe.

Kapiolani's business district, between Ala Moana Center, South King Street, and Kalakaua Avenue, is a clutter of stores, offices, apartments, restaurants, and oriental-style hostess lounges, art galleries, and antique shops.

Many interesting churches and temples lie along or just off the main streets between downtown and Waikiki.

Honolulu's Heights and Valleys

Mauka of H-1 Freeway are heights and valleys with many fine homes that overlook the central city. To see them, pick up a city map and drive the roads up to the heights named Alewa, Pacific, Makiki, Tantalus-Round Top, St. Louis, and Maunalani, and explore the valleys in between. You'll encounter interesting places:

Liliuokalani Garden, with entrances at the end of Waikahalulu Lane off North School Street and Kuakini Street, is a five-acre natural park on the banks of Nuuanu Stream with a large swimming hole fed by forceful Waikahulu Falls; it's a picnicker's delight.

Nuuanu—churches, temples, consulates. The built-up part of this valley you drive through on the way to Nuuanu Pali and Windward Oahu has become a "church row" and center for consulates and other institutions, some using former grand residences. Royal Mausoleum, 2261 Nuuanu Avenue, is the burial ground of the Kamehameha and Kalakaua dynasties.

Queen Emma Summer Palace, 2913 Pali Highway (daily 9 A.M. to 4 P.M.; admission fee). This mid-nineteenth century white frame house with classical features became Queen Emma's retreat after she was widowed in 1863 and is furnished with her possessions.

Tantalus is the city's highest, coolest residential section (its summit is 2,013 feet). Homes here are almost hidden in magnificent rain forest. On a loop that combines Tantalus Drive and Round Top Drive you climb to 1,600 feet, pass view turnouts and the beginnings of many of the easy hiking trails in Tantalus State Recreation Area. The park's Puu Ualakaa unit, off Round Top Drive, has a picnic ground and spectacular views.

National Memorial Cemetery of the Pacific, Puowaina Drive, spreads over the vast bowl of Punchbowl Crater, which Hawaiians called Puowaina (Hill of Sacrifice). Tablets in seemingly endless rows mark more than 30,000 graves of war dead from World Wars I and II, the Korean War, the Vietnam War, and members of their families. A massive monument, "Courts of the Missing," gives the names of 28,745 missing servicemen on marble slabs leading up to a 30-foot statue of Columbia, that represents a mother looking over her lost children.

Punahou School, 1601 Punahou Street, was founded in 1841 for children of missionaries and is now one of the nation's largest college preparatory schools. Its buildings range from the coral stone Old School Hall (1852) to a contemporary chapel built out over a lily pond.

Paradise Park, 3737 Manoa Road (daily 10 A.M. to 4 P.M.; fee includes admission to the park and shuttle bus from Waikiki). In this luxuriant 15-acre garden you walk down a ramp past scores of exotic birds living in one of the world's largest free-flight aviaries, take a boardwalk through a jungle of *hau* trees, visit a flamingo pond and five ethnic home-size gardens. A trained bird show, "dancing waters" show, Hawaiian crafts demonstrations, and carp feedings go on in succession through the day.

Lyon Arboretum, 3860 Manoa Road, includes 124 acres of tropical trees and shrubs (4,000 species) and is a University of Hawaii teaching-research ground. You can walk through on your own or make reservations for a guided tour given periodically.

Mid-Pacific Institute, 2445 Kaala Street, a residential secondary school, occupies a 34-acre campus overlooking the University of Hawaii. Note Kawaiahao Hall, the original building (1908) of local lava stone; Juliette May Fraser's 92-foot mosaic mural on the auditorium facade; the outstanding rainbow shower tree.

University of Hawaii, lower Manoa Valley, has more than 20,000 students and a faculty of 2,100. It excels in geophysics, tropical agriculture, ocean engineering, Asian and Pacific studies, travel industry management, biomedical sciences, astronomy, and art. Columned entrances grace the original quadrangle buildings, of which Hawaii Hall was the first (1912). A public gallery in the Art Building (Monday through Friday 8 A.M. to 4 P.M.) features faculty and student art. For self-touring information, see page 26.

East-West Center, 1777 East-West Road, was established in 1960 to promote cultural and technical interchange among peoples of Asia, the Pacific, and the U.S.A. Students come from some 40 countries and territories.

St. Louis-Chaminade Education Center, 3140 Waialae Avenue, includes a picturesque cluster of Spanish Mission-inspired buildings that dates from 1928–1929 when an early Roman Catholic boys' school, St. Louis, re-established its campus here. The Administration Building serves two schools. To the left are the main buildings of St. Louis (with 1,200 boys, grades 7 through 12) and to the right, the halls of coeducational Chaminade University which has more than 2,400 students.

Waahila Ridge State Recreation Area, at the end of Ruth Place atop St. Louis Heights, is a 45-acre park in a setting of Norfolk pines and other trees, with hiking trails, picnic tables, and group camp shelters.

TO OAHU'S EAST END

The city extends out to Makapuu, Oahu's easternmost point, and it's citylike all the way to Koko Head and Koko Crater as Honolulu's newer residential districts cover ridges, valleys, peninsulas, and shoreline along the way. For a scenic route between Waikiki and East Honolulu's main artery, Kalanianaole Highway (72), take Kalakaua Avenue, then Diamond Head Road along the coast and go through Kahala.

Kahala

Kahala Avenue, which starts from where Diamond Head Road turns inland, is shaded by splendid trees and lush shrubbery and lined with fine homes—some that are truly luxurious along the ocean front. It ends at the Kahala Hilton, handsome indeed with bougainvillea cascading over the balconies of its ten stories. You can guide yourself about using a walking tour folder available at the desk. Three chandeliers in the hotel's elegant, airy lobby contain 28,000 pieces of colored glass.

Dolphins, penguins, and turtles swim in the lagoon and its feeder streams, and you can watch them being fed at 11 A.M. and 2 and 4 P.M. each day. An antique shop, Bernard Hurtig's Oriental Treasures & Points West, carries fine quality pieces and outstanding *netsuke*, Japanese ornamental toggles.

Kealaolu Avenue will take you from Kahala Avenue to Kalanianaole Highway, along the hibiscus border of Waialae Country Club's links. But first have a look at the rest of Kahala and Kahala Mall, its big shopping center. Take one of the roads to the left from Kealaolu over to Makaiwa Street or Pueo Street and follow it inland to Kilauea Avenue which passes the mall (you can wind about on other streets, but make Kilauea your goal). Kahala Mall has department stores, supermarkets, popular restaurants, and some fine boutiques and gift shops,

many opening to its air-conditioned mall. Notice The Following Sea with exquisite crafts by American and island artists.

Koko Head and Koko Crater

Waialae Avenue, along one side of the mall, moves *Koko Head* right into Highway 72 which, with Koolau ridges and valleys to your left (many with houses) and alternating neighborhood and ocean views to the right, will convey you to Hawaii Kai. This vast development of houses, townhouses, high-rises, two golf courses, and shopping centers spreads over 6,000 acres of Koko Head and Koko Crater foothills, adjacent valleys, and Kuapa Pond (an ancient, 523-acre fishpond, now Hawaii Kai Marina).

The volcanic peak and crater are the centers of Koko Head Regional Park, consisting of natural areas, Hanauma Bay and Sandy Beach parks, and scenic lookouts. Koko Head rises to 642 feet, Koko Crater to 1,208 feet.

On the crest of Koko Head is a side road that leads to the parking area above sparkling, coconut-palm-fringed Hanauma Bay. Paths wind steeply down to the beach park (crowded on weekends). Trails along rock ledges about a foot above the sea go from the wide beach along both sides of the bay almost to the headlands, past tide pools and incredible rock formations. High tides and heavy surf can sweep across the ledges, so use caution.

Along the east shore, you scramble through an arch eroded by sea and wind from an old lava flow and end up at Toilet Bowl, a small cove named for the way incoming waves raise and lower its water level.

The bay is one in a line of craters formed during Oahu's last eruption. Over centuries, the elements opened it to the sea. Because of its great clarity and extensive underwater life, it has been made a marine preserve.

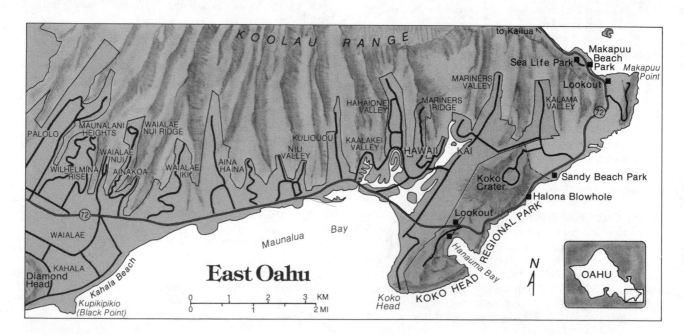

East Oahu

THE PERFECT WAVE

Though the origins of surfing are lost in prehistory, the ancient Hawaiians developed the sport to a degree unmatched anywhere in the world.

After surfing caught the imagination of *haoles* in the beginning of the 20th century, a drawback for many would-be surfers was the weight of the board (100 to 150 pounds); only the strong could surf. Experiments with reducing board weight began; the mid-1940s witnessed the birth of the modern board made of fiberglass covered with balsa. The front was scooped out and the skeg, a vertical "fin" that provides stability, was added.

Surfboards continued to evolve; modern boards have a foam core covered with fiberglass. Boards are now designed to suit every purpose, from learning on the gentle swells of south shore beaches to riding the big waves at the Banzai Pipeline. One common variation is the *paipo* board, or body board.

Surfers flock to Hawaii for the waves. With no continental shelf to slow down the swells, the velocity of a wave moving toward the beach is considerably greater in Hawaii than on the mainland. When these fast-moving swells come out of deep water and hit the shallow coral reefs, the result is an explosive wave, filled with unleashed power.

Surfers describe both the parts of the waves and the waves themselves. When speaking of the *lip*, they're referring to the leading edge of the breaking part of a wave. The *curl* is the lip of a wave when it's falling in an arc. A *hollow* wave is one in which the lip pitches out, creating a tube (a hollow curling wave or section of a wave). A *peeling* wave breaks with the curl moving across it diagonally.

The ideal shape the surfer looks for is a hollow, peeling wave. This type of wave breaks with the lip pitching out, hitting the flat water in front of the wave, and peeling left or right in a somewhat consistent manner. The place to ride is just in front of the falling lip, scribing a diagonal as the wave moves toward the beach.

No matter how many advances are made in equipment, in the end it's the wave that matters—the wave that hurls the surfer either toward the shore or under the water. Just as 15th century chiefs did, the surfer in Hawaii today waits in the water, hoping the next swell will be "the perfect wave."

Sandy swimming channels have been blasted out of the coral bottom, a favorite haunt of snorkelers. Note the coloring of the water: emerald green in the channels, purplish over coral, and deep blue beyond the reef.

Between Koko Head and Halona Blow Hole, the road snakes through a series of stratified cliffs of volcanic tuff—hardened remains of explosive showers of ash and mud once thrown out by Koko Crater and smaller vents.

From the highway, turn off to the lookout terrace above Halona Blow Hole. When waves are big, a geyser shoots up through a hole in the ceiling of a submerged lava tube. From the opposite side of the parking area, you look down upon Halona Cove, a narrow inlet between sheer cliffs with a nice beach for picnics.

Sandy Beach Park is a popular picnic and body surfing spot, but these waters are best left to experts as the very strong shore break (and resulting undertow) can be extremely dangerous.

Makapuu and Sea Life Park

The highway passes a fine windward overlook above Makapuu Beach Park, famous for its body surfing. Like neighboring Sandy Beach, Makapuu's waves and currents can be very strong. Flags advise beachgoers—red for very dangerous conditions, green for safe, and yellow for moderately rough. If you're unsure about water safety, try the surf at sheltered Kaupo Beach Park or sandy, calmer shores at Waimanalo.

Offshore is Manana Island, better known as Rabbit Island for the descendants of European hares taken there by a sugar planter in the 1880s. They live compatibly with shearwaters, noddies, and terns.

Sea Life Park. Opposite Makapuu, this fascinating park (open daily 9:30 A.M. to 5 P.M., to 10 P.M. on Thursday, Friday, and Sunday; admission fee), is home to one of the greatest varieties of marine life on exhibit. Numerous shows star dolphins, penguins, sea lions, and whales. Trained dolphins and whales engage in a wider range of activities here than they do elsewhere in captivity. The 300,000-gallon Hawaiian Reef Tank has more than 2,000 species of marine life. Take the spiral ramp from the rim to three fathoms beneath the surface for an underwater view through large acrylic windows. The Rocky Shores exhibit includes a "wave zone," whose manmade black rock shelters are washed every 90 seconds by 600 gallons of seawater, and shallow tidepools, home to sea cucumbers, feather duster worms, and cowries. Other sections to visit are the Turtle Lagoon, where the endangered green sea turtle is bred; Sea Lion Feeding Pool, where you can buy fish the animals will jump up and take from your hand; Kaupo Falls, an arborarium with indigenous plants and island waterfowl; and Seabird Sanctuary, with a breeding, nesting colony of free-flying marine birds.

Just outside the entrance are a restaurant, gift shop, and the Pacific Whaling Museum (free) displaying one of the Pacific's most extensive private collections of whaling artifacts.

Depending on how much time and driving you want to devote to sightseeing, there's a loop trip from Honolulu to the windward side and back to fit your schedule. The shortest route to the north face of the Koolau Range is by way of Waimanalo, leaving Honolulu via Highway 72 and returning on Highway 61 (or Highway 63), or vice versa. For a longer loop, cross the Koolau mountains, then go northward up the Windward Coast, along the North Shore, and back over the Central Plateau.

Crossing the Pali

To make the big circle trip you can leave the city on either of two highways that cut across the rugged Koolau Range, Oahu's 37-mile-long (59-km) eastern spine. One route, Pali Highway (61), not only leads to Nuuanu Pali Lookout, a foremost scenic attraction, but it passes through a pair of tunnels beneath this natural break in the *pali* (a line of nearly vertical cliffs) and continues as Highway 61 through Maunawili Valley to Kailua. On its windward descent it intersects with Kamehameha Highway (83), which goes north past Pali Golf Course and Hawaii Loa College to Kaneohe, and with Highway 72 from the east.

The second route, Likelike Highway (63), conquers the Koolaus with the Wilson Tunnel and passes through banana groves at the windward base of the mountains before veering *makai*. On the windward side you can turn north onto Kahekili Highway (83), an inland drive that by-passes Kaneohe and joins coastal Kamehameha Highway in Kahaluu (the route continues north as 83). This is a convenient route if you're planning to visit Haiku Gardens or Byodo-In Temple. Or you can stay on Highway 63 until it intersects with Kamehameha Highway and go north through Kaneohe's downtown and past Heeia fishpond and park. Both cross-island highways intersect with H-1 Freeway in Honolulu.

Nuuanu Pali Lookout. Marking the center of Nuuanu Pali State Wayside, Pali Lookout lies at the end of a right-hand spur road off Pali Highway, 6½ miles/10½ km from downtown. On the way, you can get a more intimate view of Nuuanu Valley's rain forest by turning off and taking the two remaining stretches of two-lane, winding Nuuanu Pali Drive (they're well-marked and return you to the highway).

From the concrete viewing platform at the lookout, a breathtaking view confronts you—usually accompanied by great blasts of chilly wind. From the 1,186-foot-high site, your eye follows the fluted palisades for several miles northwest to Mokolii Island and then travels back to Mokapu Peninsula at the opposite end of Kaneohe Bay.

The lookout also conjures up a vista for your mind's eye. In the spring of 1795, the army of Kamehameha the Great landed on Oahu's southern shore, battling the island's defenders up the Nuuanu Valley to the pali where many fell or jumped to their deaths.

The abandoned old pali road, which you see below the lookout, was a Hawaiian footpath. Improved for a horse trail in 1845, it was later widened for carriages and then for cars. A footpath goes underneath the highway to Auloa Road.

The descent from the pali opens up new vistas, including a view of 1,643-foot Olomana Peak (a green Matterhorn), highest point on the ridge between Maunawili and Waimanalo and a favorite subject for local artists.

Ho'omaluhia. Part of the sweep of green you gaze upon from Pali Lookout is Ho'omaluhia (Thursday through Monday, 9 A.M. to 3 P.M.), a 400-acre botanic garden between Pali Golf Course and Likelike Highway. The entrance is at the end of Luluku Road off Kamehameha Highway; it's also accessible via Anoi Road off Likelike Highway to Luluku. The garden has a 32-acre lake, five camping areas, and several miles of trails. You can pick up a map at the visitor center. Guided walks are given on weekends, by reservation; call 235-6636.

The Waimanalo Plain

If you've come around the island's east end, you'll start up the Windward Coast at Waimanalo, guarded by the fortresslike cliffs of the southern Koolau Range. The Waimanalo Plain is a roughly triangular area beginning as a narrow coastal strip near Makapuu and gradually broadening towards Olomana Peak and the Lanikai shoreline.

The coast here is flat, with long strips of attractive sandy beach, a few rocky areas frequented by fishermen, and houses strung out over several miles. Parks along scenic Waimanalo Bay offer good beachcombing, surfcasting, board and body surfing, swimming, and snorkeling. Kaiona Beach Park also affords access to a remnant of early aquaculture—a rock-walled holding pond that probably once held turtles for exclusive consumption by a local chief.

Mostly planted in sugarcane until 1947, much of Waimanalo's land is now used to raise fruit, vegetables, flowers, horses, and cattle.

Waimanalo's modern lava-and-sandstone Catholic church, on the *makai* side of Kalanianaole (across the street from Waimanalo Elementary and Intermediate School), has a mosaic of its patron, St. George, over the door; sculptures, a mural, and frescoes, mostly by community members, ornament the interior.

Bellows Field Beach Park (access from Tinker Road). Popular for board and body surfing, swimming, surfcasting, and strolling, the 46 acres of coral sand, coconut palms, and ironwoods are open from Friday noon to midnight Sunday for camping, and weekends and national holidays for swimming and picnicking (see page 69 for details about permits).

Past the park turnoff, Highway 72 continues northwest before forming a junction with Kailua Road/Highway 61, which meets Pali Highway. The road provides fine views as it cuts east to Kailua through verdant foothills.

Lone boat *navigates waters of Kaneohe Bay. Kamehameha Highway provides scenic route between bay and encircling cliffs, links small towns of coastal plain.*

Pageantry enlivens daily events *at Laie's Polynesian Cultural Center. University students entertain with traditions from their native homelands.*

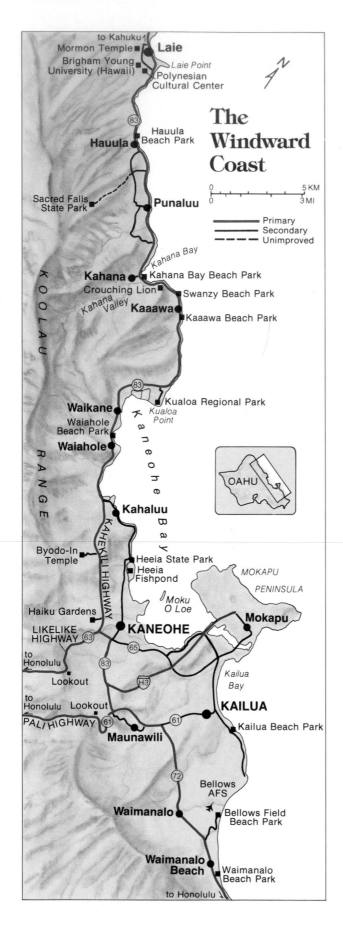

Kailua and Kaneohe

Neighboring Kailua and Kaneohe are the twin population centers of Windward Oahu. Elsewhere on this coast, small settlements and beach parks cluster alongside photogenic bays, and farms and pastures reach deep into lush valleys. Highway 83 strings these scenic pearls together en route to the North Shore.

Kailua now has high-rises and shopping centers on the fringes of its "small town" main streets. It also contains extremes of the architectural spectrum, juxtaposing an ancient temple with contemporary churches. Along Kailua Road's "church row" above town, turn off into the Windward YMCA parking area and visit Ulu Po Heiau. This temple, a state historic site, was probably built by captured warriors, but legend attributes it to *menehune*, the construction-minded little people. Walk the stone path across the huge platform and down the far side to a rock well at the edge of Kawainui Marsh, a moist, green bowl of 750 acres to be dredged and made into a park.

St. Anthony's, Kailua's largest church (114 Makawao Street), is shaped like a cross, has four patios and a massive red copper roof. Its impressive handwork includes pews made by Trappist monks and stained glass abstracts by Erica Karawina.

Kailua Bay has a sandy shoreline of several miles, from Lanikai to Mokapu Peninsula. It is lined with homes, but frequent rights of way provide beach access. Off Lanikai Beach, served by Mokulua Drive, are the Mokulua Islands seabird sanctuaries; the one shaped like a camel's back has a fine beach. Kailua Beach Park, at the ends of Kailua Road and South Kalaheo Avenue, is splendid, has Popoia (Flat) Island offshore, reachable by many swimmers. Kalama Beach Park, farther north along Kalaheo Avenue, is a favorite of body surfers.

Mokapu Peninsula, occupied by Kaneohe Marine Corps Air Station, juts out between Kailua and Kaneohe bays. It's separated from the rest of the island by two fishponds. Off the peninsula's Ulupau Crater tip is Moku Manu (Bird Island), a refuge for terns, boobies, and man-of-war birds.

Along Kaneohe Bay

Kaneohe Bay Drive continues from North Kalaheo Avenue and winds close to the shoreline of Kaneohe Bay out to the junctions of Kamehameha and Likelike highways. It offers many views of the bay as it passes Kaneohe Yacht Club, the YWCA's Camp Kokokahi, Bay View Golf Center, hillside homes, and homes with boat piers.

Kaneohe Bay is huge—8 miles/13 km long—and home for numerous recreational craft. In the south end is Moku O Loe (Coconut Island), a once luxurious private estate now partly the University of Hawaii's Hawaii Institute of Marine Biology. The bay's formerly extensive marine habitats have been greatly reduced by pollution largely from silty freshwater runoff.

Kamehameha Highway takes you past Heeia Fishpond, an ancient 88-acre fish pen with a 5,000-foot wall. Drive up on Kealohi Point in Heeia State Park for magnificent views of it against a mountainous backdrop. Glass bottom boats leave Heeia Kea Boat Harbor just north of the park to cruise over sections of an offshore coral reef.

On the Inland Road

To reach photogenic Haiku Gardens and Byodo-In Temple take Kahekili Highway (83). The gardens, a jungled estate at 46-336 Haiku Road (left turn off the highway), include a restaurant that overlooks grass houses, lily ponds, and bamboo groves.

Byodo-In Temple is the main feature of the Valley of the Temples, a memorial park in Ahuimanu Valley. A replica in concrete of Kyoto's classic Byodo-In Temple, it occupies a spectacular setting between the majestic pali and a reflecting lake enlivened by hundreds of colorful carp. (Daily 9 A.M. to 4:30 P.M.; admission fee.)

To Kahuku

Kamehameha Highway follows the shoreline closely all the way to Kahuku at the north end of the island. It passes a string of beach parks (crowded on weekends), beach cottages, modest motels or cottage resorts, a few restaurants, and some large condominiums.

Farms dot the Waiahole and Waikane valleys. Most of Oahu's sweet potatoes and almost a third of its papayas come from this area, which also produces bananas, beans, cucumbers, taro, and flowers. Scattered along the way are fruit and vegetable stands and a few souvenir stalls.

To the north, Kaneohe Bay ends at Kualoa Point, part of Kualoa Regional Park. Listed on the National Register of Historical Places, the area that includes the park was considered one of Oahu's most sacred. The point affords access to Apua and Molii fishponds (the latter is still used commercially) and a view of Mokolii (Little Dragon) Island (also known as Chinaman's Hat), all components of the park. Just beyond Kualoa Point, you'll pass the ruins of a sugar mill that ground its last crop more than a century ago.

The rock formation on the cliff north of Makaua Beach Park is known as the Crouching Lion. Supposedly, a legendary god worked as a watchman until he was so covered by vegetation he got stuck in a crouching position trying to free himself and was later turned to stone in the shape of a lion. Thus, the name of the big rock house-turned-restaurant below the cliff.

The road swings inland around magnificent Kahana Bay at the mouth of lush Kahana Valley, a 5,300-acre state park with a 5-mile/8-km trail that crosses a stream. From the beach park, shaded by false kamani and ironwoods, you can look across the water to the overgrown stone wall of Huilua, Oahu's oldest fishpond and a national historic landmark, set beneath pandanus-laden cliffs at the south end of the bay.

At Hauula, a marker points the way to Sacred Falls, which drop 80 feet from a 50-foot-wide gorge at the head of Kaliuwaa Valley. The falls form a deep swimming hole contained on three sides by plummeting, foliage-covered cliffs; it's a 2-mile/3-km walk from the parking area near the highway. Don't attempt the walk in bad weather; the last mile can be muddy. Hauula's expansive beach park has a large, walled-in swimming area. Visit charming Hauula Congregational Church and the ruins of large Lanakila Church, built in 1862 of local coral and timber.

Laie is largely a settlement of Hawaiian and other Polynesian Mormons. About 6,000 mountain-to-sea acres have been a church development project since 1864. They include the town, the impressive Polynesian Cultural Center, a lodge and restaurant, the campus of Brigham Young University-Hawaii, and the landmark Mormon Temple, set off by a formal garden. The Visitor Center is open daily from 9 A.M. to 8 P.M.

Polynesian Cultural Center

Condensing the vast span of Polynesia into walking distances, the Polynesian Cultural Center (open Monday through Saturday; admission fee) re-creates villages of Samoa, Tonga, Hawaii, Tahiti, Fiji, the Marquesas, and Maori New Zealand. Dedicated to preserving the cultural heritage of Polynesia, the center provides jobs and scholarships for students at the adjoining Brigham Young University branch campus.

You can tour the center on foot or in double-hulled outrigger canoes. Activities include a band concert, canoe pageant, festival of dances and songs of all groups, a Polynesian buffet, and in the evening the center's dramatic "This Is Polynesia" revue performed on an open air stage with a cliff backdrop and fountains for a curtain. Several different ticket packages are available.

At the daytime session (11 A.M. to 6 P.M.), luncheon is served from 11:15 A.M. to 12:30 P.M. and the main show starts at 1 P.M. Second session hours are 2 to 9 P.M. with dinner from 4:30 to 7 P.M. and the show at 7:30 P.M. Show reservations are required.

The center's villages are situated along the banks of a lagoon. At each you'll learn about the dwellings and culture and see—and even join in—demonstrations of crafts, songs, and dances. Attractions include a replica of a missionary settlement, scene of Hawaiian quilt demonstrations, and a typical plantation store. The center has a snack bar and a crafts shop.

North of the BYU-H campus (just before the Laie Shopping Center) you'll notice a Hawaii Visitors Bureau warrior marker for nearby windswept, sea-battered Laie Point. The promontory offers views of the coast and two adjacent islands; the ocean surging through the hole in one of these islands adds to the drama of this "land's end" lookout.

Just north is the state's large and lovely beach park on Malaekahana Bay with fine swimming and lawns and woods for picnicking and camping (see page 69).

Like pink islands *in a sea of green, crownlike water lilies grace pool in Waimea Falls Park. Unspoiled preserve is setting for refreshing waterfall, picnicking, hiking.*

Windward Oahu resident *presents impromptu serenade outside charming church near Hauula.*

THE NORTH SHORE

Kahuku, the fertile plain across Oahu's north tip, has changed from sugar plantation to resort area with smaller-scale agriculture. Since the plantation's final harvest in 1971, some of the acreage has been replanted with feed and truck crops. At the heart of this plain is the former sugar mill town of Kahuku whose residents are restoring the picturesque houses set among tidy colorful gardens. Many people now work up the highway at the Turtle Bay Hilton and Country Club.

On your way to the Turtle Bay resort area, you'll pass other newcomers to the North Shore—prawn ponds, windmills pumping water and generating electricity, and open markets selling the harvest of ponds and fields. The Turtle Bay development includes a large hotel, cottages, cabanas, an 18-hole golf course, riding stables, and lighted tennis courts. Next to the hotel and along the highway are two condominium villages.

Sunset Beach: Surf, Stables, and Satellites

The coast from Kawela to Waimea Bay has big winter surf (for seasoned experts only), including the famous Banzai Pipeline. Just to look at Sunset Beach waves when they run as high as 30 feet is a thrill. However, don't get more involved than being a spectator; even the currents of water swirling on the beach are too strong from about October to April.

On the *mauka* side of the highway near the beach, you'll pass the Waialee Livestock Research Farm, operated by the University of Hawaii. In the Paumalu section, you'll see Comsat—largest, most versatile earthstation for international commercial satellite transmissions; one dish antenna is 10 stories tall. Call a day in advance to visit on weekdays. To reach the facility, take Comsat Access Road from Highway 83.

As the highway continues southwest, you pass a marker that points to a cliff formation in the likeness of George Washington's head; legend says it's a prince turned to stone while chasing a lover to whom he had been unfaithful.

Puu O Mahuka. To reach Oahu's largest ancient temple, turn left from the highway onto Pupukea Road and take the right-hand spur road at the first junction. Inside the walls of this large heiau, human sacrifices were made. Here, too, a famous Hawaiian priest forecast that the islands would be overrun by strangers from a far-off land.

The view from here extends from Waimea Bay and Stream far below all the way to Kaena Point.

Wet and Wild Waimea

As you leave the Pupukea area behind, Highway 83 rounds a bend, providing your first glimpses of Waimea Bay. Rising above the last cluster of buildings on the left is the tower of an early rock-crushing facility. The tower and other buildings were later renovated as Saints Peter and Paul Mission. On the cliffs to the left of the highway grow sisal plants, wild descendants of a 1907 attempt to commercially harvest the leaves and stalks for hemp and fencing.

Waimea Falls Park (daily 10 A.M. to 5:30 P.M.; admission fee). A half-mile up the north side of the Waimea River from the highway is Waimea Falls Park. You can ride in open-air minibuses or walk a 1-mile/1.6-km-long trail through the Waimea Valley to the 45-foot waterfall for which the park was named. Bus drivers describe the arboretum and botanical garden along the way; for walkers, plants and trees are labeled. Guided walking tours are given throughout the day.

The 1,800-acre park also is a Hawaiian games site where guides demonstrate and teach the sports of long ago; visitors are welcome to try the games themselves. You can tour a Hawaiian living site, a recently excavated ancient burial temple, and the appropriately lei-shaped Lei Garden. Traditional hulas are presented several times each afternoon. Cliff diving from 55 feet above the pool takes place at 11 A.M., 12:30, 2, and 3:30 P.M.

Hikers can explore 7½ miles/12 km of trails that burrow deep into an unspoiled valley where there are fern grottoes and koa, guava, orange, coffee, mountain apple, and mango trees. Peacocks, geese, ducks, and jungle fowl roam freely in the park. Near the park entrance, there's a restaurant, snack bar, and country store. Free moon walks are conducted two nights each month at 8:30 P.M. when the moon is full.

Waimea Bay Beach Park. Just south of Waimea River Bridge is Waimea Bay Beach Park with its generous stretch of sand. Usually calm during summer, the bay roars to life in winter. Often two or three stories tall, the waves attract expert surfers. Because of their height and accompanying rip current, these waters are extremely hazardous from October to April.

From Waimea Bay to Haleiwa, you feast on more views of the unprotected coast, see attractive beach homes around Kawailoa, additional surf breaks (Chun's Reef and Laniakea), and a modern dairy farm that has provided a thatch-roofed picnic shelter and children's animal farm for the public.

Haleiwa Ages with Charm

Explore Haleiwa, a mix of old plantation and fishing village, grown a little Bohemian. Though Haleiwa lost out as the Waialua District's main settlement when newer Waialua grew up around the mill, the village has bounced back yet preserved much of its charm, its character now given some permanence by a protective ordinance.

There are new houses; some old buildings with character have had face lifts; and Haleiwa Shopping Plaza has

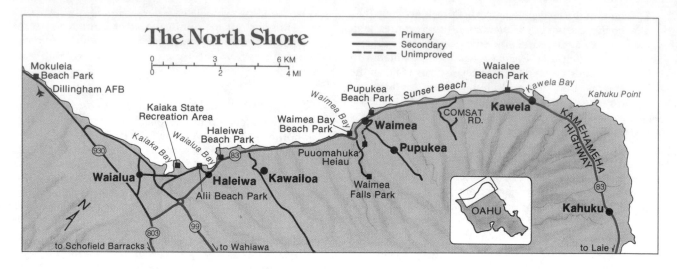

The North Shore

been designed to harmonize with neighbors that have stood here more than half a century.

Haleiwa Beach Park. The highway skirts Haleiwa Beach Park. The park's generous expanses of grass, sand, and coconut palms fringe the head of Waialua Bay and face the Mokuleia shore and the head of the rugged Waianaes. As you cross the narrow, arched bridge over Anahulu Stream, look inland at a few small boats resting under a cover of trees or outward at many craft moored in the boat harbor.

You'll pass a couple of restaurants, pint-sized bank, restored old wooden courthouse, new shopping complex, and archaic buildings that house pool halls, souvenirs, art galleries, and small markets that do a whopping business in "shave ice"; Matsumoto's has an island-wide reputation.

Waialua Church. A Kamehameha Highway stop should be Waialua Protestant Church, also known as Liliuokalani Church, the fifth (built in 1961) sanctuary on the old mission site. It has the ancient bell, a memorial archway, and the clock the queen presented in 1890—the hours are the 12 letters of her name. Ancient gravestones date from the 1830s. The church was enhanced recently with 15 memorial stained glass windows by Erica Karawina that symbolize Biblical verses.

Haleiwa Road. You can turn off the highway just south of the Anahulu bridge and drive Haleiwa Road. A spur to the right, at the end of the boat harbor, leads to Alii Beach Park, at one end of a long, broad ribbon of sand bordering winter surfing ground. On the same spur, Waialua Bay's 800-foot rock breakwater is popular with surfer-watchers and fishermen who turn out in crowds for the *hahalalu* runs that occur between July and December.

Summer seas are calm at Alii Beach Park (best swimming is at the southern half) and farther along at the beach in front of Jodo Mission and the Japanese language school. Haleiwa Road also passes a charming little Hawaiian Protestant church, graceful fire station, and former elementary school that residents plan to restore for an arts center. Next to the school a spur road goes to Kaiaka State Recreation Area on Kaiaka Point where picnicking and fishing are popular; there's swimming just down the beach.

From Haleiwa Road, Paalaa Road will take you back to the main highway, past taro patches, banana groves, and the Shingon Mission (note its fine Japanese roof).

Waialua and Mokuleia

Take Haleiwa Road or Kamehameha Highway to Waialua Beach Road, then turn onto Goodale Avenue and drive past the Waialua recreation field to Waialua's tree-shaded center. Go west on Kealohanui Street past Waialua's mill to see Hongwanji Buddhist Temple. Turn *mauka* on Puuiki Street and drive through a plantation camp with tiny houses and bright gardens and a pretty wooden church to Farrington Highway (930).

Farrington goes west to a vacation house colony, Dillingham Field (private planes and gliders), a beach park for camping, and organization camps. The road then becomes a dirt road around Kaena Point (see page 65; tough going even for 4-wheel-drive vehicles). Farrington goes east to Thomson Corner, where routes 930 and 803 join.

In a cane field on the Haleiwa side of the junction, you'll see the stack of the old mill of 1880s vintage. Continue south on a cane road from the end of Highway 803 and look in another field for ruins of a large Catholic church and graves marked with crosses or oriental characters. The church's successor is the 1923 Spanish-style St. Michael's on Goodale Avenue.

ACROSS THE CENTRAL PLATEAU

The cool, 1,000-foot plateau between the Waianae and Koolau ranges contains some of the state's best farm land, still planted primarily with pineapple and some sugarcane. Hub of the area is Wahiawa, shopping center for approximately 40,000 agricultural workers, suburbanites, and service families from nearby Schofield Barracks and Wheeler Air Force Base.

Two routes cross the plateau from the North Shore. From Weed Circle at Haleiwa's edge, you can take highways 99 and then 80 (together called "Kamehameha Highway") through Wahiawa. Highway 803, from Thomson Corner near Waialua, passes Schofield Barracks, bypassing Wahiawa; it begins as Kaukonahua Road and then becomes Wilikina Drive. Kamananui Road (99) connects the two routes north of Schofield Barracks and Wahiawa. Both routes climb through cane, then pineapple fields, and provide good views of the Waianae Range's 4,020-foot Kaala, Oahu's highest peak; Kolekole Pass, the only break in the Waianae mountains; and the more distant Koolau Range.

As you drive uphill to Wahiawa or Schofield, you'll view Kolekole Pass on your right. It was here, on December 7, 1941, that two flights of Japanese planes flew through the Waianae Range to bomb Schofield and nearby Wheeler Air Force Base on their way to Pearl Harbor. The pass is 1,700 feet high.

Southbound on Kamehameha Highway

About 7 miles/11 km along Kamehameha Highway, you come to the Dole Pineapple Pavilion, which has freshly picked pineapple for sale; Helemano Plantation next door with fruit, vegetable, and flower garden, bakery, country store, and a lunch room featuring fresh produce, bakery treats, and ethnic food favorites; Poamoho Village, an old-time plantation camp; and Del Monte's Variety Garden, exhibiting some 30 species of the bromeliad family (of which pineapple is a member).

Just north of Wahiawa, in the middle of a pineapple field and surrounded by a grove of eucalyptus and coconuts, are the Kukaniloko Birth Stones upon which royal children were once born. The stones are accessible from a dirt road off Kamehameha Avenue; the turnoff is opposite Whitemore Avenue (Highway 804).

Wahiawa

In Wahiawa visit Wahiawa Hongwanji Mission, a Buddhist temple (1067 California Avenue; it intersects with Highway 80). A healing stone, housed in a concrete shelter near the low end of California Avenue, is usually laden with flowers, fruit, and votive candles placed there by local people who believe in the stone's curative powers.

Wahiawa Botanic Garden. Open daily from 9 A.M. to 4 P.M., the garden at 1396 California Avenue contains plants that thrive in cool, wet regions, including a collection of aroids (relatives of the calla lily and jack-in-the-pulpit) and ferns. Paths lead around nine planted acres and to some fine picnic spots.

Turn off California and drive the few blocks of North Cane Street, Wahiawa's first main street and location of its one-time railroad depot. The pastel-painted wooden buildings, some with balconies, are vintage 1910.

Schofield Barracks

Home of the 25th Infantry Division, Schofield Barracks began in 1909 as a cavalry base and island fortification center and was the army's largest post until World War II. Drive in Macomb Gate from Wilikina Drive. (For your visitor pass, you'll need proof that you have automobile insurance covering public liability and personal indemnity.)

On the base you'll drive tree-shaded roads past graceful, quadrangular-shaped, three-story barracks buildings known as "quads." Of Second Renaissance Revival style, they were built between 1914 and 1933.

Exhibits in Tropic Lightning Museum (Monday through Saturday, 10 A.M. to 4 P.M.) trace the history of Schofield and of the 25th Division, featuring the battle records of the regiments that served on the base and in three wars. Out front stand some representative American tanks and cannons from World War II and a 7-foot dragon statue, emblematic of the 14th Infantry's Peking assault during the 1900 Boxer Rebellion.

Kolekole Pass. The pass is about 5 miles/8 km from Macomb Gate. You can drive almost up to it on a road that snakes through luxuriant forest. Just below the sentry post at the Kolekole Lookout, you can park and walk two short trails: one (right of the road) to the base of a white steel cross erected for Easter sunrise services; the other (above the parking area) to Kolekole Rock, which old-timers say represents Kolekole, the female guardian of the pass.

Both paths have lookouts for a grand view over the Central Plateau.

The road over the pass that drops quickly around hairpin turns through Lualualei Valley to the Waianae Coast is restricted because it passes Lualualei Naval Magazine.

Kemoo Farm. If you're going just to the museum at Schofield, park at Kemoo Farm, across the highway from Macomb Gate, and walk over, along a Norfolk Island pine-lined drive; it's easier than finding your way and a parking place on the base. Consider stopping anyway at Kemoo's rustic-style restaurant and country store with snack bar set amid the eucalyptus trees that fringe Lake Wilson, Wahiawa's fish-stocked reservoir. The restaurant's Wednesday and Sunday "plantation day" luncheons with Hawaiian entertainment attract many Honolulu residents.

...Across the Central Plateau

To Pearl Harbor through Mililani

South of Wahiawa, Kamehameha Highway changes its numbers back to Highway 99. It intersects Wilikina Drive (page 61), skirts Wheeler Air Force Base, cuts through forested hills, and sweeps past patches of new houses. Highway 99 then bridges deep Kipapa Gulch before it reaches continuous residential and commercial development near Pearl Harbor.

Wheeler Air Force Base. Wheeler, shared by both army and navy, is preserved in its parklike, pre-World War II form. Near the main gate stands a replica of a P-40, the aircraft in use on that fateful December 7th. You'll also find plaques commemorating two of the earliest mainland-to-Hawaii flights, both in 1927.

Mililani. The highway bisects Mililani, a totally planned "new town" rising on 3,500 former pineapple acres. Now about half-built, it houses more than 23,000 people. Wide streets have islands of trees (mostly shower trees). There's a bikepath-walkway system, a continuous string of parks with two recreation centers, a golf course (open to the public), and attractive shopping centers.

At Meheula Parkway, turn left and drive to the furnished homes complex, a showplace of single family homes being offered in the islands. There are always ten or more open, ranging in size from two to five bedrooms. Visitors as well as residents enjoy going through them.

You'll have Pearl Harbor (see page 64) in view on the long downhill drive. Then the highway passes part of that huge navy base, meeting the H-1 Freeway between Waipahu and Pearl City. Pearl City Tavern, at the corner of Kamehameha Highway and Lehua Avenue, has been a landmark for some 40 years. Its huge menu includes Japanese dishes and seafood specialties. There's a fine bonsai collection on the roof.

An alternate route. If you've lost track of the time while touring the Central Plateau, you may want to take the fast H-2 Freeway south to the Waipahu/Pearl City area, where you can pick up the east-west corridors, H-1 Freeway or Kamehameha Highway (99). You can catch the six-lane H-2 from Wilikina Drive (Highway 99) or Kamehameha Highway (80 at this point) just south of Wahiawa.

Kunia Road

Another route from Schofield and Wahiawa to Waipahu is scenic Kunia Road (Highway 750), starting from Wilikina Drive (Highway 99). The road descends through pineapple fields and then sugarcane beneath the forested windward slopes of the Waianae Range on the right. It passes Del Monte's big shed where workers pack fresh pineapple into containers to be shipped to mainland markets, and Kunia village, noted for its highland gardens— a mix of temperate zone and tropical flowers—and for its annual spring show of orchids and the oriental arts of bonsai and ikebana.

Below Kunia, Highway 750 gradually winds to the southeast, joining the H-1 Freeway in Waipahu and then intersecting Farrington Highway.

Pearlridge and Aiea

Between Kamehameha Highway and Moanalua Road is Pearlridge Shopping Center, a huge, air-conditioned complex with department stores, specialty shops, and eating places common to several large island centers. A monorail connecting two sections of the shopping center runs at 5-minute intervals between the rooftop of the first mall and the third level of the second mall.

Below the shopping center, the swampy watercress fields of Sumida Farm are a welcome patch of green in the midst of all the urban congestion. From the parking lot at the shopping center, you can watch pickers in rubber boots and waterproof aprons working patches of the 11-

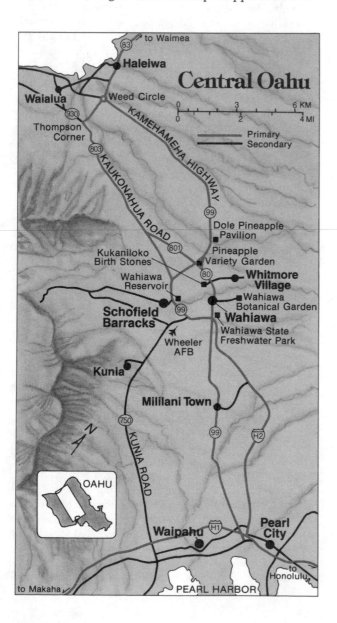

Pearl Harbor's *U.S.S.* Arizona *Memorial spans hulk of ship in which 1,102 men were entombed; Navy boats ferry visitors from shore. Nearby attractions include* U.S.S. Utah, *a submarine museum, and a plaque honoring Apollo XI splashdown.*

Pineapple *and neighboring sugarcane fields dominate the Central Plateau. For a close look at the plant and its family tree, stop by Pineapple Variety Garden. You can sip the juice at the Dole Pineapple Pavilion.*

acre family farm started in 1928. Workers walk on tiles that divide the flooded fields. One-third of the state's watercress crop (1½ tons a day) is grown here. Island watercress is taller and milder than its mainland counterpart.

Take Moanalua Road from Pearlridge to Aiea's center and drive uphill on Aiea Heights Drive, past Hawaii's only sugar refinery. All island-grown sugar consumed locally is processed here; all other raw sugar goes to Crockett, California, for processing.

At the top of the road, about 3 miles/5 km up, a lovely state park contains the ruins of Keaiwa Heiau, an ancient healing temple. The park has picnic and camp grounds, magnificent groves of Norfolk pines, and plants grown by the early Hawaiians for medicinal uses. An easy 5-mile/ 8-km trail loops through the area.

To reach Honolulu from Aiea, you can stay on Moanalua Road (Highway 78), which becomes freewaylike from Halawa Interchange to Middle Street and then becomes H-1. Or you can return to the city on Kamehameha Highway; it passes Pearl Harbor's gates, joins with Nimitz Highway, and passes the airport under H-1.

Aloha Stadium. Two other "temples" in Aiea are dedicated to recreation. The first is 50,000-seat Aloha Stadium, built in 1975 to convert from baseball to football configurations: movable grandstand sections ride on a cushion of air. Home teams include the AAA baseball Hawaii Islanders and Western Athletic Conference-member University of Hawaii Rainbow Warriors. The facility also hosts all-star football games (Pro Bowl and the collegiate Hula Bowl), Aloha Bowl, high school gridiron contests, and rock concerts. The stadium's exits from the H-1 Freeway and Moanalua Road (Highway 78) are well marked.

For an experience visit the tree-shaded stadium parking lot on Saturday or Sunday from 6 A.M. to 3 P.M. The Aloha Swap Meet draws second-hand merchandise of every description; there's also a huge assortment of flowers, produce, and handicrafts.

Castle Park. Hawaii's first major amusement park, Castle park, is just south of Aloha Stadium. Open Monday through Thursday from 10 A.M. to 10:30 P.M., until 12:30 A.M. weekends, the 16-acre grounds offer a water flume ride, river rafting, miniature golf, electronic arcade, scaled-down Grand Prix racing, restaurant, and snack bar.

Pearl Harbor

The December 7, 1941, attack on Pearl Harbor propelled the United States into World War II and the Hawaiian port into the American consciousness. But long before the "Day of Infamy" and battle cry "Remember Pearl Harbor," this area was well-known to military strategists and the Hawaiian population.

A strategic harbor. Competing powers in the islands, particularly the United States, viewed the former Pearl River lagoon as the most significant natural port in the North Pacific; the region became a major issue of negotiation in a series of 19th century treaties increasingly favorable to American interests.

Sacred home of sharks. Hawaiians believed that the site was the home of a beneficent shark queen and her subjects, so they viewed with apprehension the initial dredging of the harbor channel. This occurred without mishap, despite destruction of a fishpond and fish god shrine, because navy workers ceremoniously buried the image stones. But in 1913, offended sharks had their revenge; the first drydock collapsed before completion, an event attributed by some to the dock's construction over the home of the shark queen's son.

Arizona Memorial. Best known of the vessels sunk or severely damaged in the 1941 attack, the U.S.S. *Arizona* is the final resting place for 1,102 servicemen. The 1962 memorial, a white concrete bridge, seems to float above the water-shrouded battleship; oil still seeps from the ship's holds.

Visitor center. An onshore visitor center and museum (open daily 8 A.M. to 5 P.M.; free) houses materials on World War II naval history and wartime Hawaii; at the information desk, you'll receive a number (first come, first served) for a free shuttle-boat ride to the memorial (preceded by a film on the attack).

The boats operate from 8 A.M. to 3 P.M. daily except Monday. Shuttles may be canceled during inclement weather; call the center (422-2771) for information. Children must be 45 inches tall; those under 12 must be accompanied by an adult. Bare feet and bathing suits are not allowed. (Boat cruises from Waikiki do not stop at the Arizona Memorial.)

You can reach the center from Kamehameha Highway (99), turning west onto Arizona Memorial Place.

Other historical attractions. A crosswalk from the visitor center takes you to the U.S.S. *Bowfin,* a storied World War II diesel submarine now restored as a museum. It's open daily, 9:30 A.M. to 4:30 P.M.; there's an admission fee.

The Pacific Submarine Museum in the Pearl Harbor Submarine Base contains "hands-on" exhibits of undersea vessels from World War I to the present. Open Wednesday through Sunday 9:30 A.M. to 5 P.M., the museum is accessible from the Nimitz Highway (92); stop at Pearl Harbor's Nimitz Gate for a pass and further directions.

On Ford Island, beyond the Arizona Memorial, stand monuments to a disparate pair of events. One honors the dead aboard nearby U.S.S. *Utah,* another victim of the Pearl Harbor attack (civilians must be guided by an armed forces member or dependent); the other monument acknowledges the return to *terra firma* of Apollo 11's astronauts following the dramatic first moonwalk mission in July 1969.

THE WAIANAE COAST

To the west of the Waianae Range, amid large plains, deep valleys, and steep ridges, lies leeward Oahu's scenic and historic Waianae Coast. Ancient ruins, remains of plantation communities, military and industrial sites, and fast-growing resort and urban developments all call this coastline home. Much less traveled, particularly by visitors, than the rest of the island, the Waianae Coast lacks the commercial atmosphere too often associated with well-worn paths.

To reach the Waianae Coast from Honolulu, take the H-1 Freeway; its elevated sections provide a sweeping view of plains, mountains, and ocean. Your first stop might be in Waipahu, at Waipahu Cultural Garden Park, 94-695 Waipahu Street, where a village typical of Old Waipahu is being re-created amid taro patches and ethnobotanic plants and a picnic ground below Oahu Sugar Company's big mill. A visitor center has exhibits on life in the town decades ago. (See map on page 62.)

You can visit Ewa, as compact and pretty a plantation town as you'll find, by taking Fort Weaver Road (Highway 76) south from Farrington or from the Kunia turnoff from H-1 and turning west into Renton Road. Part of Oahu Sugar now, Ewa and its camps were built in the 1920s and 1930s by Ewa Sugar Company, whose abandoned mill is still a landmark. Renton Road is divided by trees, passes graceful houses, pretty churches, handsome company buildings, and ends at the working yard of the Hawaiian Railway Society with 40 pieces of rolling stock including the restored Waialua No. 6, a plantation engine built around 1918 from spare parts.

As H-1 rounds the Waianaes to merge into Farrington Highway, you'll see the large refineries on the coast that mark Campbell Industrial Park and the new deep draft harbor for the largest ships afloat.

In Waianae Shopping Mall is E'ala, a native Hawaiian cultural center and gift shop with exhibits on the coast's historic sites (call or stop in and ask about guided tours). E'ala's double-hulled voyaging canoe is berthed at Pokai Bay at the entrance of Ku'ili'o'loa Heiau, a temple 200 feet long, 50 to 70 feet wide.

Along the highway shore at Makaha, you can see the attractive homes and apartments, a shopping center, and two beach parks—Mauna Lahilahi, and Makaha (the great winter surfing mecca). Inland is one of Oahu's largest tourist and residential developments outside Waikiki, the Sheraton-Makaha Resort and Country Club. Makaha Valley's deeper recesses are being left in their natural state for hiking and riding. Ask permission at Sheraton Makaha to visit Kaneaki Heiau, restored to the way it looked in the 18th century, when it was used as a war temple. The platform atop its dry-laid rock walls has grass houses, prayer towers, and a sacrificial altar.

At Makua is dramatic Kaneana Cave whose inner reaches are blocked by cave-ins. Hawaiians of long ago believed the cave led to spirit dwellings of dead chiefs. The country traveled by miles of coral-and-gravel road around Kaena Point is state park; however, the road is tough going, even with 4-wheel-drive vehicles.

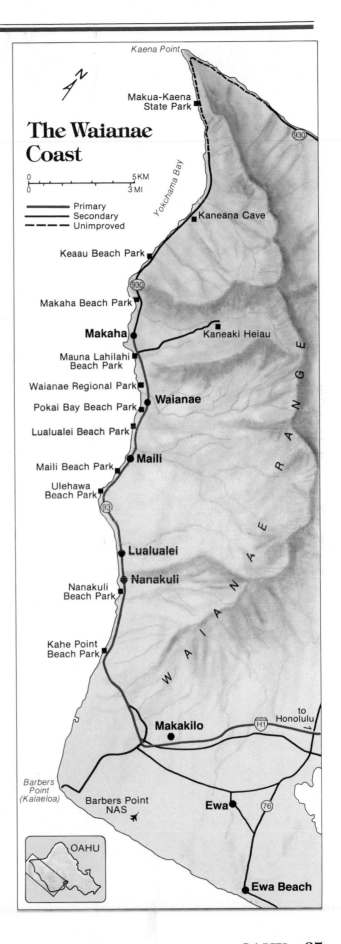

The Waianae Coast

Silhouettes *of kiawe trees break the wide expanse of sea in this view from Keaau Beach Park.*

Pink glow *lights up sky and water as sun sets beyond Mauna Lahilahi at Mauna Lahilahi Beach Park.*

OAHU RECREATION GUIDE

 Oahu, the most populous island, provides a wealth of recreation activities for visitors. For further details on any activity listed below, consult your travel agent or the Hawaii Visitors Bureau (2270 Kalakaua Avenue, Honolulu, HI 96815).

Most large hotels also offer sports activity desks for their guests. Here, it's easy to arrange tee times, reserve tennis courts, and make arrangements for snorkeling or scuba diving expeditions. Transportation is also provided for some of these activities, either by the hotel or the company.

Flightseeing. Get above Honolulu's busy streets, enjoy a bird's-eye view of the more distant Windward and Waianae coasts, or make a day of it and island hop. Choices range from self-piloted hang gliders to chartered helicopter jaunts. You'll find a wide range of itineraries and prices. It's important to check carefully for the best deals.

Plane. (All at Honolulu International Airport unless noted.) Adventure Store, World War II AT6 half-hour flights from Dillingham Field following path of Pearl Harbor bombing; Panorama Air Tours, one-day, eight island flight with ground tours of Hawaii, Maui, Kauai, including meals and ground transportation; Scenic Air Tours Hawaii, one-day, eight-island flights with ground tours of Hawaii, Maui, Kauai, including meals and ground transportation, and seven-island tours including Molokai, Maui, and Kauai. The latter companies also provide tours to single island destinations.

Helicopter. Hawaii Pacific Helicopters, tours from Ala Wai Helipad in Waikiki, Turtle Bay Hilton on North Shore, and Sheraton Makaha; Kenai Helicopters, specialized tours, charter, and group rates; Royal Helicopters, flights over Waikiki, Pearl Harbor, Windward/Pali, circle-island routes, charters.

Glider. Glider Rides (Honolulu Soaring Club, Inc.), Dillingham Airfield (Mokuleia), piloted sailplaning above the North Shore in 3-seat aircraft (1 or 2 passengers).

Hang glider. Hawaii's Airsport and Tradewinds Hang Gliding offer instruction and certification, use Makapuu and North Shore sites. Telephone for reservations.

Golf. All the courses listed below are open to the public. Yardages are from the regular (white) tees.

Public courses. Ala Wai Golf Course, Honolulu, 18 holes, 6,111 yards; Pali Golf Course, Kaneohe, 18 holes, 6,493 yards; Kahuku Golf Course, Kahuku, 9 holes, 2,699 yards; Ted Makalena Golf Course, Waipahu, 18 holes, 5,946 yards.

Resort/commercial courses. Hawaii Kai Golf Course, Honolulu, 18 holes, 6,350 yards (championship course), 2,386 (executive course); Honolulu Country Club, Honolulu, 18 holes, 6,182 yards; Moanalua Golf Club, Honolulu, 9 holes, 3,042 yards; Olomana Golf Links, Waimanalo, 18 holes, 5,856 yards; Bay View Golf Center, Kaneohe Bay, 18 holes, 2,231 yards; Turtle Bay Hilton & Country Club, Kahuku, 18 holes, 6,366 yards; Hawaii Country Club, Kunia, 18 holes, 5,664 yards; Mililani Golf Club, Mililani Town, 18 holes, 6,800 yards; Sheraton Makaha Resort West Golf Course, 18 holes, 6,400 yards; Makaha Valley Country Club, Makaha, 18 holes, 6,251 yards; Pearl Country Club of Hawaii, Aiea, 18 holes, 6,491 yards.

Military courses. Active and retired members of the armed forces, their families, and civilian guests accompanied by a military sponsor may play at eight military courses on Oahu: Hickam Air Force Base, 18 holes, 6,746 yards; Navy-Marine, 18 holes, 6,510 yards; Fort Shafter, 9 holes played as 18 with changing tees, 5,194 yards; Kaneohe Marine, 18 holes, 6,346 yards; Leilehua, 18 holes, 6,400 yards; Barbers Point, 18 holes, 6,455 yards; Ford Island, 9 holes, 1,340 yards; Kalakaua, 18 holes, 6,344 yards.

Tennis. In addition to the public and resort or commercial courts listed below, many condominiums have courts for guest use. The big military bases have a generous supply of courts for active, reserve, and retired servicemen, their families, and civilian guests.

Public courts. These facilities are available for use at no cost. More than 150 courts are located in parks and playgrounds around the island; more than half are within Honolulu's city limits. The Parks and Recreation Department can give you information about facilities and clinics or other instruction. Listed here are courts close to Waikiki: Kapiolani Park has 4 lighted courts at the Kapiolani Tennis Courts on Kalakaua Avenue and 9 courts (unlighted) at Diamond Head Tennis Center on Paki Avenue; Ala Moana Park has 10 lighted courts.

Resort/commercial courts. Honolulu: Hawaiian Regent, 1 court; Honolulu Tennis Club, 4 lighted courts, free shuttle service to/from Waikiki hotels; Pacific Beach Hotel, 2 courts; Oahu Club, 6 lighted courts; Outrigger Malia, 1 court; Westin Ilikai, 5 courts (1 with lights). Kahuku: Turtle Bay Hilton & Country Club, 10 courts (4 with lights). Makaha: Sheraton Makaha Resort & Country Club, 4 lighted courts.

Swimming. Swimming is generally safe in reef-protected areas. Beaches aren't necessarily marked as unsafe, though, so check before entering the water in any area where you are unsure of currents.

Ocean swimming. The beaches listed here, most of them beach parks, are usually safe for swimming: Ala Moana and Magic Island, all sections of Waikiki from Duke Kahanamoku Beach to Diamond Head, Kaalawai, Waialae and Kahala Hilton, the close-to-shore areas of Hanauma Bay, Kaiona, Waimanalo, Bellows Field, Lanikai shore, Kailua, Kalama, Kualoa, Kaaawa, Kahana, Punaluu, Hauula, Malaekahana, Kuilima Cove (at Turtle Bay Hilton), Kawela Bay, Haleiwa, Mauna Lahilahi, Pokai Bay, Kahe (Tracks Beach), Nimitz, Oneula, and Ewa.

Spots that look inviting but are hazardous are Halona Cove (rocks), Koko Head Sandy Beach (treacherous waves and currents), Makapuu (powerful waves, some undertow), Waimea Bay, and Sunset Beach (dangerous riptides and very strong undertow except when absolutely placid). Except for Kawela and Pokai, any of the north and west side beaches from Kahuku to Barbers Point can become dangerous when the sea is agitated.

Freshwater swimming. For a quiet paddle or a brisk workout when the beach looks bad, there are many swimming pools open free to the public in city parks.

Surfing. Oahu has the highest surf in the world—30-foot swells at Waimea Bay and Sunset Beach that challenge the most experienced surfers. But for beginners, there are excellent surfing beaches with calmer conditions. You should be a strong swimmer since you will spend more time paddling in the water than riding on it. Private lessons are available along Waikiki Beach.

Board surfing. Beginners can learn at Waikiki (though summer waves sometimes reach 8 feet), the Kalama shore, Chun's Reef, Nimitz, and Oneula Park.

Point Panic, Ala Moana, Magic Island, Diamond Head, Black Point, and Koko Head have higher summer surf. Challenging winter surf is found at Sunset Beach, Banzai Pipeline near Ehukai Beach Park, Waimea Bay, Haleiwa, Yokohama Bay, Makaha, and Maili (for experts only).

Body surfing. For gentle waves, try Kuhio Beach Pier at Waikiki, Waimanalo, Bellows Field, and Kalama. When the waves are small, you can switch from board to body surfing at Black Point, Koko Head, Ehukai Beach Park, Makaha, and Nimitz. For body surfing in big waves, head to Makapuu.

Windsurfing. Kailua and Lanikai are excellent grounds for all windsurfers, beginners to advanced. Tricky Diamond Head and "Backyards" at Kawailoa Beach are for the skilled. Aloha Windsurfing in Waikiki, Kailua Sailboard Company and Windsurfing Hawaii in Kailua, and Surf N Sea in Haleiwa offer lessons and rent equipment.

Beachcombing, tidepooling, and reef walking. To see Oahu's marine life without putting on diving gear, wait until the tide goes out and walk on lava rocks or coral reefs. Wear tennis shoes and remember gloves if you handle any rocks. Leave the rocks and reef as you found them and turn back any rocks that you may move (exposure to light can kill marine life).

Low-tide walking. Areas of Fort Kamehameha near the airport, Waialae Beach Park, Kaneohe Bay, Kualoa Point, Kaaawa Beach Park, Punaluu Beach Park, Chun's Reef, Kaiaka Bay, Mokuleia Beach Park, and Ewa Beach Park. The Waikiki Aquarium offers periodic beach walks.

Skin and scuba diving. Explore Oahu's underwater world of brilliantly colored fish and beautiful coral reefs. Snorkeling and diving equipment can be rented in Honolulu and other major beach areas; several diving companies offer skin and scuba diving excursions. Some also offer instruction, certification courses for scuba diving, and night diving excursions.

Diving spots. Good diving spots lie along the Waianae Coast beaches, the North Shore beaches in summer (par-
ticularly Shark's Cove at Pupukea), off Rabbit Island and Magic Island, Maunalua Bay, and Hanauma Bay, a marine life conservation district (see the interpretive display in the beach pavilion).

Diving companies. Some 20 diving companies are listed in the Oahu *Yellow Pages* under "Skin Diving—Equipment, instruction, tours."

Military personnel or dependents may rent from the Special Services departments on the bases.

Boating. From beach service stands at several places along the Waikiki strip you can take off on an hour-long sail offshore aboard a small speedy catamaran or take an outrigger canoe ride—you'll surf in on three waves and likely do some of the paddling. All of the beach stands have surfboards for rent and offer surfing lessons, and some may also rent *paipo* (belly) boards, air mattresses, kayaks, and surf skis.

The *Yellow Pages*, under "Boats," lists companies that rent catamarans and other craft you can sail yourself. The Honolulu Sailing Co. in Kaneohe is a major concern that offers bareboat or skippered charters, instruction, and boats from 20-foot day sailers to 90-foot yachts.

Popular water skiing spots are Keehi Lagoon and Hawaii Kai Marina, and the *Yellow Pages* (under "Water Skiing") lists companies that can supply equipment or take you out.

Mainland yacht club members are welcomed at the Hawaii Yacht Club and Waikiki Yacht Club at Ala Wai Yacht Harbor (see page 29), and Kaneohe Yacht Club on Kaneohe Bay. Active or retired military personnel can look to the Pearl Harbor Yacht Club on the U.S. Naval Base, the Pacific Yacht Club at Hickam Harbor, or the Kaneohe Marine Corps Air Station Marina; they have sailboats of various sizes available for rent.

See also Boat Tours, page 25, and Fishing and Skin Diving in this section.

Fishing. Fishing areas abound on Oahu. No matter what type of fishing you prefer, you're sure to find something to suit your fancy. No license is required for saltwater fishing, but one is required for freshwater fishing. Contact the Division of Conservation and Resources Enforcement, 1151 Punchbowl Street, Honolulu.

Fishing locations. Most charters will take you trolling off the Waianae Coast, off Koko Head's choppy water, around the Penguin Banks near Molokai, or along the Windward Coast, notably in the open sea off Kaneohe Bay.

Waianae's deep and inshore waters are excellent for spearfishing. North Shore areas are good in some summer months. Best spots for spin fishing, surfcasting, and poling from lava ledges are the rocky coast beyond Koko Head, Koko Head Sandy Beach, Waimanalo Beach, some parts of Kaneohe Bay, and selected spots along the entire north and Waianae coasts.

In late summer *'oama, moi-li'i,* and *hahalalu* (baby goat fish, threadfin, and scad respectively) come into shallow sandy beaches to spawn—at Waikiki, Ala Moana, Waimea Bay, Pokai Bay, Ewa Beach. People wade in up to their hips and catch dozens with a simple bamboo pole and line. Some fish like mullet and *moi* favor the brackish water near the mouths of streams. You can fish for them and net crabs from highway bridges near the ocean at Haleiwa and Waialua and the banks of the Ala Wai and Kahaluu canals and Nuuanu Stream.

For freshwater fishing on Oahu, Lake Wilson (Wahiawa Public Fishing Area) is well stocked with bass, bluegill, sunfish, tilapia, and tucunare. Nuuanu Reservoir Number 4 has channel catfish, Chinese catfish, and tilapia, and is open for fishing on a limited basis. Check with the Division of Aquatic Resources, 1151 Punchbowl Street, Honolulu, for the freshwater fishing seasons.

Charter companies. Most fishing charters leave from Kewalo Basin, a few from Waianae Boat Harbor. You can get a list from "Fishing Parties" in the *Yellow Pages.*

Horseback riding. Koko Crater Stables, Honolulu, trail rides through botanical garden in Koko Crater; Kualoa Ranch, Kaaawa, one and two-hour rides into Kaaawa Valley, picnic rides, reservations required; Gunstock Ranch, Laie, one and two-hour ranch rides, full-day rides available; Turtle Bay Hilton Stables, Kahuku, one-hour rides along beach and in woods; Sheraton Makaha Resort Riding Stable, Makaha, one-hour trail rides into scenic Makaha Valley; Barbers Point Riding Stables, Barbers Point, hourly rides Wednesday through Sunday, evening and hay rides by arrangement.

Bicycling. Rental bikes (the majority are 10-speeds) are plentiful in Waikiki; check "Bicycles" in the *Yellow Pages.* The city has a number of bike routes and bikeways that ease riding through traffic-congested areas you must travel if you're using two wheels for transportation or to reach quiet residential areas that are a pleasure to explore by bicycle. For information on them call Honolulu's Department of Transportation Services, Traffic Safety Education section.

If you're planning cross-country trips you should probably bring your own bicycle. A day trip up Nuuanu Valley to Pali Lookout offers forest scenery and good views; the round trip from downtown is 12 miles/19 km. You can detour twice into the jungle on two ½-mile meandering segments of the old road, Nuuanu Pali Drive.

Ride from Waikiki to Hanauma Bay for great snorkeling and swimming; round trip from Waikiki is about 23 miles/37 km.

A good ride of two days or more is to circle all or part of Oahu. Continue past Hanauma Bay, up the Windward Coast, and along the North Shore. From Haleiwa, turn inland and uphill to Wahiawa; then head down to Pearl City, Aiea, and Honolulu. This trip is just over 100 miles. If you start this ride on the Pali Highway out of Honolulu, you can cut about 15 miles/24 km off the trip. Reversing the direction of the round-the-island trip allows you to avoid riding into the wind over the long Windward Coast,

but either way it's a long climb through the island center to Wahiawa. Along the entire coast are camping areas and occasional hotels, condos, and tourist cottages.

Hiking, camping, off-road touring. Oahu's mild weather tempts all out-of-doors enthusiasts, and the hiking and camping are plentiful.

Hiking trails. Both the Koolaus and the Waianaes are crisscrossed by trails, many of which are described on a map available free from the State Division of Forestry and Wildlife, 1151 Punchbowl Street, Honolulu. Many trails cross private or restricted areas and are off limits. Before going on any trail, check with the Division of Forestry for the latest conditions and for information on obtaining permission to hike. Better still, join a local hiking club for a day's outing.

Here are a few trails easy and safe enough to do on your own: Judd Trail, a short loop trail to Nuuanu Valley past Jackass Ginger Pool; the interconnecting trails (about a dozen) in the Tantalus State Recreation Area through forested land from Manoa to Nuuanu valleys (the Makiki Environmental Education Center, 2131 Makiki Heights Drive, Honolulu, has a good map and interpretive booklets); Diamond Head summit trail; and the Moanalua Valley trail—call Moanalua Gardens Foundation for information and to make reservations for periodic guided hikes.

Other state parks and recreation areas with good hiking are Waahila Ridge State Recreation Area, Keaiwa Heiau State Park (it has the Aiea Loop Trail), Sacred Falls State Park, Kaena Point State Park, and Kahana Valley State Park (for which a permit is required from the division office at 1151 Punchbowl Street).

Camping. Camping is permitted at these city and county beach parks for a maximum of five consecutive days—they're closed on Wednesday and Thursday: Makapuu, Kaiona, Waimanalo, Kualoa, Kaaawa, Kahana Bay, Punaluu, Hauula, Haleiwa, Mokuleia, Keeau, Lualualei, Nanakuli, and Kahe Point. Camping is permitted on weekends at Bellows Field and Swanzy. You'll need to get a permit to camp from Honolulu's Department of Parks and Recreation, 650 South King Street.

Two state parks offer beach camping, Malaekahana State Recreation Area and Sand Island State Park; Keaiwa Heiau State Park campgrounds enjoy cool mountain air. Camping at all three is by permit from the Division of State Parks and is limited to five consecutive days (they're closed Wednesday and Thursday). Ho'omaluhia Botanic Garden offers camping to participants in its outdoor education programs. Call about reservations.

Family camping is permitted at some of Oahu's private camps (see Yellow Pages), including Camp Kailani at Kailua Beach, operated by the United Methodists; Mokuleia Episcopal Church Camp; Camp Puu Kahea at Waianae, run by the Southern Baptists; the YWCA's Camp Kokokahi on Kaneohe Bay; and Camp Hauula, run by the Catholic Youth Organization.

KAUAI

• LUSH, GREEN, QUIET ... BUT THIS COMPACT ISLE CONTAINS SURPRISES •

Only an artist with an extensive palette could identify the myriad shades of green in the lush vegetation covering most of Kauai. One glance tells you why it is called the "Garden Island."

Hawaii's oldest island, Kauai was created by an ancient volcano, Waialeale, which rises to 5,243 feet at its highest peak, Kawaikini. Once volcanic activity stopped here thousands of years ago, other forces of nature softened and changed the land. Torrential rains of 400 to 600 inches a year falling on Waialeale eroded gorges up to 3,000 feet deep along its flanks and sent streams large enough to be called rivers flowing to the sea.

Rain, wind, and powerful wave action have sculptured Kauai's northwest coast into a series of bold precipices that drop off steeply to the ocean and into verdant valleys worn between them. The deep gulches of the Na Pali Coast and Waimea Canyon border the Kokee Plateau (3,000 to 4,000 feet high) and its huge Alakai Swamp—so nearly level that heavy rains drain off slowly and drop over the tableland cliffs in the form of high waterfalls. Most of this vast, nearly inviolate region is protected in state parks.

You'll see striking contrasts by following the shore of this small (550 square miles/1,430 square km) circular island, Hawaii's fourth in size. The long stretch of windward coast from Na Pali around to Wailua is damper, cooler, and greener than the lee side from Koloa to Polihale. Rainfall varies from over 50 inches a year on the north shore to about 20 inches at Kekaha in the southwest.

Past, Present, and Future

The waves of Polynesian immigrants came early to Kauai, and this was the first island visited by Captain Cook in 1778. It was the only one of the islands not conquered by King Kamehameha. After Kamehameha's two attempts to reach the island had been thwarted, Kauai's King Kaumualii voluntarily submitted to the all-island rule in 1810. A few years later, a Russian emissary almost persuaded him to break away from Kamehameha and put his island under Russian protection. The remains of a Russian fort at Waimea Bay are a reminder of the 19th-century rivalry between the United States, Great Britain, France, and Russia for control of the islands—a rivalry that was largely responsible for Hawaii's remaining independent until 1898.

Hawaii's first successful sugar plantation was started at Koloa in 1835. Today, sugar defers to tourism as Kauai's leading income producer, and some cane fields have been taken out of production in favor of other crops such as papaya and guavas, now cultivated in the stretch from Moloaa to Kilauea. Bananas, macadamia nuts, and more than half the state's crop of taro are grown on Kauai, too.

Most of Kauai's 45,000 residents live in small towns with charming lanes of old, wooden buildings. But the growing tourism industry has brought development in the form of expanding resort clusters, principally in the Hanalei, Wailua, and Poipu areas.

You'll find a unique sense of community in Kauai. It was fostered by a hurricane that slammed into the island in November 1982, leaving a trail of devastation in its wake. But the storm was barely spent when rebuilding and replanting began. Today traces of the storm are difficult to find, but the residents' pride in their island is very apparent.

Land of Legend

Everywhere on Kauai you'll hear tales of the *menehune*. Whatever happenings early storytellers couldn't explain, they attributed to the legendary people—short, stocky, and very strong—who were skilled workers in stone and who completed each job in a single night or never returned to it. The island has *heiau* (temples), dams, ditches, and trails, supposedly built by the industrious race.

Legend also says that Pele, the fire goddess, tried first to make a home on this island for herself and her lover, Lohiau, then king of Kauai. But, after several unsuccessful attempts to dig a dry pit where she could start her fire, she continued south to the other islands.

70

Pristine pocket beach along rugged Na Pali Coast

THE ESSENTIALS

Kauai lies 72 miles/115 km northwest of Oahu. It's a 27-minute flight between Honolulu and Lihue airports via Aloha or Hawaiian airlines. Princeville Airways flies regularly between Honolulu, other island cities, and Princeville on Kauai's north shore. United Airlines has direct service from the mainland to Lihue. Travelers whose schedules prohibit a more lengthy stay can visit Kauai on one-day flightseeing tours from Honolulu.

Getting Around

Formidable cliffs—Na Pali, on the northwest side of Kauai—prevent a circle trip completely around the island by car. Most visitors break Kauai sightseeing into two main excursions: the coast from Lihue north to the road's end near Haena (80 miles/128 km round-trip from Lihue); and the south shore, including a side trip to Kokee Park and the lookouts above Waimea Canyon and Kalalau Valley (100 miles/160 km round-trip from Lihue).

Tour companies visit all of these areas. If you drive these trips yourself, plan a day for each to allow time to stop often, tour a garden or museum, have a swim and picnic, and take side trips—to Koloa and Poipu (if you're staying elsewhere), Lawai Valley, Kukuiolono Park, the Wailua Homesteads, or a boat trip up the Wailua River to Fern Grotto.

Cars, campers, 4-wheel-drive vehicles. You'll see all major car rental agencies at the Lihue Airport. In addition, you'll find cars, campers, and 4-wheel-drive vehicles from a number of island-only companies at the airport, in Lihue town, or at main resort areas. It's wise to reserve transportation in advance; you may also qualify for discounted rates.

Bus and shuttle services. Aloha Bus provides service daily (except Sunday and holidays) between The Market Place at Waipouli and Lihue Shopping Center, Kauai Surf, and Lihue Airport. With advance reservations, you can stop en route at Coco Palms, Kauai Resort, and Kapaa Shopping Center.

Where To Stay

Kauai has four main resort areas: the Lihue-Nawiliwili region, Wailua-Kapaa just to the north, Hanalei at the north shore, and the Poipu Beach area along the south shore.

In Lihue, you'll find several small apartment and motel facilities. At nearby Nawiliwili, accommodations include condominiums and a motel. The Westin Kauai, part of the 800-acre Kauai Lagoons development, fronts Kalapaki Beach on the north shore of Nawiliwili Bay. The 847-room mega-resort (tennis, golf, health spa, shops, 16 restaurants) includes lagoons and carriage trails.

Resorts, hotels, condominiums, and motel units stretch between Hanamaulu and Kapaa. Many hotels in the area are clustered within walking distance of other hotels, shops, and restaurants. Among the largest are the Coco Palms (full resort in a century-old coconut palm grove), Islander on the Beach, Kauai Beach Boy, Aston Kauai Resort (at Wailua River), Kauai Sands, Sheraton Coconut Beach, and Kauai Hilton & Beach Villas (north of Hanamaulu).

Along the north shore, you'll have a choice of the Sheraton Mirage Princeville or condominiums at Princeville. Hanalei Bay Resort (most resembles a hotel), Hanalei Colony Resort (on the beach), Pali Ke Kua, and The Cliffs at Princeville are among the largest. This resort area offers 45 holes of golf on two courses.

In the Poipu Beach area, several resort hotels (Stouffer Poipu Beach, Sheraton Kauai, deluxe Stouffer Waiohai) are strung along the beach. Among the nearby condominiums and apartment hotels are Aston Makahuena at Poipu, Kiahuna Beachside, Kiahuna Plantation, Lawai Beach Resort, Nihi Kai Villas, Poipu Crater, Poipu Kai, Poipu Kapili, Poipu Shores, Sunset Kahili, Waikomo Stream Villas, and Whalers Cove. Most have pools; several have tennis courts. The Kiahuna Golf Club's 18-hole course is open to the public.

In Kokee State Park, you can stay in completely equipped cabins rented by Kokee Lodge or arrange off-season use of YMCA, YWCA, and Methodist Church camps by writing to organization headquarters in Lihue. You can also camp at Polihale and Kokee state parks as well as at county parks throughout the island.

Camping permits are required for both park systems. County fees are $3 for adults; children are free. There's no charge for state permits. For information and permits, contact local offices in Lihue at the addresses on page 89.

Touring the Island

Tour companies schedule trips to Kauai's main attractions. Tours can be booked through travel desks of major hotels or directly with the following activities centers: Island Adventure (Lihue), See Kauai (Hanalei), and South Shore Activities (Koloa). Among the possibilities are beach parties, horseback rides, half-day sightseeing tours, and helicopter trips. For river boating excursions, see page 76 on boat trips up the Wailua River from Wailua Marina to the Fern Grotto or refer to pages 88-89.

The Shopping Experience

Though Kauai lacks the wide range of stores you'd find on Oahu, it does offer some intriguing small shops in such historic towns as Hanamaulu, Hanapepe, Koloa, and Lihue, as well as a few interesting shopping complexes: The Market Place at Coconut Plantation (Wailua River region), where machinery and relics remind you of its former sugar mill existence; Ching Young Village Shopping Center (Hanalei), a center that encompasses the Native Hawaiian Trading and Cultural Center; Kilohana (Lihue), a shopping complex/museum on a 1935 sugar-cane estate; and Kukui Grove Center (Lihue), a

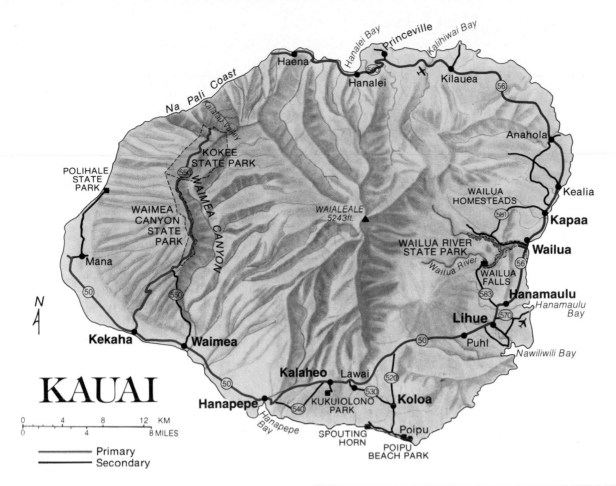

KAUAI

0 4 8 12 KM
0   4   8 MILES

——— Primary
——— Secondary

modern mall. You'll also find shops in most major resort hotels. Souvenir shopping and bargain hunting is perhaps best among the vendors' tables at Spouting Horn.

Probably the best craft shopping is for the delicate Niihau shell leis. These exquisite shells are collected, hand-sorted, and fashioned into leis by the residents of the privately owned island off Kauai's coast (see right).

Dining and Entertainment

Kauai's restaurants offer a wide variety of cuisine, ranging from fast food to gourmet dining. J.J.'s Broiler (Lihue) has a "Slavonic steak" house specialty. At Plantation Gardens (Poipu) you dine in a 19th-century manor set among showy gardens. Luaus take place several times a week at most major hotels. For the most authentic Hawaiian cuisine, try the Friday night feast at Tahiti Nui (Hanalei). You'll also find an array of Mexican, Chinese, and Italian restaurants around the island.

Entertainment generally centers around resort hotels; don't miss the nightly torch lighting ceremony at Coco Palms. For late-night activity, residents go to Club Jetty on the wharf at Nawiliwili Harbor.

On pages 88–89, we've included a guide to the island's recreational facilities. For information and addresses of specific accommodations, excursions, and attractions, contact the Hawaii Visitors Bureau, 3016 Umi Street, Lihue, HI 96766.

KAUAI'S INTRIGUING NEIGHBOR

Because Niihau, the small island off Kauai's leeward coast, was off limits to tourists until recently, it has acquired an air of mystique. Today, 50-minute helicopter tours from Kauai offer bird's-eye views of the island plus a brief stop on a deserted beach.

The Sinclair family bought the island from King Kamehameha V in 1864 and established a cattle and sheep ranch. Descendants of the family still operate the estate; only relatives of the some 200 Hawaiian workers are permitted lengthy island visits. Life remains much as it was in the 19th century: no electricity (except at the ranch house and school), television, telephones, shops, or restaurants. Employees supplement the staples provided by the ranch with fish and home-grown vegetables.

In October the entire population combs the beaches for tiny shells from which they carefully sort and fashion their famous leis. The shells are fashioned into complex designs that can take weeks to string. Look for them in some of Kauai's better gift stores.

One of the state's oldest plantation towns, Lihue is the business center of Kauai and the seat of Kauai County, which includes the privately owned island of Niihau off Kauai's southwest coast (see page 73). It's also the first place most visitors see after landing at the airport, 2 miles/3 km from downtown.

Nawiliwili Harbor, 2 miles/3 km downhill, is Kauai's chief port. Down in a gulley in another direction stands the Lihue Plantation Company mill, one of the state's largest (and last) sugar mills.

Around Town

Lihue still exudes a small-village atmosphere. Here you'll find the handsome state and county office buildings, Courthouse, and Hawaii Visitors Bureau office (3016 Umi Street). Though now eclipsed by Kukui Grove Center at Puhi, Lihue Shopping Center on Rice Street has a mall and eating spots. The Haleko Shops section across Rice Street on Haleko Road reflects the architectural preferences of the Germans who owned Lihue Plantation until World War I. The four restored two-story, concrete duplexes house stores and a restaurant. Shrines and sculpture dot the garden—including the Lihue Horse Trough, a marble fountain bought in Italy and shipped around Cape Horn in 1909 by Pastor Hans Isenberg, a German immigrant and brother of a plantation founder.

On a hill overlooking the mill, Lihue Cemetery's rows of simple tombstones contrast sharply with a stately white marble monument erected in 1911 in honor of the Rice family, island pioneers. The monument was exhibited at Bremen and Paris art galleries before it was shipped.

Back of nearby Lihue Union Church rests a little Hawaiian cemetery nestled in a grove of plumeria trees. On a neighboring hill perches Lihue Lutheran Church, built in 1883 with an ornate altar and pulpit like a church of old Germany.

Kauai Museum. A visit to the two-building museum complex at 4428 Rice Street will help you get your bearings before further island exploration. In the William Hyde Rice Building a 6-minute film gives a bird's-eye view of areas seldom seen by the average visitor. You'll see an elaborate display of island history from its volcanic genesis some 60 million years ago up to the end of the 19th century, when Hawaii was annexed by the United States.

The Albert Spencer Wilcox Building (handsome historic landmark and former town library) houses changing exhibits of Hawaiiana and Hawaii's ethnic heritage. Its shop sells outstanding imports from the South Pacific, as well as Kauai and Niihau handcrafts.

Kauai Museum is open weekdays from 9 A.M. to 4:30 P.M., Saturdays until 1 P.M. There's an admission charge.

Grove Farm Homestead Museum. Time seems to stand still when you enter Grove Farm Homestead's 80-acre grounds. It's one of Hawaii's earliest sugar plantations and a living memorial to the Wilcox family who lived here from 1864 to 1978. Descendants of missionaries, the family also restored the Waioli Mission House in Hanalei.

Unhurried, 2-hour, guided tours offer visitors a look at carefully preserved buildings and grounds. In addition to viewing a vast repository of Hawaiiana, you'll learn how a sugar plantation operated. The tour covers the

Reached by boat, *Fern Grotto provides natural setting for Hawaiian serenade.*

well-furnished main house, outbuildings, Kaipu Camp (one of the last collection of workers' dwellings on the island), gardens, orchards, and groves of grand trees dating back to the days of Kalakaua. Along the way, you'll hear fascinating family tales, sip mint tea, and eat the sugar cookies that Hisae Mashita, family cook, has been preparing for four decades.

Tours begin promptly at 10 A.M. and 1:15 P.M. Monday, Wednesday, and Thursday. Because the sizes of the groups are limited, reservations must be made well in advance of your visit. For information and reservations, write to Grove Farm Homestead, P.O. Box 1631, Lihue, HI 96766, or call (808) 245-3202. Upon confirmation of your reservation, you'll be given directions to reach the homestead. A modest admission is charged. One tip: Wear shoes that slip off easily; you'll be removing them indoors.

Nawiliwili Bay

As with any deep-water port, Nawiliwili's business centers around ships, docks, and wharves. But there's a lot of activity and local color. If a freighter is being loaded, you can watch raw sugar moving by conveyor from a bulk plant into the hold. Harborside Club Jetty is a good spot to watch the flotilla of fishing and pleasure craft. Note also the restored Hotel Kuboyama.

At the ocean end of the harbor, the Westin Kauai and the 36-hole Kauai Lagoons Golf & Racquet Club look over Kalapaki Beach and the bay to the Hoary Head Mountains and their green-clad peak, Haupu. Inland, at the mouth of Huleia Stream, you'll get a fine harbor view from Niumalu Beach Park.

Menehune Garden. Located near the harbor on Highway 58, the Menehune Garden is dominated by a giant weeping banyan. In its shade stand a replica of a primitive Hawaiian house and a stage where ancient Kauai chants and dances are performed, Hawaiian instruments are demonstrated, and food and medicinal plants growing in the garden are explained. You can walk the paths with or without a guide; all plants are labeled. Open daily, there's a small charge.

Alakoko (Menehune) Fishpond. There's not much to see from the roadside lookout on Niumalu Road off Highway 58; it's the lore surrounding the serene pond that attracts visitors.

According to legend, the pond was built for a princess and her brother by menehune under their usual conditions—that no mortals watch them and that they complete the wall in a single night. But the royal pair could not restrain their curiosity. By the light of the moon, they watched the little people, lined up in a double row as far as they could see, passing rocks from hand to hand to workers at the dam. But they watched a little too long and were discovered by the menehune, who turned them into the twin pillars of stone you see on the mountainside

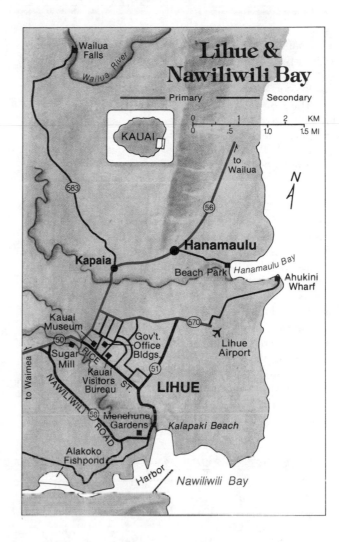

above. Having used up their time, the menehune had to leave two gaps in the wall. Chinese mullet raisers later filled these in, and the resulting pond is still in use.

North to Hanamaulu Bay

Two routes lead to Hanamaulu Bay. Highway 570 continues for another mile past Lihue Airport to Ahukini Landing. From the remains of the extensive wharf, you'll see fishers and get a look at the windswept eastern coast. Highway 56 leads to the bay through Kapaia, the turnoff for a 4-mile/6-km drive inland to Wailua Falls, where about a half dozen white ribbons of water plunge over a high canyon wall in the river's upper reaches. A trail descends the steep bank below the falls to a pool.

At Kapaia, also note the picturesque stores (former plantation houses), modern Hongwanji Buddhist temple, and Spanish-style Immaculate Conception Catholic church. Kapaia Stitchery, south of town, is the best place to find traditional Hawaiian quilt patterns and fabrics.

Hanamaulu, another plantation village, presents classic false-front facades on its post office and store; inside the latter is a free museum.

Midway along Kauai's east coast lies Wailua, former home for Hawaii's royalty, the *alii*. In those days no visitors were allowed without specific invitation, and royal children had to be born here to be recognized as high chiefs. Today, it's a favorite tourist destination.

The mouth of the Wailua River marks the supposed landing site of Tahiti's first migrants. Seven sacred heiau once lined the river from its mouth to its source, the slopes of Waialeale. You'll hear stories of the royal years during the popular boat ride upriver to Fern Grotto.

Wailua River State Park

Several recreational and historic areas comprise Wailua River State Park. The Lydgate area of the park complex contains picnic sites and campgrounds, a beach, lava-rimmed ocean pool, and remains of a temple of refuge that once sheltered fugitives. Shore boulders with petroglyphs are sometimes exposed on the ocean side of the highway bridge.

On the north side of the river, Highway 580 heads inland. This route was the ancient Highway of the Kings; commoners were forbidden to use it, and rulers were carried over it because their feet were considered too sacred to touch the ground.

Kaumualii Park, alongside the river in a coconut grove, is a pleasant spot for a picnic.

The Poliahu area of Wailua River State Park is about 2 miles/3 km inland along this road. Here you'll find Holo-Holo-Ku, one of Kauai's oldest heiau, which bears a remarkable resemblance to a Tahitian temple. Partially restored, it contains reproductions of idols and a priest's grass house, a sacrificial rock, and royal birthstones. A trail up the hillside leads to an interesting Japanese graveyard.

At the top of the hill, stop at the site of Poliahu Heiau and the king's home. A trail goes down to the Bell Stone, which resounds musically when struck with a rock. This method was once used to signal Malae Heiau and to herald the birth of royal children. Just beyond is a view point over magnificent Opaekaa Falls and, across the road from it, a good view of the river far below.

The road continues into Wailua Homesteads, a region of small farms, ranches, and fruit and macadamia nut orchards. Stop at Alexander's Nursery, a mile from the falls—it's a fascinating, disorganized collection of just about everything that grows in Kauai's home gardens. Call ahead to visit the University of Hawaii Agricultural Experiment Station, which contains early Hawaiian medicinal plants and other varieties.

Roads crisscross the hills back of Kapaa and Kealia. Instead of reversing course, you can continue through this pastoral countryside, returning to the main route along Highway 581.

TWO TROPICAL BOTANICAL DELIGHTS

Cupped in a lush valley on the fertile south shore of Kauai, the Pacific Tropical Botanical Garden makes a delightful plan-ahead excursion for gardening buffs. Chartered by Congress in 1964 as a private, non-profit organization for tropical botanical and horticultural research and education, the center recently opened to the public. Volunteer guides lead 2-hour tours through the gardens four mornings a week.

Most tours sample two very different gardens that share the natural greenhouse of the Lawai Valley: the hardworking 186-acre research garden, and the gracious older garden of the 100-acre Allerton Estate. Tours pass through most of the major collections of the botanical garden, including 500 species of palms (planted from seed in 1971 and now standing 25 feet high), 50 varieties of bananas, and 100 of the 115 known species of exotic flowering coral tree (*Erythrina*). As an added attraction, you'll see and hear a variety of native birds.

From the nursery, a path leads into the cool green Allerton Estate gardens. This end of the valley served as a retreat for Queen Emma (bride of King Kamehameha IV) in the 1880s, then was cleared for agriculture before being purchased by Robert Allerton in 1938.

Using ancient Hawaiian taro terraces and old stone walls as key landscape elements, the Allertons directed springs and streams into pools and fountains graced by sculpture.

You are never far from the sound of water. Paths shaded by leafy umbrellas of monkeypod and tamarind trees wind through emerald groves of bamboo, past flaming thickets of red-flowered ginger. Rubber trees tower nearly a hundred feet overhead.

On Tuesday, guides take you down to the houses at Lawai Bay. Here are Queen Emma's cottage (she planted the bougainvillea swathing the hill behind the cottage) and the open-veranda home of Allerton's son, architect John Gregg Allerton.

Tours of the Pacific Tropical Botanical Garden and the Allerton garden are 9 and 10:15 A.M. Tuesday and 9 A.M. Thursday. Tours of the botanical gardens only are Wednesday and Saturday at 9 A.M. Reservations are a must. For reservations and ticket price, call (808) 332-7361 or write Pacific Tropical Botanical Garden, Box 340, Lawai, Kauai, HI 96765.

To reach the gardens, take Koloa Road west from Koloa 2½ miles/4 km to Hailima Road; turn left ½ mile to the visitor center.

Smith's Tropical Paradise. Ethnic villages located on 31 acres of tropical gardens and lagoons behind the Wailua Marina feature life styles from Japan, the Philippines, Portugal, Korea, China, and Polynesia. You can walk through, if you wish, or take a narrated tour by tram. The admission fee includes the tram ride. Smith's Tropical Paradise is open daily from 9:30 A.M. to 4:30 P.M.

Fern Grotto. The road inland along the river's south bank goes to Wailua Marina and ends at Smith's Tropical Paradise. Boats leave the marina daily between 9 A.M. and 4 P.M. for the short trip upriver to the Fern Grotto. As you glide between river banks covered with *hala* (pandanus), *hau* (jungle trees with hibiscuslike flowers), and rare *pili* grass that was once used for Hawaiian houses, boat captains entertain with fascinating legends about the area. Caves in the bluffs were royal burial grounds.

At the upstream landing, a short trail leads through dense jungle growth to the Fern Grotto, a cool, damp, 40-foot cavern trimmed with a trickling waterfall and lush, feathery ferns. The grotto forms a natural amphitheater and provides fine acoustics for the Hawaiian chorus serenade. Night excursions up the river include dinner and special pageantry.

Boats operate about every half hour. Both tour operators offer similar programs. A restaurant, shops, and other attractions allow you to linger at the marina before or after your trip. More than a half-million people visit the grotto each year; if you're allergic to crowds, plan to take the earliest trip.

North of the river. Just north of Wailua River, the century-old lagoon of Kauai's last queen and a large coconut grove planted in 1896 are part of the grounds of the Coco Palms Hotel. The elaborate torch-lighting ceremony that takes place nightly among the lagoons is well worth watching.

Kamokila Hawaiian Village, 2 miles/3 km east on Highway 580, is a re-creation of a Polynesian grass-hut village that stood on this site centuries ago. Tours include Hawaiian quilting and lei-making demonstrations.

The East Shore

Between the Wailua River and Kapaa, the highway skirts Wailua Bay and bisects a large coconut grove in the midst of the Coconut Plantation development, an 80-acre site with hotels, restaurants, and a shopping complex called The Market Place. Shops are set amid waterways, pools, fountains, trees, flowers, and the relics of a sugar mill.

Kapaa. Modern architecture combined with intriguing 19th-century balconied wooden stores—Kapaa is well worth a walking tour. Notice the restored Seto Building and the venerable Kauai General Store. The small plantation town's churches and temples represent a wide range of faith: Buddhist, Church of Christ, Episcopal, Mormon, and Seventh-Day Adventist.

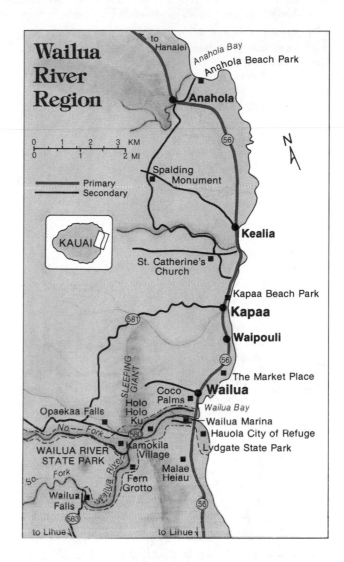

Between Kapaa and Anahola. The highway to Anahola bypasses wonderful scenery; to reach it, take stretches of the old winding road, spurs down to the sea, or the several roads that go inland from Kapaa and Kealia. The road uphill south of Kapaa Stream bridge goes to St. Catherine's Catholic Church, a square structure with ceramic murals and frescoes by Jean Charlot, Tseng Yu-ho, and Juliette May Fraser. The view back should cause you to reach for your camera.

You can continue from the church into Wailua Homesteads. Or turn right just past the building, go down into Kealia Valley, and follow the stream—and perhaps picnic on its bank under a monkeypod tree. The good road ends at the University of Hawaii agricultural station.

Just north of Kapaa the Hawaii Visitors Bureau marker indicates the fruit stand where you'll find papaya, guava, and other island delicacies.

Anahola. People still gossip and snooze on front porches in Anahola, a traditional Hawaiian homestead area. There's a pretty red-roofed church on the hillside and an inviting park alongside the tree-lined bay.

Deterred by rumors about wet weather and the quiet pace, many tourists plan only a day's outing to Kauai's North Shore. This doesn't bother residents and repeat vacationers. They prefer to keep the area secluded. They're delighted to have horses available at nearby stables and are pleased that Hanalei Valley's one-way bridges stop the tour buses.

But clear, sparkling days do occur. When first-time visitors see postcard-pretty valleys and cliffs halted only by the sea, stroll through bucolic Hanalei town, snorkel at Ke'e Beach, play a round of golf at Princeville, or watch the sun set over Hanalei Bay—the secret is out.

Between Anahola and Kilauea, rerouted Highway 56 bridges gulches and streams; the old road winds down through Moloaa Valley. From it, a turnoff leads to the remains of a little village virtually wiped out in the 1946 tidal wave. Much of this region's former pineapple and sugarcane land now grows papayas, guavas, and seed corn.

The old town of Kilauea contains some handsomely restored houses, unusual stores located in old plantation buildings, a historic schoolhouse, and a couple of intriguing churches. St. Sylvester's Catholic Church is an octagon with an interior designed as a "church in the round" that contains Jean Charlot frescoes. Rugged Christ Memorial Church is built of stone with a craggy lava rock facade and glowing stained glass windows.

Kilauea Lighthouse, now automated, sits on a peninsular bluff high above the sea, commanding rugged seascape views in both directions. The tower, on the state's northernmost point, contains the first light sighted by ships heading east from the Orient. Its clamshell lens is the world's largest.

The peninsula, known as Kilauea Point, is now a wildlife refuge for endangered seabirds. It's also the spring and summer resting place for red-footed boobies. These amusing birds are quite unafraid of people, so you can photograph at close range. Hordes of shearwaters and frigate birds with their impressive 7-foot wing spans make the point their home. An information center and a 20-minute self-guided walking tour introduce visitors to this 129-acre refuge. The lighthouse is open Sunday through Friday from 10 A.M. to 4 P.M.

Beyond Kilauea, you can reach Kalihiwai Bay and Anini Beach by turning back onto the old road after you cross the main highway bridge across Kalihiwai Valley. Stop on the Kilauea side for a valley view that takes in some sparkling waterfalls.

Anini Beach, down a side road from the old coastal route, is a little like Tahiti: some tumbledown shacks and comfortable summer cottages line a long ribbon of sand with a backdrop of cliffs festooned with mangoes, *hau*, hala, palms, bamboo, and parasitic vines. The water is shallow out to a protecting reef popular for torch fishing.

Mirage Princeville Resort

The main highway passes Mirage Princeville at Hanalei. This recreational resort community contains the cliff-hugging Sheraton Mirage Princeville, single-family homes, condominiums, cottages, and two championship golf courses perched on a bluff overlooking the ocean. A small shopping center fronts the highway.

In spite of continual construction (mainly additional luxury condominiums), Mirage Princeville Resort maintains a low profile, following the island height restriction of "no building taller than a coconut palm." Several restaurants offer good views of Hanalei Bay.

Prestigious Mirage Princeville's 11,000 acres were once part of Kauai's oldest ranch. Princeville Ranch, established in 1853 by British minister R.C. Wyllie, provided much of the island's beef.

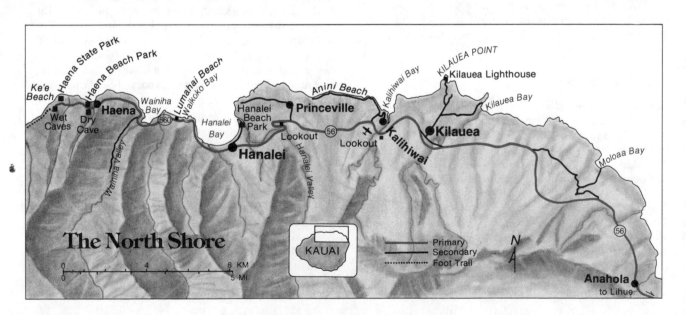

Muumuus brighten *Sunday scene at Hanalei's Waioli Hui'ia Church; Social Hall next door was the original mission church.*

Hanalei Valley

Just past Princeville, you'll catch your first view of Hanalei Valley. From the lookout, you gaze down on taro patches bisected by the silvery Hanalei River and rimmed with precipitous green mountains. The backdrop of neighboring Waioli Valley is often laced with waterfalls. As the highway starts its winding descent, you'll get a different view—across the valley to crescent-shaped Hanalei Bay, bounded by a green headland. Soon you'll cross the first of many historic bridges between Hanalei town and the end of the road. Though you may have to wait for oncoming traffic, these crossings enhance the area's appeal.

From the bridge where the highway reaches the valley floor, you can follow a spur road along the river bank for several miles into the valley. Yellow ginger, purple ground orchids, guavas, and pomelo now abound in an area once cultivated for oranges.

Hanalei is still quiet and peaceful, but change is coming. Though the Ching Young Store, a landmark since 1906, has been replaced by a shopping complex, much of the past remains.

Hanalei has humble bungalows, comfortable summer homes, some tourist apartments, a courthouse, post office, two general stores, eating places, a photogenic lily pond, museum, and five churches. It's also the headquarters for the inflatable boat tours of the Na Pali Coast. Note Waioli Social Hall, the original mission church, built in 1841; it's an example of the best in Hawaiian architecture. Pretty, pale green Waioli Hui'ia Church next door dates from 1912. Behind is the mission home, a two-story, white building with verandas; built in 1836, it has been restored and contains many original furnishings (tours conducted Tuesday through Saturday 9 A.M. to 3 P.M., Sunday 11 A.M. to 3 P.M.; closed Mondays; free).

Modern St. William's Catholic Church across the road has a Hawaiian longhouse shape and tile murals by Jean Charlot. Hanalei Museum, in a plantation cottage (open daily in summer; check hours for other seasons), features turn-of-the-century furniture, agricultural tools, and artifacts of various ethnic groups. A snack bar with tropical fruit juices and ice creams is located right behind the museum.

Hanalei also has a splendid beach—but because of treacherous currents, swim only by the pier, past the beach park near the end of the shore road.

To Road's End

One of the most photographed bays in the islands is Waikoko, at the eastern end of the Lumahai shore. From the marked view point on the highway, a trail descends the hala-laden cliffs to a small, rock-edged cove where you can picnic (swimming is not recommended). The Lumahai sands (sift through them for olivines) stretch west a long way.

At Wainiha Bay, take the road that climbs above the river to the powerhouse for a sampling of heavily wooded Wainiha Valley, strung with perpetual waterfalls that begin in Alakai Swamp.

The Wainiha General Store is your last chance to pick up picnic supplies before road's end. At the Hanalei Colony Resort, just beyond, you'll find a restaurant, bar, and art gallery.

The Haena region, once heavily settled, is now sprinkled thinly with old-timers' ramshackle homes and vacationers' cottages—old and new. Every rock, cave, and cliff speaks a legend; beaches are little roamed; mountain peaks are jagged but clothed in foliage and softly overhung with clouds. You will pass Maniniholo Dry Cave, which legend says was made by menehune as they dug seeking a supernatural being who had stolen their fish. Waikapalae and Waikanaloa Wet Caves are said to have

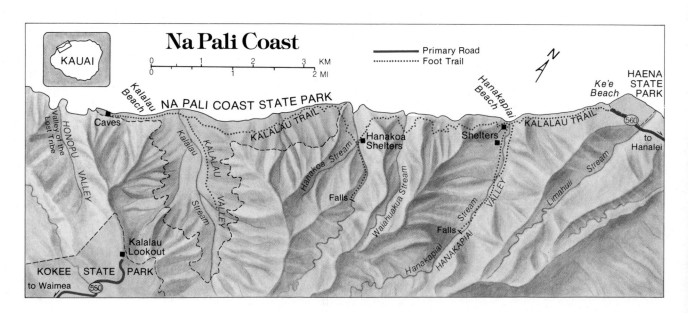

been dug by the fire goddess Pele while she was trying to find herself a home on this verdant island.

Even though it's not usually safe to swim off Haena Beach Park, idyllic Ke'e Beach at the end of the road (location for the movie *Thorn Birds*) is placid most of the year. Just east of it there's a tiny roadside pool in Limahuli Stream. At low tide you can walk a mile from Haena State Park to Ke'e along the sandy shore (take shoes because of a few rocky spots). Ke'e's backdrop is the triangular Makana (Fireworks Cliff).

Above the sandy cove you can hike up to ruins of the Hula Heiau, a platform from which the traditional dance was performed centuries ago.

The Na Pali Coast

From the northern end of Ke'e Beach, you can glimpse the spectacular Na Pali Coast. Ridges of cliffs rising 2,000 to 3,000 feet from the sea embrace a series of deep, jungled valleys from here all the way to Mana.

Until helicopter excursions began (see page 82), few people had viewed these uninhabited valleys, some accessible only from the sea in fair weather. Although the flights over the valleys are exciting, they show only a small sampling of what these valleys—from Hanakapiai west to Milolii—hold. Some of the scenery may look familiar; parts of *Fantasy Island* and *King Kong* were filmed along this coastline.

You can view Na Pali from an inflatable boat any time when the weather is favorable. Because sandy beaches disappear when big swells pound the shore, landing on this coast is usually impossible in winter. For boat trips, see page 89. A few valleys are accessible by hiking over the 11-mile/18-km Kalalau Trail. To camp in any of the Na Pali valleys, permits are required and camping limits are in effect (see page 89 for camping information).

Hanakapiai, the first valley, is a steep but easy 2-mile/3-km walk. If you go just ¼ mile along the trail that starts from the end of Highway 56, you will be rewarded with a splendid view back down upon Ke'e Beach and the Haena reefs. The trail on to Hanakapiai is resplendent with hala, ti, kukui, guavas, and wild orchids, has spectacular Na Pali overlooks, and reaches a broad beach. A 1¼-mile/2-km loop, a spur off the main trail, goes into the valley across ancient taro terraces, through a mango grove, and past ruins of a coffee mill where there's a shelter.

Out of Hanakapiai the trail climbs steeply and does not drop to sea level again until it reaches Kalalau Beach. Footing is good, but the going is either up or down (no level places to ease leg work) and the weather is hot. About 6 miles/10 km along is Hanakoa, a good rest stop or a destination in itself. A path leads from a rustic cabin to a wonderful swimming pool with waterfall in Hanakoa Stream. From across the stream, a short spur goes up to Hanakoa Falls, a cascade at the rear of a fork of the valley.

From Hanakoa on, the country gets drier. You encounter sisal, lantana, and cattle. The trail enters Kalalau, the largest valley, near the main stream. At this point,

you're more than a mile from the favored campsite on its mile-long beach—near a small stream with waterfall "shower" and bathing pool. As you cross the valley, note the branch trail that climbs inland near Kalalau Stream and offers good valley exploring. You can follow the main stream all the way to Davis Falls. Some like the beach dry caves for sleeping; everyone wades and splashes in the wet caves. In summer, you can partly swim, partly wade to neighboring Honopu, the legendary "Valley of the Lost Tribe," where remains have been found of an ancient Polynesian settlement that unaccountably vanished.

With ice cream cone in hand, *barefoot boy isn't distracted by ancient surfboard propped against the Hanalei museum wall.*

FLIGHTSEEING BY HELICOPTER —
A VIEW FROM ALL SIDES

A bird's-eye glimpse of a plummeting waterfall, a fingertip pass over a jungle-clad mountain slope, a leisurely look at wave-sculptured lava cliffs, a peek into a desolate crater—these are all part of flightseeing Hawaii by helicopter.

You'll glide, whirl, and swoop through hidden canyons and over inaccessible beaches, flit across sugar, taro, and pineapple fields, and soar by tiny hamlets of civilization that punctuate the verdant landscape. The view from a helicopter is one of the best ways to see the islands' dramatic topography.

Service and destination. Helicopter flights are available on five islands: Oahu, Kauai, Maui, Molokai, and Hawaii. Kauai is certainly the capital with nearly a dozen companies offering flights ranging from 30-minute overviews of coastline and canyons to circle-island tours that might include a touchdown on a deserted beach or a sunset flight. There's even a helicopter trip to mysterious Niihau, Kauai's island neighbor generally off limits to tourists. Companies operate from the Poipu, Lihue, and Hanalei areas.

On Oahu, you can view sprawling Honolulu from the air, put Pearl Harbor into perspective, climb above Diamond Head and into the Punchbowl, and skim across the Pali on a circle-island itinerary. Service is provided by several companies from a Waikiki helipad.

A look at the Maui countryside might include a flight across the channel to neighboring Molokai or Lanai, sunrise over Haleakala, or a spin across the island for a picnic lunch in Hana. Eight companies offer a choice of flights; sunset tours are popular. On Molokai, you can fly over Kalaupapa and along the Pali Coast, which has the world's highest sea cliffs as measured from the ocean floor.

The diversity and size of the Big Island is better grasped from the air. Helicopters sweep along the Kona and Kohala coasts, peer into Mauna Loa crater, and venture across the mountains to picnic in sheltered Waipio Valley. Flights leave from the Kona and Kohala coasts, Hilo, and Hawaii Volcanoes National Park.

Cost. How much you'll pay to hover over Hawaii depends on the length of the flights, itinerary, and number of people. Though extensive flightseeing is not inexpensive, you may receive extras such as champagne, snacks, or meals. Some companies provide free hotel pickup and delivery.

Additional information. Helicopter companies are listed in the "Recreation Guide" section for each island. For reservations and more details, check with your hotel's activities desk or call the company directly; telephone numbers are listed in the island Yellow Pages.

Helicopter hovers *near base of waterfall on Kauai's rugged Na Pali Coast. You can swoop, glide, and dip into the state's hidden scenic treasures on all major islands.*

THE SOUTH SHORE

Today, the South Shore is the destination for vacationers who seek plentiful sunshine, broad beaches, calm seas, and riotous plant life. In earlier days, the southern region played host to King Sugar. Some of the picturesque old plantation communities and mills still stand among the cane fields, but luxurious resorts, restaurants, shops, golf courses, and tennis courts have blossomed, turning the area into a site from which it's hard to wander.

To reach the South Shore from Lihue, follow Highway 50. Highway 520 branches off to historic Koloa and the resort areas around Poipu Beach. A network of roads between Poipu and Hanapepe takes you through a number of places of interest in the region south of the main highway.

En Route to Koloa

Within the first 8 miles/13 km out of Lihue, look for these attractions: wild ginger along the roadside; the marvelous old post office–store, new community college, and Kukui Grove Center at Puhi; the turnoff to Kipu Ranch at the foot of Haupu peak; Halfway Bridge over the Huleia River; Knudsen Gap, between the Hoary Head Mountains and Kahili peak at the end of the island's central mountain mass. Highway 520 to Koloa starts off through a magnificent cathedral grove of fragrant eucalyptus.

Koloa—Site of the First Sugar Mill

Stretch your legs in the plantation town of Koloa, 3 miles/5 km from the junction of highways 50 and 520. It's a historic village with big trees and charming wooden buildings. You'll see the stone mill stack of Hawaii's first bona fide plantation.

Visit three quaint-but-thriving temples (Hongwanji, Jodo, and Odaishi) and the restored church of Koloa Mission (1834), and ask the way to St. Raphael's Church south of town. Kauai's oldest Catholic mission (1841) has an impressive 1856 masonry church, coral stone houses, graveyard, outdoor altar, and tiny lava rock chapel seating eight.

In and Around Poipu

As you drive downhill to the sunny coast, you may encounter some confusing road forks. To reach Poipu beaches, resorts, 18-hole golf course, and restaurants, take Poipu Road to the left. The road passes Poipu Beach Park and ends at Makahuena Point. At the park, you'll find a shallow cove with gentle waves for youngsters. To the west, in front of several hotels, there's smooth water for swimmers and surf suitable for boards. In the opposite direction (east) from Poipu Beach is Brennecke's Beach, popular for body surfing until the 1982 storm. The road ends at the crater where Kauai's last eruption occurred.

Following Hoonani Road from Highway 530 brings you to Koloa Landing, departure point for diving and snorkeling tours. Whalers—as many as 50 at a time—used to winter at Koloa Landing; hotel buildings now sit on the cove's west bluff.

There's plenty to do in the Poipu area if you tire of water sports: golf at Kiahuna Golf Club, tennis, bike riding, horseback riding, whale watching (December through April), or perusing hotel shoreside shops or the ones at Kiahuna Shopping Village.

Kukuiula Bay and Spouting Horn

Turn right at Lawai Road to reach Spouting Horn and the Kukuiula shore. The road to Kukuiula Bay passes Prince Kuhio Park, where a monument marks the birthplace of Hawaii's long-time delegate to Congress.

Beyond Kukuiula Bay, a photogenic sampan harbor, the road ends at Spouting Horn, where the sea pushes up like a geyser through a shoreline lava tube. The moaning sound that comes from beneath the lava is said to be the cries of a legendary lizard, Lehu, who crawled into the tube long ago and became entrapped.

From Spouting Horn's lookout you can gaze across the water to the south shore of Niihau, just 17 miles/27 km away. This private island is the home for some 200 pure Hawaiians.

En Route to Hanapepe

To continue along the southwest coast, you'll need to return to Koloa. Highway 530 meanders through the pastoral Lawai Valley in the few miles between Koloa and Highway 50. Lawai, site of the Pacific Tropical Botanical Garden (see page 76), still contains the remnants of the Kauai pineapple cannery.

From Kalaheo, drive up to Kukuiolono Park, formerly the estate of the founder of McBryde Sugar Plantation. A favorite of picnickers, the park also provides a 9-hole hillside golf course, Japanese garden, display of Hawaiian legendary boulders, and inspiring views out over Lawai to the sea.

Beyond Kalaheo, a sign directs you inland to Olu Pua Gardens, previously a plantation manager's estate. Visitors receive a printed map with a suggested walk through the eight gardens that make up the complex: jungle path to native and orchid areas, hibiscus garden, oriental garden, palm garden, sunken garden, succulent garden, blue garden, and kau kau (food) garden. All plants are identified. The garden is open from 8:30 A.M. to 5 P.M. daily; there's a moderate charge.

The Charm of Hanapepe

From Hanapepe Canyon Lookout, you can scan the green valley nestled between red cliffs. You view taro patches and farm plots at the lush canyon's mouth.

A side road loops through the town, reminiscent of the Old West, which follows the winding Hanapepe River.

...The South Shore

Intriguing wooden buildings overhang the river bank; a narrow old bridge crosses the stream. A drive through the farms on the dead-end road back of town gives you the feeling of old rural Hawaii.

Turn off on Highway 543 to Salt Pond Park, a clean crescent of sand beside a reef-protected bay. Before reaching the park, you pass the ponds where coarse luau salt is still made in dry weather by evaporating sea water. Salt obtained in this way was used by early Hawaiians to preserve meat and fish and by traders to cure furs.

Kaumakani, another plantation village, rewards curious visitors with a quaint post office and the Kaumakani Methodist Church, uphill of the highway northeast of town.

Historic Waimea

Despite its small population (around 1,500 people), Waimea is west Kauai's center for commercial activity. This role isn't unexpected given the region's history; it was a seasonal court of chiefs in pre-Western times and the setting for exploration, trade, and missionary settlement by the English, Americans, and Russians.

Much of the town's attraction stems from an intriguing cultural mix, most readily apparent in architectural diversity. Kauai's first mission was established on the Tsuchiya Road grounds in 1820. The Waimea Foreign Church, constructed in 1853 of coral and sandstone, stands nearby between mission and Oriental cemeteries. A third house of worship was built by Reverend George Rowell, who also initiated the Waimea Hawaiian Church on Highway 50.

Other historic buildings include the Ako Store (a general store across from the Hawaiian Church), the Mar-vin Koahi house (circa 1880), and the island's oldest home, the Gulick-Rowell House on Huakai Road. The latter, a New England–style structure with limestone walls and gable roof, was started in the early 1830s by missionary Peter Gulick.

Well-preserved remains of Fort Elizabeth, built by the Russians in 1817, cover the bluff above Waimea River and Bay. Waimea was Captain Cook's first Hawaiian landing place. Both the fort and landing site are national historic landmarks. The fort, built in an irregular star shape about 400 feet across, flew the Russian flag briefly, mostly as a trading post. Hawaiian troops then occupied it until 1853. The state has reconstructed the fort trappings and added parking and rest room facilities.

Drive the narrow river road through town for 1½ miles/2 km to Menehune Ditch, once a long watercourse allegedly built by the little people. You pass taro and farm plots, a poi factory, and an unusual Shingon temple. The temple's 88 bullet-shaped outdoor shrines honor soldiers killed in World War II.

Polihale State Park

The sleepy town of Kekaha has a beach park for picnicking (swimming is dangerous along this shore). Offshore, you'll see privately owned Niihau.

From highway's end at Mana you can follow signs along several miles of cane roads to 140-acre Polihale State Park at the south end of Na Pali. This is a developed park (rest rooms, showers, picnic shelters) where you can camp, hike across dunes or along the base of the bluffs, and swim in summer—in the sea if it's calm or, if not, in Queen's Pond, an often-exposed brackish water channel in the beach.

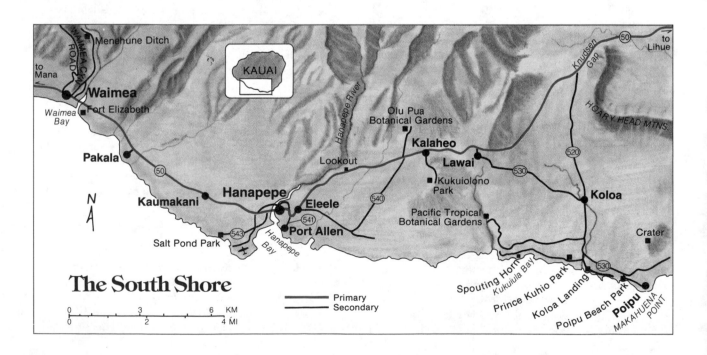

The South Shore

THE NEW WORDS YOU'LL HEAR

As you might expect, the English spoken in the islands has been augmented with words and expressions from languages native to Hawaii's various ethnic groups. You'll hear people pronounce vowel sounds in English words as they would in Hawaiian, Japanese, or one of the Romance languages.

You'll also hear pidgin English—shortcut communicating that may be unintelligible. Most islanders can and usually do speak good English; they just enliven their talk with Hawaiian words and occasionally interject pidgin vocabulary.

Since names of most places and streets are Hawaiian, some knowledge of the pronunciation rules of this language will prove helpful. The Hawaiian alphabet contains only 12 letters: the 5 vowels plus 7 consonants (h, k, l, m, n, p, and w). Words seem to overflow with vowels, but pronunciation is not difficult if you remember to pronounce every letter separately. The vowel sounds are *a* as in "arm," *e* as in "end," *i* as in "machine," *o* as in "old," and *u* as in "rude." Consonants have the same sounds as in English except for the *w*. Some Hawaiians always pronounce it as a *v* unless it is preceded by an *o* or *u*; others do so only when it is the next to last letter in a word. In diphthongs (*ei, eu, oi, ou, ai, ae, ao, au*), stress the first member (*lei*).

If you see a glottal stop mark, or hamza, it indicates, in the Polynesian language, that the letter *k* has been omitted; there is a definite break in sound between the letters it separates.

Here are some frequently used words and phrases. Gourmets and anglers will also find helpful the list on page 145.

'ae	yes
ahui ho	until we meet again
ahupua'a	land division
aikane	friend (slang)
'aina	land, earth
akamai	wise, smart
ala	road, path
ali'i	royalty, a chief
aloha	greetings, welcome, farewell, love
aloha nui loa	much love
'a'ole	no
auwe	alas! ouch
ha'ina	end of song
hale	house
hana	work
hana hou	encore
haole	Caucasian
hapa	half, part
hapai	to carry, be pregnant
Hauoli la Hanau	Happy Birthday
Hauoli Makahiki Hou	Happy New Year
heiau	temple
hele mai	come here
hikie'e	large couch
holoku	fitted ankle-length dress with train
holomu'u	fitted ankle-length dress
ho'olaule'a	celebration
huhu	angry
hui	club, association
hukilau	to fish with a seine
iki	small, little
ipo	sweetheart, lover
kahili	feather standard
kahuna	priest, expert
kai	sea
kala	money
kama'aina	native born
kanaka	person, man
kanalua	doubtful, hesitant
kane	male, husband
kapakahi	crooked, lopsided
kapu	forbidden, keep out
kaukau	food (slang)
keiki	child
kokua	help
kona	lee side
kuleana	right, property, responsibility
kumu	teacher
lanai	porch, veranda
lei	garland, wreath
lomi (or lomilomi)	rub, press, massage
lua	toilet
mahalo	thanks
maika'i	good, fine
makai	toward the sea
make	dead
malihini	stranger, newcomer
malo	a loin cloth
manu	bird
manuahi	free, gratis
mauka	inland
mauna	mountain
mele	song
Mele Kalikimaka	Merry Christmas
menehune	dwarf, legendary race of dwarfs
moana	ocean
moemoe	sleep (slang)
momona	fat
mu'umu'u	long or short loose-fitting dress
nani	beautiful
ne'i	this place
nui	big, large, great
ohana	family
'okolehao	ti-root liquor
'okole maluna	bottoms up
'ono	delicious, tasty
'opu	belly, stomach
Pake	Chinese (slang)
pali	cliff, precipice
paniolo	cowboy
pau	finished
pa'u	wrap-around skirt
pehea'oe	how are you?
pikake	jasmine
pilau	putrid
pilikia	trouble
pohaku	rock, stone
popoki	cat
pua	flower, blossom
pua'a	pig, pork
puka	hole, door
pupu	shell, hors d'oeuvre
pupule	crazy, insane
tutu	grandmother
tutu kane	grandfather
wahine	female, wife
wai	fresh water
wikiwiki	fast, hurry

You can combine visits to the "Grand Canyon" and a crisp mountain plateau in one trip to Waimea Canyon and Kokee state parks. It's a year-round destination by tour bus or on your own. In summer months, many people stay to enjoy the outdoor life—to camp, fish streams, pick plums, and hike luxuriant forest trails among such native flora as the *iliau* tree (a member of the sunflower family), *mokihana* berry, and lobelias found only in Kauai.

You reach this wilderness on Kokee Road from Kekaha, or by Highway 550 (Waimea Canyon Road) from Waimea. Highway 550 travels the canyon rim, where it is joined by Kokee Road. The highway then climbs arid, scrub-covered hills above Waimea Canyon for 12 miles/ 19 km to the main lookout.

If you're driving, check your gas gauge; the last station is in Kekaha. Bring a light wrap, since temperatures are lower in the higher elevations.

Waimea Canyon's Chasm

From Waimea Canyon Lookout at 3,400 feet, you can see most of the 2,857-foot-deep gorge that cuts into the Kokee Plateau. The canyon has a monumental quality as unexpected on a tropical island as the crisp, invigorating mountain air. It resembles the Grand Canyon in character, if not in size, with the addition of the blues and mossy greens of lush vegetation to complement the reds and browns of exposed volcanic rock walls. Clouds usually hang over the rim, their moving shadows heightening the impression of vastness.

About 1½ miles/2 km beyond the entrance to 1,866-acre Waimea Canyon State Park, there's a small parking area at the start of the Kukui Trail, which drops in switchbacks down the west wall of Waimea Canyon and ends at the Waimea River (a drop of over 2,000 feet in 2½ miles/4 km). At the start of the Kukui Trail is the Iliau Loop Trail, an easy, ¼-mile nature walk. Twenty native plants are identified, including the iliau, which blooms in June and July. The loop offers excellent vistas of the canyon and distant Waialae Falls.

From Puu Hinahina Lookout, farther up, your eyes can follow the canyon out to the coast and pick up Niihau across the sea to the west. Just above the lookout, you pass a paved spur that goes 4½ miles/7 km down Makaha Ridge, through typical reforested country, to views of the Na Pali Coast.

Kokee State Park

The highway climbs 8 scenic miles/13 km past several waterfalls and streams on its way to 4,345-acre Kokee State Park, a center for camping and hiking.

Around the park headquarters, you'll find Kokee Lodge, with restaurant, cabins, shops, and camp and picnic grounds. Adjacent Kokee Museum features exhibits of flora and fauna, geology, and petroglyphs.

Kokee is the starting point for about 45 miles/72 km of hiking trails, some of which go into the surrounding

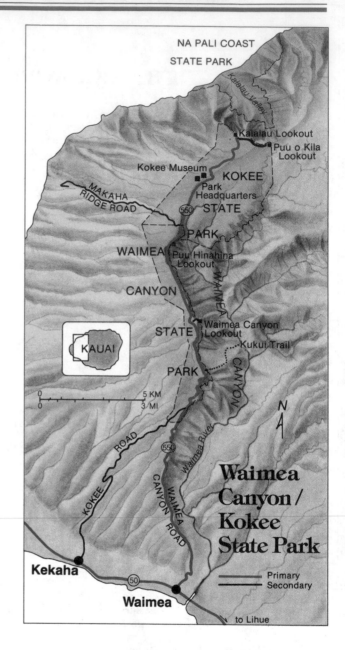

forest reserve. Many of the trails are under a mile, making them popular picnic sites. Some of the longer trails include treks into the Alakai Swamp between Kokee and Mt. Waialeale, and over ridges separating valleys of the Na Pali Coast. Hurricane Iwa damaged many trails when winds struck in 1982; check with park headquarters before setting out. Hikers should register at headquarters for all trails. In dry weather, dirt roads that provide access to trail heads can be driven in ordinary passenger cars.

Past the park headquarters, Kokee Road becomes Kalalau Road on its climb to Kalalau Lookout, a 4,000-foot-high view point over broad, green-carpeted Kalalau Valley and the shimmering blue sea at its mouth. If a cloud obscures the view, as it often does, wait a while—it may lift. (Caution: No hiking is permitted from the lookout into the valley.)

Spouting Horn *shows off. Geyserlike spray is accompanied by sorrowful moaning of a legendary lizard said to be trapped in the lava tube below.*

Visitor overlook *offers grand views of Waimea Canyon. Shifting cloud shadows constantly change colors of the lava slopes.*

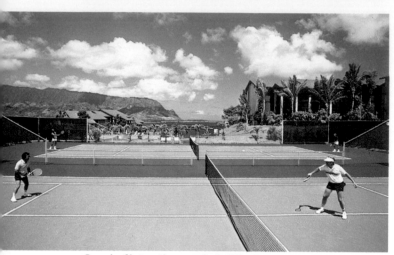

Scenic distractions *make it difficult to keep your eyes on the ball at Princeville's tennis courts.*

It's been said that the only flaw in Kauai's reputation is a lack of activities. Nothing can be further from the truth—Kauai is much, much more than an island-sized arboretum. The following listing offers a general look at Kauai's recreational attractions. For further details on any activity, consult your travel agent, your hotel desk, or the Hawaii Visitors Bureau (Lihue office: P.O. Box 507, Lihue, HI 96766).

Flightseeing. One of the best views of Kauai's dramatic topography, particularly the almost inaccessible Na Pali Coast and central island peaks and valleys, is from the air. Most companies offer circle-island tours and charter flights; all fly from Lihue Airport with additional flights from other sites as noted.

Plane. Panorama Air Tour and Scenic Air Tours Hawaii (originating at Honolulu International Airport).

Helicopter. Bruce Needham Helicopters (Hanapepe), Island Helicopters, Jack Harter Helicopters, Kauai Helicopters, Kenai Helicopters, Menehune Helicopters, Niihau Helicopters (tours to Niihau from Port Allen near Hanapepe), Ohana Helicopters, Papillon Helicopters (also Princeville and Port Allen), Will Squyre's Helicopter.

Glider. Tradewinds Glider Flights.

Golf. All the courses listed below are open to the public. Yardages are from the regular (white) tees.

Public Course. Wailua Municipal Golf Course, Wailua, 18 holes, 6,631 yards.

Resort/commercial courses. Kukuiolono Golf Course, Kalaheo, 9 holes, 2,981 yards; Kiahuna Golf Club, Poipu, 18 holes, 5,669 yards (Robert Trent Jones, Jr. course); Princeville Makai Golf Course, Hanalei (Ocean Nine, 3,460 yards; Woods Nine, 3,460 yards; Lake Nine, 3,488 yards); Robert Trent Jones, Jr. course, in *Golf Digest* Amer-

ican Top 100; Mirage Princeville, Prince Golf Course, Hanalei, 9 holes, 3,176 yards (Robert Trent Jones, Jr. course with 9 more holes under construction); Kauai Lagoons Golf Course and Kiele Lagoons Golf Course, Lihue (two 18-hole Jack Nicklaus courses under construction).

Tennis. Public and resort or commercial courts are listed below. Many condominiums also have courts for guest use. Check with your travel or rental agent.

Public courts. Waimea, next to Waimea High School; Hanapepe, near Hanapepe Pavilion; Kalaheo, Kalaheo School; Koloa, next to the fire station (near Highway 52); Lihue, next to Convention Hall; Kapaa, next to Kapaa Ball Park. All public facilities have 2 lighted courts.

Resort/commercial courts. Poipu: Kiahuna Tennis Club, 10 (7 with lights); Stouffer Waiohai and Poipu Beach, 6; Poipu Kai, 8; Sheraton Kauai, 3 (2 with lights). Nawiliwili: Westin Kauai, 8, stadium court. Wailua: Aston Kauai, 2; Coco Palms, 9 (2 with lights); Kauai Beachboy, 1; Sheraton Coconut Beach, 3. Princeville: Hanalei Bay Resort, 11 (3 with lights); Princeville Tennis Center, 6.

Swimming. The most difficult aspect of swimming on Kauai may be choosing which beach.

Ocean swimming. Salt Pond, Kukuiula, Poipu, Kalapaki (Nawiliwili), Hanamaulu, Lydgate (in man-made ocean pool), Wailua (at Kapaa end), Anahola, Anini, Hanalei (at pier), Ke'e.

Freshwater swimming. Hanakoa Valley pool, Kokee's Kawaikoi Stream, Limahuli Pool, Wailua River.

Surfing. Check water conditions with residents, companies renting surfing gear, or your hotel's activities desk.

Surfing equipment. Surf'n' Cycle, Koloa; Bea's Activities, Sea Sage Diving Center, Lihue; Aquarius Beach Center, Aquatics Kauai, Waipouli; Pedal'n' Paddle, Hanalei.

Board surfing. Poipu shore, Nawiliwili (Kalapaki Beach), Wailua Bay, Hanalei Bay.

Body surfing. Poipu shore, Kalapaki Beach, Wailua Bay, Hanalei Bay, Ke'e Beach.

Beachcombing, tidepooling, and reef walking. You can see a lot of the island's marine diversity without even donning mask and snorkel.

Low-tide walking sites. Polihale, Salt Pond, Poipu, Hanamaulu, Anahola, Moloaa, Anini, Lumahai, Haena.

Skin and scuba diving. Not all of Kauai's gardens are above sea level. For the underwater world, you'll find everything from introductory classes to interisland dive trips.

Diving spots. Poipu, Anahola, Moloaa, Anini, Ke'e end of Haena.

Diving companies. Fathom Five Professional Divers, Koloa; Kauai Divers, Koloa; Sea Sage Diving Center, Kapaa; Aquatics Kauai, Kapaa; Dive Kauai, Kapaa; Ocean

Odyssey, Kapaa; Wet-N-Wonderful Ocean Sports, Kapaa. Most diving companies offer instruction, certification, rentals, and dive trips. For further information, write Dive Hawaii, Box 90295, Honolulu, HI 96835.

Boat cruises, charters, and rentals. Just about any kind of craft can be rented on Kauai.

Poipu-Lihue. Blue Water Sailing, Eleele, snorkeling; Capt. Andy's Sailing Adventures, Koloa, snorkeling and sunset cruises; Island Adventure, Lihue, kayak trips; Lady Ann Charters, Lihue, snorkeling, sightseeing; Momona Sailing, Eleele, snorkeling, sailing, sunset cruises; Na Pali Coast Cruise Line, Eleele, snorkel cruises, zodiac trips, sunset cruises; Na Pali Kai Tours, Eleele, Na Pali snorkel cruises; Nawiliwili Marine, Lihue, kayak rental; Playtime Charters, Hanapepe, Na Pali snorkel cruises; Ramblin' Rose Charters, Koloa, Na Pali snorkel cruises.

Hanalei. Blue Odyssey Adventures, Na Pali snorkel cruises; Captain Zodiac Raft Expeditions, raft snorkel trips; The Hawaiian Z-Boat Co., Na Pali snorkel and sunset cruises; Kauai Charter Boat Service, snorkel and moonlight cruises; Na Pali Adventures, snorkel and dinner cruises; Na Pali-Kauai Boat Charters, Na Pali raft and boat trips, sunset and south coast cruises, fishing; Ocean Ventures (Kilauea), Na Pali raft snorkel trips; Paradise Adventure Cruises, snorkel and sunset cruises; Raft Riders, Na Pali raft snorkel trips; Sea Kauai, raft snorkel trips; Seascape Kauai, Na Pali snorkel cruises; Whitey's Boat Cruises, Na Pali snorkel cruises.

Fishing. Kauai offers all types of fishing, from freshwater to deep-sea. Contact the State Parks Division of the Department of Land and Natural Resources (3060 Eiwa St., Lihue, HI 96766) for spearfishing regulations and freshwater licensing and limits; there are no saltwater licenses or limits.

Saltwater fishing locations. Spearfishing: reefs off Poipu and Kukuiula, Nualolo and Milolii valleys, and from Hanalei to Kalihiwai. Surfcasting: good all around Kauai. Pole fishing: along harbor piers to catch 'aweoweo (red bigeye) and hahalalu (young bigeye scad) in late summer.

Freshwater fishing locations. Kokee: Choose from 13 miles of fishable streams and a 15-acre reservoir. Trout fishing requires an additional permit (free at park headquarters). Many ponds and reservoirs have bass, bluegill, tilapia, catfish, and carp. Lihue: contact Bass Guides of Kauai. Wailua: sites include a 30-acre reservoir and smallmouth bass fishing in Wailua River tributaries.

Fishing charters. Poipu-Lihue: Bass Guides of Kauai, Coastal Charters Kauai, Gent-Lee Fishing & Sightseeing Charters, Lady Ann Charters, Sportfishing Kauai. Hanalei: Seabreeze Sportfishing Charters, Seascape Kauai. Anahola: Alana Lynn Too Charter Fishing.

Horseback riding. Sightseeing from the saddle can range from hour-long rides to overnight events: Highgates Ranch, Wailua; Pooku Stables, Hanalei.

Hiking, camping, and mountain touring. You can experience Kauai in a variety of ways.

Hiking information. For maps, guides, and other information, contact Hawaiian Geographic Society, 217 S. King St., Honolulu, HI 96813; Hawaii Trail and Mountain Club, Box 5032, Honolulu, HI 96814; Hawaii Sierra Club, Box 22879, Honolulu, HI 96822; Department of Land and Natural Resources, Box 1671, Lihue, HI 96766.

Camping information. For campsite specifics and permits, contact the State Parks Division, 3060 Eiwa St., Lihue, HI 96766; for county parks, Kauai County War Memorial Convention Hall, 4191 Hardy St., Lihue, HI 96766.

Mountain touring and camping. Kauai Mountain Tours, Poipu, conducts four-wheel-drive trips through Waimea Canyon, Kokee State Park. Beach Boy Mobile Holidays, Lihue Airport, offers campers for rent.

Poipu's sunny shores *invite watery sports—swimming, snorkeling, surfing, diving, and boating.*

Beach near Kalama Park, Kihei

MAUI

- WHAT'S YOUR PLEASURE ?
JUST NAME IT ... THE VALLEY ISLAND
CAN PROVIDE IT •

The minute you get off the plane at Kahului Airport, Maui introduces itself to you through one of its more subtle specialties—breezes, from sea and valley, that somehow are *Maui* breezes, different in certain indefinable ways from those of any other place. Varying from gentle morning breezes to brisk afternoon tradewinds, they frequently carry the delicate fragrances of the tropics. Chances are that you will notice and appreciate them throughout your stay—and remember them always.

"Maui No Ka Oi"

Hospitable Maui has a slogan, *Maui No Ka Oi,* "Maui is the best." Certainly few destinations rival the island's warm, friendly atmosphere, and it is a place of almost endless discovery. An increasing number of visitors return year after year.

Hawaii's second largest island (729 square miles/ 1,888 square km) offers superb beaches, fine golf and tennis facilities, and a world of family activity. There is plenty for hikers, bikers, joggers, horseback riders, garden enthusiasts, whale watchers, shoppers, bird lovers, gourmets, or just plain tired-out visitors wanting to relax and "unwind."

Sightseeing ranges from the heights of Haleakala to the scenic and invigorating upcountry ranchlands to the historic former whaling town of Lahaina—attractions so different from one another that the visitor may wonder "Can this be the same island?"

Until the late 1960s, Maui was known primarily for its agriculture, despite the fact that Kaanapali, on the west Maui coast, was already beginning to develop into the island's first major resort area. In recent years several other resort areas have been developed, increasing tourism dramatically. Agriculture, though still strong, has declined to some extent; many island residents (permanent population numbers 78,000) whose forebears worked in the pineapple and cane fields now find employment in resorts, restaurants, and retail stores.

How Two Islands Became One

Maui began existence as two separate land masses. Centuries of erosion from their slopes formed the isthmus that joins them today. From that isthmus Maui gained its nickname, the "Valley Island." Cane fields now blanket the irrigated plain between the mountains, and sugarcane and pineapple cover the foothills. And spread out from where the plain meets the ocean to the north are Maui's two largest towns, Wailuku and Kahului.

On the 5,788-foot summit of the West Maui Mountains, Puu Kukui, more than 400 inches of rain falls annually, making it second to Kauai's Waialeale as Hawaii's rainiest peak.

On the other side of the isthmus, the great mass of the dormant volcano Haleakala rises to 10,023 feet. Its cool, grassy slopes provide grazing for cattle and other livestock, and vegetables and flowers are grown here for commercial markets.

At the foot of Haleakala's eastern slope, standing in contrast to the changing picture throughout most of Maui, is gentle old Hana—where an always-easy pace combines with geographical remoteness to make the area seem almost like an island in itself.

Aloha Airlines, Hawaiian Airlines, Princeville Airways, and Air Molokai-Tropic Airlines connect Kahului daily with other island destinations. Princeville Airways also flies in to Hana and Kapalua-West Maui. United Airlines offers direct mainland flights between Kahului and Los Angeles, San Francisco, and Chicago. Delta Air Lines provides direct service from Los Angeles. American Airlines offers through service to Maui from several mainland cities. Charter flights are also available.

Getting Around

A quick glance at a map might lead you to believe that a circle trip around the island is possible. It's not advisable, though, since certain stretches of road on the northern and southeastern extremities of the island are unimproved and can be dangerous, particularly during and after heavy rains.

It takes at least 3 days to travel Maui's main roads and visit principal attractions. But you're in for some long hours of driving if you try to cover everything from one hotel base.

From Kahului, it's about 40 miles/64 km to the top of Haleakala and about 50 miles/80 km to Hana; these trips take longer than the distances indicate, though, because part of the route is over narrow, winding roads. Minibus tours to these two destinations are particularly popular.

Most of Maui's highways are excellent; auto exploring or simply getting from one place to another is pleasant and relatively easy—except for early morning and late afternoon commute hours. Because many roads are narrow by mainland standards, drivers generally prefer compact to larger models.

Car rental. There are more than 30 car rental agencies at Kahului airport and vicinity, with a wide choice of makes, models (including 4-wheel-drive vehicles and campers), and prices. You'll also find rental agencies in the resort areas.

Bus and shuttle services. Grayline-Maui and Roberts offer shuttle service (reservations only) between Kahului Airport and major resort areas. Taxi and limo service is also available, but costly because of the distances involved.

Shoreline buses operate throughout the day between Kahului, Wailuku and West Maui with stops at hotels along the route. Kaanapali Trolley (free) roams the spread-out resort area of Kaanapali. The Lahaina Kaanapali & Pacific Railroad (page 102) runs for 6 miles/10 km between Kaanapali and Lahaina stations.

Where to Stay

Most Maui vacationers head for one of three regional bases: Lahaina and Kaanapali on the west coast, Napili Bay and Kapalua on the northwest coast, or the southwest oceanfront areas from Kihei south to Wailea. The Kahului-Wailuku area in northcentral Maui makes a good base for visitors on business; it is also a convenient hub for those interested primarily in sightseeing.

In west Maui, the resort region extends from Lahaina, with its colorful Pioneer Inn, to the luxurious Kapalua Bay Hotel and condominium villas. Kaanapali Beach Resort has six deluxe hotels, all on sandy swimming beaches: Hyatt Regency Maui, Kaanapali Beach Hotel, Maui Marriott, Royal Lahaina, Sheraton Maui, and Westin Maui. Six condominiums are also available. Napili Bay has many informal resorts. All along the coast are apartments, apartment hotels, condominiums, and cottages. Wherever you stay in west Maui, you will be only a few minutes away from four 18-hole golf courses—two at Kaanapali and two at Kapalua.

Maui's southwest coast, on the leeward side of Haleakala, has undergone continual development, particularly since the mid-1970s. You'll find some popular "traditional" places, such as the Maui Lu Hotel, still very much in business. But many new condominiums and apartments are strung out along the coast. Farther south, Wailea has two resort hotels (Inter-Continental and Stouffer's Wailea Beach) and three condominium villages, plus two 18-hole golf courses.

Past Wailea, at Makena is the Maui Prince Hotel, an 18-hole golf course, and a condominium complex.

Elsewhere on the island. Hana's prestigious Hotel Hana-Maui is set in 20 acres of gardens; also in Hana are the Hana Kai-Maui Resort and a small inn, Heavenly Hana. In Kula, up on Haleakala's slopes, you'll find accommodations at Kula Lodge and Silversword Inn.

SUN & SURF SAFETY

Visitors to Hawaii will have a safe and more enjoyable stay if a few simple rules are heeded:

- To avoid wrecking your vacation with a sunburn, expose yourself gradually to Hawaii's tropical sun. An hour at midday may be too much for fair-skinned people. Protect your skin with a good suntan lotion.
- Inquire locally about safety of a beach—currents, tides, drop-offs—before entering water.
- Duck or dive *beneath* breaking waves just before they reach you.
- Coral cuts are easily infected. Avoid swimming or snorkeling near coral in shallow water. Protect your feet with sneakers or similar gear when walking on reefs.
- Don't get mesmerized when snorkeling—you may suddenly find yourself far offshore.
- If you find yourself in trouble in the water, don't waste your breath with pointless yelling; remain calm and stay afloat until help arrives.
- Never turn your back on the ocean when you're near the shoreline.
- Never swim alone.

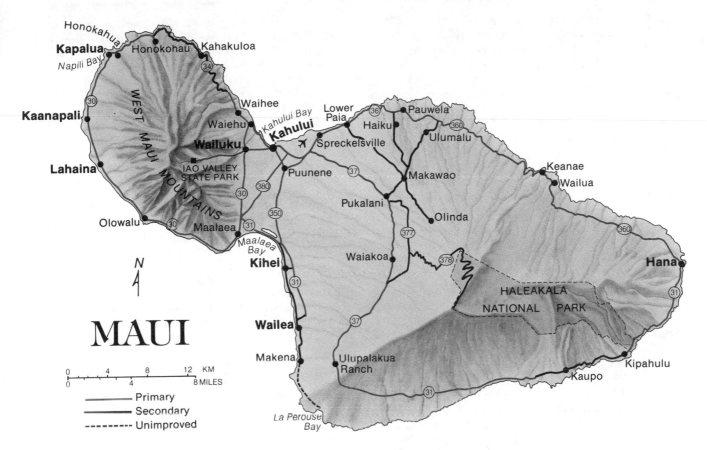

Touring the Island

Tour companies offer a wide variety of excursions, including minibus trips to Hana, Lahaina, Iao Valley, and up-country to Haleakala. Special activity tours include horseback riding, sailing, a variety of cruises, whale watching (winter months only), trips to the best snorkeling waters, and flightseeing by small plane or helicopter.

Shopping—Almost a Recreation

For anyone who enjoys shopping, Maui offers myriad stores, boutiques, and art galleries. Even those who generally don't may find some pleasant surprises, such as the wide variety of seashells and coral available in specialty stores and souvenir shops. When you're grocery shopping, make it a point to try Maui Potato Chips and Maui's sweet Kula onion.

Most areas boast one or more large shopping centers. *Kahului:* Kaahumanu Center, Kahului Shopping Center, Maui Mall; *Lahaina:* Lahaina Market Place, Lahaina Shopping Center, Mariner's Alley, Wharf Shopping Complex, Dickenson Square, The Cannery; *Kaanapali:* Whalers Village; *Kihei:* Azeka Place, Kihei Town Center, Rainbow Mall; *Wailea:* Wailea Shopping Village; *Pukalani:* Pukalani Terrace Center.

Resort hotels have some excellent shops, as do several of the small towns. Makawao, especially, is an off-the-beaten-path shopping experience.

Dining and Entertainment

Maui's profusion of restaurants cover the gamut from budget-priced fast food to the finest and most expensive cuisine. Many are right on the ocean shore, and diners can—if they wish—reserve a table with a view. Outdoor dining is another Maui specialty; the lanai settings (particularly at some of the hotels) make it difficult to determine whether you're dining indoors or out. Brunches, often with champagne, are a specialty at some hotels and restaurants.

Casual attire for evening meals is generally acceptable; before dining at one of the more fashionable places, though, it's wise to check as to any special clothing requirements. When in doubt, wear slacks instead of shorts, shoes rather than sandals.

There's plenty of music and entertainment to choose from, especially at the resort hotels. Late-night activity is particularly lively in and around Lahaina's bustling waterfront and at Kaanapali. Luigi's, at Azeka Place in Kihei, is a popular disco spot.

See pages 120–121 for a guide to Maui's recreational facilities. For information and addresses of specific accommodations, excursions, and attractions, contact the Maui Visitors Bureau, 172 Alamaha St., Suite 100, Kahului, HI 96732.

Maui's business and commerce centers around Wailuku and Kahului, adjoining towns at the northern end of the isthmus separating the West Maui Mountains from Haleakala.

Wailuku, older of the two towns, is charmingly situated on the slopes of the West Maui Mountains at the mouth of Iao Valley. Narrow, hilly streets, wooden shops, tree-shaded residential lanes, and the handsome buildings in its historic district give the town a look of the past in spite of a growing number of modern office buildings. Wailuku is the seat of Maui County (which includes Lanai and Molokai). You can't miss seeing Kalana O Maui, the 9-story county office building that towers over its older neighbors in the government complex.

Kahului, 3 miles/5 km downhill alongside Kahului Bay, is Maui's deep-water port. Several hotels and three shopping centers face Kaahumanu Avenue, the main thoroughfare. Kahului Airport is just east of town.

A few minutes drive northwest of Wailuku is Waiehu Golf Course, a scenic and challenging 18-hole layout with an ocean setting. Just beyond is Waihee, a small plantation settlement. From here, the road winds through and around the West Maui Mountains (see page 104); many stretches are unimproved.

Three routes cross the isthmus from the island hub to Maalaea Bay at the south. From Wailuku, Honoapiilani Highway (Highway 30) skirts the West Maui Mountains and leads to Lahaina, Kaanapali, and the other west Maui resort areas. Monkeypod-lined Puunene Avenue (Highway 350) goes to Puunene Mill (headquarters of Hawaiian Commercial & Sugar Company). Alexander & Baldwin Sugar Museum, in the mill's plantation office, is open Monday through Saturday; there is a small admission fee. Highway 350 then continues south to Kihei and Maui's southwest shore. Highway 380 runs southwest from Puunene to Highway 30, and then heads to Maalaea Bay and on up to Lahaina and points north.

Kahului...Port City

Kahului, Maui's port city, is rapidly expanding with new business and commercial developments. There are several excellent restaurants; Ming Yuen attracts devotees of Chinese food from all over the island.

Kanaha Beach Park runs along the beach just above the airport. You can picnic here beneath large shade trees and enjoy a panoramic view across the water. To reach the park, turn off the airport road at the Department of Water Supply baseyard near the terminal, then turn right on Alahao Street.

Kanaha Pond, between the airport and Kahului, was an ancient royal fishpond. Now it's Hawaii's most important native and migratory waterfowl bird refuge, particularly for the Hawaiian stilt. Its low water levels also attract a variety of migratory shorebirds.

Kahului Harbor, Maui's deep-water port, has the state's first bulk sugar plant and acts as a fueling base for several hundred Japanese fishing boats each year. Adjacent Hoaloha Park is a pleasant picnic spot.

Three shopping complexes, Kahului Shopping Center, Maui Mall, and Kaahumanu Center front a half-mile stretch of Kaahumanu Avenue. Kahului Shopping Center, oldest of the three, is gradually giving way to newer Maui Mall and Kaahumanu Center, but its well-worn benches in the cool shade of burgeoning old monkeypod trees are still a favorite gathering place for local residents. The three centers offer an assortment of shops, ranging from small boutiques and specialty stores to department stores and supermarkets. Here, too, are several restaurants, snack bars, and take-out counters featuring local foods. Special entertainment is staged frequently at all three centers; check local papers for events and times.

Maui Community College, part of the University of Hawaii, occupies a 78-acre site along Kaahumanu Avenue midway between Kahului and Wailuku. About 2,100 students are enrolled.

Central Maui Park will include an area from the west end of Kahului Harbor to Wailuku's edge. This proposed 190-acre park will incorporate the War Memorial recreational complex, future housing for Maui Community College students, and a cultural center and museum, harbor,

Central Maui

— Primary
— Secondary

0   2   4 KM
0 1 2   MI

MAUI

Maui County Zoo, picnic areas, and sports area. It will also provide a network of bikeways and pedestrian paths.

Halekii and Pihana Heiau State Monument is reached from Waiehu Beach Road about 2 miles/3 km from Kahului; turn off on Kuhio Place, just past the bridge over Iao Stream, and follow the markers to the hilltop site. From the parking area, there's a good view down over central Maui and Kahului Harbor. Halekii, a 150 by 300-foot temple of worship, was used during the reign of Kahekili (1765–1795). A diagram at the site explains its partially restored stone walls, terraces, and post holes. Pihana, 300 feet farther up at the end of a path, was a sacrificial temple consecrated in 1779.

Maui Jinsha, in Paukukalo off Highway 34, is a beautiful and fascinating Shinto shrine. Sacred objects are located in a separate little building; both it and the shrine have traditional roof symbols—protruding horns and a barrel-shaped ridge piece.

Wailuku...a mix of old and new

The best way to explore Wailuku's narrow, hilly streets is on foot. Many of the interesting new and old buildings are clustered in a compact area along High Street, between Main and Aupini streets. The Wailuku Historic District is on the west side of High Street. Walk some of the side streets to see older residential areas with small, tidy homes and colorful gardens. To view handsome homes on nicely landscaped hillside lots, drive up to Wailuku Heights; the road to it branches off the Iao Valley Road.

Government buildings line High Street. Most conspicuous is 9-story Kalana O Maui, the county office building. Adjacent to it, at the corner of High and Wells streets, sits the venerable 1907 Court House. Federal offices occupy the building on the opposite corner of Wells Street; just beyond, at High and Main streets, is the state office building.

Iao Needle, *a Maui landmark, juts up from floor of verdant valley. Iao Stream cascades in foreground.*

Kaahumanu Church *was Maui's first Christian congregation (1832). Present church building was constructed in 1876.*

Happy Valley on Highway 33, a part of old Wailuku reached by driving north on Market Street, has balconied living quarters above open-front shops and taverns.

The Wailuku Library, housed in an attractive, low, white stucco building on High Street across from the county office building, contains an excellent Hawaiiana room.

Kaahumanu Church, built on High Street in 1876 of plastered stone, is third church building of Maui's first Christian congregation (1832). Its handsome spire, set off against a dramatic mountain backdrop, is a much-photographed subject. The church's name honors Hana-born Queen Kaahumanu, favorite wife of Kamehameha I.

Early Hawaiian Christian Cemetery, just above High Street on the Iao Valley Road, has been restored and landscaped. It contains the graves of a number of early Hawaiian Christians, including that of the first ordained Hawaiian minister to serve Kaahumanu Church.

Hale Hoikeike, off Iao Valley Road, is a museum consisting of two buildings: the home built in 1841 by Edward

Bailey, head instructor of the Wailuku Female Seminary; and the kitchen–dining room of the school, an 1838–39 addition to its original building (now gone). The Bailey home has beams of hand-hewn sandalwood and 20-inch-thick stone walls covered with a mixture of plaster and goat hair. It contains historical exhibits, changing ethnic displays, and an exhibit of the 19th-century paintings of Edward Bailey.

The Church of the Good Shepherd, 2140 Main Street, is a 1911 Episcopal sanctuary of stone, with interior details of native woods and an unusual stained glass window behind the altar.

Wailuku Union Church, a small Gothic-style church on High Street, was built in 1911 to replace its 1867 predecessor.

Ka Lima O Maui, 95 Mahalani Street, is a rehabilitation center where you can buy Hawaiian craft products and nursery plants.

Iao Valley

From Wailuku you can drive for 3 miles/5 km into Iao Valley, never straying far from Iao Stream. The road (Highway 32) is a continuation of Wailuku's Main Street. Two miles/3 km from Wailuku, it passes Kepaniwai Heritage Gardens, a Maui County park with formal gardens and pavilions representing cultures that were instrumental to the growth of Hawaii. The name recalls a bloody battle fought here in 1790 in which Kamehameha I defeated the forces of the king of Maui. So many warriors were killed, says the legend, that their bodies choked the stream. This gave the park its name—Kepaniwai—which means "damming of the waters."

The road ends in Iao Valley State Park, dominated by 2,250-foot Iao Needle, a green-mantled remnant of erosion that rises sharply for 1,200 feet from the north valley wall. From the parking lot at the end of the road, you can follow well-marked paths through an impressive collection of exotic plants and trees down to the stream, up to a shelter view spot for a look farther into the hushed ravine, and to the top of the ridge for a commanding vista of the Needle, the valley floor, and, in the distance, Kahului Bay.

Maui Plantation

At Waikapu, 3 miles/5 km south of Wailuku on Highway 30, this 60-acre plantation presents the story of Hawaiian agriculture in a unique and fascinating way. A tram takes you through acres of tropical crops—coffee, pineapple, guava, mango, and macadamia nuts. In the market and restaurant you have a chance to touch, sniff, and sample the plantation's harvest. Open daily from 9 A.M. to 5 P.M., admission is free; there is a fee for the tram ride and for the lively luau held Monday and Wednesday at 5:30 P.M. (reservations suggested).

WEST MAUI: LAHAINA / KAANAPALI

This stretch of west Maui has for years been one of the most popular vacation destinations on the island. Devotees point out, quite rightfully, its scenic beauty and excellent beaches. Of at least equal importance are the well-preserved historical attractions which acquaint the visitor with the region's sometimes brawling and always fascinating past. Many vacationers (especially repeat ones) find everything they need or want right here and never stray far from this concentration of resort facilities.

Kahului to Lahaina

From Kahului Airport, you'll drive about 6 miles/9 km on Highway 380 to its junction with Highway 30; from there, it's another 17 miles/27 km to Lahaina.

Shortly after you join Highway 30, a road veers left toward Maalaea, a settlement with several condominiums, stores, restaurants, and a wharf and boat harbor. There's a sweeping view across Maalea Bay.

Lahaina waterfront *is a bustling place by day or night. Historic Pioneer Inn is at left.*

Giant bronze Buddha, *at Jodo Mission near Mala wharf, was erected to mark hundredth anniversary of the arrival of first Japanese plantation laborers in 1868.*

Sugar Cane Train *(see page 102) puffs merrily along, transporting rail fans and sightseers between Kaanapali and Lahaina town. Trip offers scenery ranging from oceanscapes to cane fields to golf fairways; a singing conductor helps keep things lively.*

...West Maui: Lahaina/Kaanapali

Highway 30 follows a picturesque route along the tops of seashore cliffs; at a scenic lookout, a plaque features information on the humpback whale. The highway then descends to the narrow Olowalu plain, where cane fields slope up to mile-high mountains broken by Ukumehame Gulch and other deep gashes.

Monkeypod trees shade quiet Olowalu, a small community with a few homes, a French restaurant (Chez Paul), and a little general store that seems typically Hawaiian. A half mile to the north lies a good hunting ground for "Hawaiian diamonds" (high-grade quality). Surfing waves boom offshore here and also farther north at Launiupoko State Park.

Between Maalaea and Lahaina, Ukumehame and Puamana county parks and Papalaua and Launiupoko state parks are good places for a picnic.

Lahaina...Historic Waterfront Town

Modern Hawaiian history has its roots deeply embedded in Lahaina ("*cruel sun*," as translated from early-day terminology). Kamehameha the Great established a residence here after he conquered Maui in a bloody battle in Iao Valley. Some of the first missionaries from Boston came ashore at Lahaina in 1823. And Kamehameha III lived here when he granted religious freedom and drew up Hawaii's first laws and constitution.

In the middle 1800s, whalers came by the thousands to winter in this little port, anchoring their ships offshore. Humpback whales migrating to their Hawaiian breeding grounds from the Aleutians still make whale watching a popular winter pastime. Tour boats leave from Lahaina and Maalaea harbors for a close-up look at these leviathans, some of which swim right up to the boats. The best months to see whales are January through April, though you may spot some stragglers as late as June.

Lahaina is still partly the town it has been for a century and a half—streets are narrow, sidewalks few, trees old and spreading, family gardens a tropical hodgepodge. Most houses are simple cottages. Some shopping still takes place in false-front wooden buildings.

But Lahaina no longer exists as it did more than 20 years ago. when its primary purpose was to sell staples to west Maui's cane and pineapple workers. New shopping complexes, restaurants, and bars (some in recycled buildings) are constantly being added to the scene. Condominiums seem to spring up overnight. Today, Lahaina town is a popular and often crowded visitor destination.

Restoration activity. Lahaina is a national historic landmark, and its center is under Maui County Historic District protection.

Most of the additions and changes are in keeping with the town's restoration program, a joint effort of state and local government and the Lahaina Restoration Foundation. Weathered buildings (particularly on Front Street) are being refurbished, harmonious new building encouraged, and restoration and rebuilding underway for a few

(Continued on page 102)

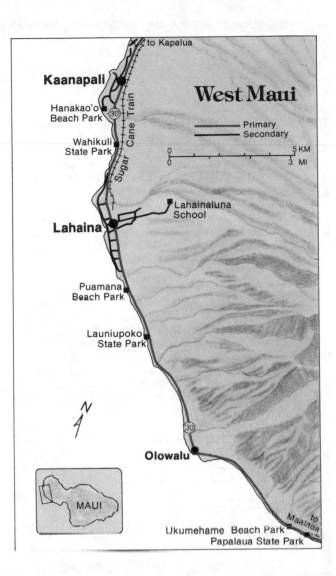

West Maui

Primary
Secondary

0   5 KM
0   3 MI

to Kapalua
Kaanapali
Hanakao'o Beach Park
Wahikuli State Park
Lahainaluna School
Lahaina
Puamana Beach Park
Launiupoko State Park
Olowalu
Ukumehame Beach Park
Papalaua State Park
to Maalaea

MAUI

SCRIMSHAW — WHALERS' ART

The meticulous art of scrimshaw—the carving or engraving of ivory, bone, and whales' teeth—goes back hundreds of years. Scrimshaw shops in Lahaina offer a wide variety of old and new pieces, ranging from a few dollars to collector's item prices.

Among the finest scrimshanders were the sailors who manned the whaling ships; many a whale's tooth took shape under the skilled hands of these seafarers who found scrimshaw to be a good way to pass the often lonesome weeks and months at sea. But since the Endangered Species Act of 1973 prohibited importation of whale products into the United States, scrimshanders have turned to other media, especially fossil ivory.

STROLLING THROUGH LAHAINA'S VIVID PAST ...

Fortunate is the history buff who visits Lahaina, because here—in one compact area—the flavor of the past can be sampled in reasonable time and with minimum wear on the shoes. A publication containing expanded information about the historical attractions mentioned on these pages can be obtained from Baldwin Home or other museums.

①Masters' Reading Room, built in 1834 by missionaries and ship's officers, was restored by the Lahaina Restoration Foundation in 1970. Coral block and fieldstone construction was preserved.

②Baldwin Home Museum includes Dr. Baldwin's dispensary-study and restored Baldwin Home, the New England style residence of medical missionary Dwight Baldwin and his family from 1836 to 1868. Built in 1834–35 of plastered coral and hand-hewn 'ohi'a beams, the home contains original furnishings and other period pieces. Dr. Baldwin's medical kit and theological books, and some early physician's implements are displayed in the dispensary. Museum is open daily; there's an admission fee.

③Site of Richards house, earliest coral stone house in the islands. William Richards was the first Protestant missionary to Lahaina. He traveled in the United States and Europe as envoy of Kamehameha III.

④Site of taro patch, visible as late as the 1950s, where Kamehameha III once worked to show his subjects the dignity of labor.

⑤Hauloa Stone is believed to have been used by early Hawaiians as a healing place.

⑥The "Brick Palace," thought to be the first Western style building in the islands, was built at the command of Kamehameha I.

⑦Carthaginian, a museum afloat, is a 93-foot replica of a 19th century brig. A project of the Lahaina Restoration Foundation, the ship contains a "World of the Whale" exhibit; there's an admission fee.

⑧Pioneer Inn was west Maui's only visitor accommodation until the late 1950s. The original building was constructed in 1901; the amusing house rules of that time are posted in the rooms. A wing added in 1964 reflects the same architectural style.

⑨Banyan Tree, planted in 1873 to commemorate the 50th anniversary of the arrival of Lahaina's first Protestant missionaries, is the largest banyan in the islands. It covers an entire square (about two-thirds of an acre) behind the Courthouse. At sundown, mynah birds strike up a chorus you won't soon forget.

⑩Courthouse was built in 1859 with stone from the demolished Hale Piula (15).

⑪Old Fort, next to the Courthouse, is a reconstruction of the ruins of a fort built here in the early 1830s and used chiefly to confine unruly seamen. The original fort was torn down in the 1850s to supply stones for the construction of Hale Paahao (21).

⑫Harbor is not a natural one, as is Honolulu's. Whaling ships were forced to anchor in deep water offshore; smaller boats ferried the crews into town.

⑬Site of old Government Market, where natives traded with sailors during the whaling days, is said to have earned its nickname: Rotten Row.

⑭Holy Innocents' Episcopal Church was built in 1927; Episcopal services at Lahaina actually date back to 1862, when the first services were held in Hale Aloha. The church has a unique painting of the Madonna and Child for which a Lahaina mother and infant posed.

⑮Site of Hale Piula, an old courthouse until damaged beyond repair by a gale in 1858. Its stones were used to build the present courthouse (10).

⑯Maluuluolele Park was once the site of a pond with an island where several Maui chiefs were buried.

⑰Wainee Church was the first stone church in the islands, circa 1830. Windstorms and fires have destroyed it several times since. The current church, dedicated in 1953, was renamed Waiola, "Water of Life."

⑱Wainee Cemetery, planted with fragrant plumerias and ancient palms, has gravestones with inscriptions dating back to 1823. Keopuolani, queen of Kamehameha the Great, is buried here.

⑲Hongwanji Mission has been a meeting place for Buddhists since 1910, when they erected a small temple. The present building dates from 1927.

⑳Site of house of David Malo, renowned Hawaiian scholar and philosopher who fought hard to preserve old Hawaii against growing outside control. A graduate of Lahainaluna Seminary, his gravesite is at the top of nearby Mt. Ball.

㉑Hale Paahao, the old prison, has walls of coral block taken from the old waterfront fort (11).

㉒Episcopal Cemetery contains the grave of Walter Murray Gibson, flamboyant and extravagant adviser to King Kalakaua in the 1880s.

THE DAYS OF KINGS, MISSIONARIES & WHALERS

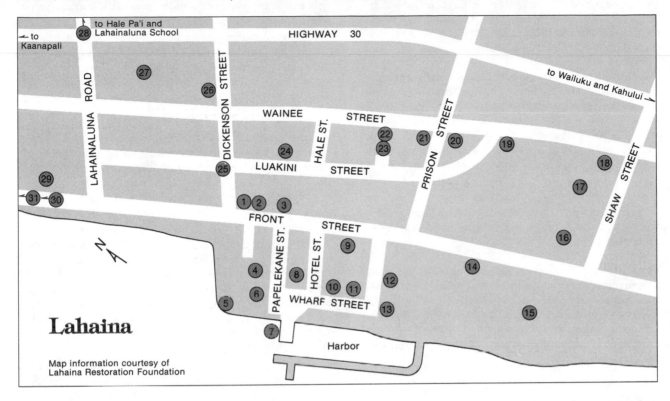

Lahaina

Map information courtesy of Lahaina Restoration Foundation

(23) **Hale Aloha,** built in 1858 and used as a church and school for many years, fell into ruins but was restored in 1974.

(24) **Shingon Buddhist Temple** has the simple, wooden architectural style typical of houses of worship built during the plantation era when Japanese laborers were brought to Hawaii.

(25) **Luakini Street** was the route of the funeral procession of Princess Nahienaena, who died tragically at age 21 in 1837.

(26) **Maria Lanakila Church** was built in 1928. It replaced an 1858 frame structure established after the celebration of Maui's first Catholic Mass on Lahaina beach in 1841.

(27) **Seamen's Cemetery** has only one inscribed marble slab and the fragment of another remaining. Buried here are a cousin and a shipmate of author Herman Melville.

(28) **Hale Pa'i and Lahainaluna School** are across Highway 30 and 1½ miles/3 km up the hill. (Just before you begin the climb, you pass the old Pioneer Mill Company, which dates from 1860.) Hale Pa'i, a print shop at Lahainaluna Seminary founded by Protestant missionaries in 1831, produced Hawaiian textbooks and Hawaii's first newspaper. The school, the oldest educational institution west of the Rockies, now serves as the public high school for the Lahaina area. Hale Pa'i was restored in 1980–82 by the Lahaina Restoration Foundation. An exhibit features a replica of the early press and facsimiles of early printing. The museum is open to visitors daily except Sunday.

(29) **Wo Hing Temple** is affiliated with the Chee Kung Tong, a Chinese fraternal society with branches all over the world. Recently restored, the temple has a small museum. The Chinese were among the earliest immigrants to Hawaii and became a powerful force in the commerce of Lahaina and throughout the islands.

(30) **Seamen's Hospital** was precisely that, during the whaling era from 1840 to 1865. But it also has served as a girl's school, vicarage, and residence—and once as a hideaway for Kamehameha III. It was completely reconstructed in 1972.

(31) **Jodo Mission** contains the Japanese Cultural Park, commemorating the first immigrants. Here you'll find a giant bronze Buddha imported from Japan, a temple, pagodas, and a bell tower.

structures from each period of Lahaina's 19th-century history—from early monarchy days through the beginnings of plantations and the influx of workers from the Orient. The famed old sea wall (a favorite place for watching sunsets) was restored in 1980. Wo Hing Temple on Front Street, built in 1912, underwent extensive renovation in the early 1980s (see page 101).

A walking town. Lahaina town is just the right size for walking. Nearly flat, it stretches out for 2 miles/3 km along the water but is only 4 blocks deep. Most of the historic places lie between Lahainaluna Road and Shaw Street (see pages 100–101) and are within a couple of blocks of Front Street; walking tour maps of Lahaina town are available at the Baldwin Home Museum.

You can cover most of Lahaina's in-town points of interest in about 1½ hours. If you have less time, explore the area along Front Street and the boat harbor, the departure point for fishing charters and a wide variety of boat cruises.

Night life. For those seeking evening entertainment, Lahaina offers musical sounds and a general air of jollity. If you are visiting Maui in late October, don't miss the Halloween pageantry; just walking down Front Street is an experience you won't soon forget. To really get the most out of it, contrive a costume of some sort and join the celebration.

Lahaina to Kaanapali

The drive from Lahaina to Kaanapali on Highway 30 is short—less than 3 miles/5 km. The widened highway encourages cyclists. Just north of Lahaina, you can see the remains of a royal coconut grove, planted in 1827 by the wife of Maui's governor, Hoapila. Young palms are now taking the place of the older ones as they succumb to wind and age.

Two excellent beach parks, Wahikuli and Hanakao'o, are popular with local residents. Both offer sandy beaches, picnic tables, and changing rooms.

Kaanapali Beach Resort

As you approach the first of three entrance roads to the resort, you look out over the manicured greens and fairways of one of Kaanapali's two championship golf courses, the Kaanapali South Course. One clubhouse, just inside the turnoff, serves both the South and North courses. Parts of both courses climb to higher elevations and offer spectacular views.

This multifarious resort, which even maintains its own airstrip, includes 600-plus developed acres and six deluxe beachfront hotels. Several condominiums face the ocean, and others flank the golf fairways. Kaanapali is a popular tennis center; most hotels and condominiums have courts. There are numerous restaurants, cocktail lounges, snack bars, swimming pools, shops, and a variety of nightly entertainment.

Free trolleys provide shuttle service around the resort, to and from the Sugar Cane Train's Kaanapali Station (see below), and the Whalers Village and Museum. The latter, a multilevel, 8-acre complex of buildings and open plazas, combine displays of whaling artifacts with shops, art galleries, and eating places.

"THE SUGAR CANE TRAIN"

One of the most unusual attractions in the islands is the 1890-style, open-sided train of the Lahaina Kaanapali & Pacific Railroad, which chugs along a 6-mile/10-km route, taking you back in time to the turn of the century when narrow-gauge trains were common on Hawaii's major islands.

The train runs on 36-inch, narrow-gauge, German-made tracks that were used by the Kahului Railroad before it stopped operating in 1966. It puffs its way through fields of sugarcane, crosses a 400-foot-long trestle, runs alongside the 4th hole of Kaanapali's south golf course (watch the golfers gawk!), and follows part of the roadbed of the cane haul line that traveled to and from Lahaina's Pioneer Mill between 1882 and 1952. As the train rolls along, passengers are entertained by a singing conductor.

Cars with wooden seats are modeled after coaches that King Kalakaua had built to his order in England around 1888. The steam engine, "Anaka," incorporates parts of five early Hawaiian locomotives, including brass-trimmed domes and headlight and a mahogany cab. It and the backup engine, "Myrtle," were rebuilt to 1890–1910 vintage from derelict Porter locomotives sitting on track in Carbon, Ohio.

There are five scheduled departures daily from the Victorian style stations at Lahaina and Kaanapali and the boarding platform at Puukolii. Earliest is 9:35 A.M. from Puukolii; last train, at 4:10 P.M., is one-way only from Lahaina to Puukolii. Tickets may be purchased at train stations or at tour and activities desks. Jitneys transport passengers to and from Lahaina town or the Kaanapali hotels.

NORTHWEST MAUI: NAPILI / KAPALUA

Less than a 10-minute drive north from Kaanapali, two vacation destinations attract an increasing number of visitors each year: Napili Bay and Kapalua. These adjacent regions have their own special characteristics, yet the two areas share at least one important asset—a spectacular view across brilliant blue ocean to the neighboring islands of Molokai and Lanai.

For those who enjoy auto exploring, the rugged north coast is right "next door."

Kaanapali to Napili Bay

North of Kaanapali, Highway 30 takes an inland route above the apartments, condominiums, and cottages lining both sides of the lower road, which travels through Honokawai to Kahana before joining the highway. A little more than a mile farther you come to Napili. Several condominiums and informal resorts with kitchen facilities preside over a lovely curve of sandy beach. Northern-

Kapalua Beach (*formerly Fleming Beach*), *fronting Kapalua Bay Hotel, combines scenic beauty and safe swimming.*

Kapuna program, *where senior citizens work with youngsters to keep old traditions alive, is popular with all ages—as witness this group with heart-shaped leaves picked from taro fields.*

most of these is the Napili Kai Beach Club, seven separate two-story wings scattered over 10 acres; here, on Napili Beach, the Tea House of the Maui Moon is a popular spot for dining and night life.

Kapalua Resort

Just to the north of Napili lies Kapalua Resort, one of the island's primary vacation destinations since its inception in the mid-1970s. The Kapalua Bay Hotel, the resort's central feature, stands just back from Kapalua Beach. There are also several vacation villas and residential communities.

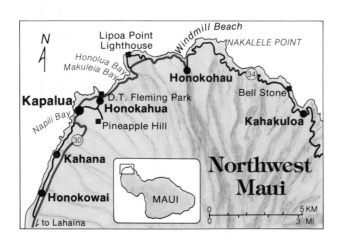

Kapalua's 750 landscaped acres include two 18-hole golf courses. The Village Course, opened for play in 1981, combines a challenging hillside layout with dramatic views from just about anywhere. Kapalua's original golf links, the Bay Course, ranges from the lower slopes down to the water's edge and features tropical landscape planting.

Tennis courts are located in a secluded garden area. Kapalua Bay offers plentiful watersports—windsurfing, scuba diving, snorkeling, and just plain swimming. Riding stables are only a 5-minute drive away, at Rainbow Ranch.

Kapalua to Honokahua

Beyond Kapalua Bay are several excellent beaches favored—and sometimes nicknamed—by local people: Oneloa (Beach Camp) Beach; D. T. Fleming Park (Ball Park or Stable Point), fronting 600 feet of white sand *makai* of Honokahua village (swimming and surfing for experts only); Makuleia Bay (Slaughterhouse Beach); and Honolua Bay. Because of their wealth of underwater life, Makuleia Bay and most of Honolua Bay have been designated by the state as a marine life conservation district.

Around the West Maui Mountains

The narrow, twisting, up-and-down road around the north end of the West Maui Mountains follows the course of an old royal horse trail and bears the extravagant title "Kahekili Highway." This isn't a good wet-weather drive; pavement ends just 5 miles/8 km east of Honokolau Bridge and begins again about 2 miles/3 km farther. Check car rental insurance coverage before making the trip.

Between a lighthouse at the island's north point and Honokohau, you cross weathered sandstone bluffs of various hues. There's a blowhole on the jagged coast. Windmill Beach, usually windy and rough, is splendid for diving on glassy days.

Honokohau is a jungle of fruit trees. Drive down into the valley a little way to see taro cultivated beside the stream and orchids on the slope. Just before you dip down into Kahakuloa village, try to get a ring from a roadside boulder known as the Bell Stone; you're supposed to listen on one side while someone bangs a rock against the other. (Results are dubious, but the stone is well worn from many trial bangs.)

Kahakuloa village stands at the mouth of a green valley in the middle of cattle country; a bold headland guards the southern approach. Amid the cluster of iron-roofed, wooden shacks fringed by a patchwork of taro, you'll find two picturesque churches—one Catholic and one Protestant. Villagers still pound poi, raise pigs, fish, beat the washing on rocks in the stream—but, at night, watch television.

Beyond Kahakuloa, the road winds along cliffs above fern gulches that stretch to the sea.

KIHEI & WAILEA

Until the early 1970s, Maui's southwest coast—from Maalaea Bay through Kihei and on south to Makena—was a quiet rural area where the only break in the lazy routine was a visit to Azeka's store, the post office, or Kihei's original and still charming resort, the low-rise Maui Lu. But, with its exceptional weather and multiplicity of excellent beaches, this region was destined to become the major tourist destination that it is today. It seems—to local residents who remember a kiawe-tree-covered area where seldom was heard the sound of a jackhammer—to have happened almost overnight.

This part of Maui is dry and usually sunny, receiving less than 10 inches of rainfall annually. Had it not been for this scarcity of water, tourism would have come to the region much earlier. When plans were laid for the Wailea resort area just south of Kihei, a major project was undertaken to import water from the rainy West Maui Mountains. By the early 1970s, condominiums and apartment hotels were under construction all along the coast; this development has continued, not only near the water but inland to the lower slopes of Haleakala.

Kahului to Kihei and Wailea

Highway 350 from Kahului Airport crosses central Maui from ocean to ocean; the drive takes about 25 minutes, depending on traffic conditions. Along the way you pass through miles of cane fields, with views of Maui's two mountain masses on either side—Haleakala to the left, the West Maui Mountains to the right. Kihei is most easily reached by following the highway all the way to Kihei Road, which runs the gamut of condominiums south along the ocean to the Wailea Resort turnoff. For a more direct route to Wailea, turn left from Highway 350 shortly before it reaches the ocean, onto the newer and faster Highway 31. You can also take this route to Kihei; several turnoffs lead down to Kihei Road. Or, if you are staying at the extreme southern end of Kihei, turn *makai* (toward the ocean) when you reach Wailea and then buttonhook back northward on Kihei Road.

Kihei—One Beach After Another

For sunny weather, sandy beaches, and good ocean swimming, Kihei (and south through Wailea and Makena) cannot be topped anywhere else on the island—or, for that matter, anywhere in Hawaii. Beach parks along this coast are popular with visitors and local residents alike. Reserve Kalama Park's pavilions in advance; they're usually crowded with festive groups on weekends and holidays. Kamaole Beach Park, just to the south, actually includes three separate beaches, with picnic tables, showers, and changing rooms.

A popular family vacation destination, Kihei has condominiums (more than three dozen) for just about any budget. Spaced throughout the region are several excellent restaurants. The popular Kihei Prime Rib features evening piano entertainment; its upstairs location gives

Early birds *enjoy stroll on a magical morning at Kamaole Beach Park #1. West Maui Mountains lie in distance.*

Gourmet favorites *such as 'ula 'ula and* ulua *come to end of the line at Maalaea's busy wharf.*

LOVABLE GIANTS—THE HUMPBACK WHALES

Breaching whale, seen close-up, is an awesome sight

With the arrival of winter each year, two groups of visitors make their presence known in Maui: the prime tourist season begins, and the humpback whales, having summered in Alaska and the Bering Sea, return to Maui's waters to breed, calve, and tend their young. First sightings usually occur in early December; by late May, all but a few stragglers will have departed.

The humpbacks are, to put it mildly, a sight to see. Once you've viewed them—particularly at close range from the deck of a whalewatcher cruise boat—you will begin to understand why the people of the islands have an ongoing love affair with these huge but gentle mammals.

Fewer than a thousand humpbacks remain in the North Pacific—about 600 of them visit Hawaii annually—but these are a small fraction of their numbers before they became prey to commercial hunters. Back in the mid-1800s, when as many as 450 whaling ships anchored in Lahaina each winter, perhaps 15,000 humpbacks inhabited the North Pacific. Though protected by international convention since 1966, the humpback population continues to decline. Both the Pacific Whale Foundation, headquartered in Maui, and the University of Hawaii are devoted to research, conservation, and education programs focused on whales (also dolphins and porpoises).

Humpbacks are 10 to 15 feet long at birth, weighing from 1 to 3 tons. During the first few weeks they gain about 200 pounds a day, due largely to the high percentage of fat in the mother's milk. When full sized, they average 45 feet in length, often weighing over 40 tons. Their long flukes (tails) have markings underneath which differ with each humpback; researchers who track their comings and goings can identify each individual from these "fingerprints."

Scientists have revealed that some male humpbacks "sing," or at least produce noises ranging from shrieks to low growling sounds that travel for miles in the water. Research continues as to what this might signify.

What to Watch for

Whalewatchers soon learn the meanings of four key terms: "breaching," "spy hopping," "fluking," and "fluke-slapping."

A whale "breaches" when it comes bursting out of the water head-first—maybe because it's disturbed about something or perhaps just having fun. If you see part of the whale's head out of the water for more than a couple of seconds, it's "spy hopping"—having a look-see above the surface. "Fluking" means that the whale is diving; the tail emerges and quickly submerges again. If its tail slaps against the surface in the process (an awesome "thwack"), the whale is "fluke-slapping."

...Kihei & Wailea

diners a good vantage point for watching sunsets. Paradise Fruit, almost a local institution, serves up a completely different kind of eating experience with its old-Hawaii atmosphere, heroically proportioned sandwiches, and blender-mixed tropical fruit concoctions.

Wailea Resort

One of Maui's three world-famed luxury resorts, this 1,450-acre complex includes the Inter-Continental and Stouffer's Wailea Beach hotels, three condominium villages, private homes, five beaches, shops, and restaurants. Guests enjoy tennis, volleyball, snorkeling, sailing, windsurfing, scuba diving, and lessons in hula. Three of its 14 courts are grass—hence Wailea's nickname "Wimbledon West." The resort will be home to three hotels when Four Seasons opens in 1989.

There are two scenic and challenging 18-hole golf courses, the Blue (original) and the Orange. The Orange is considered to be a bit more demanding, with tighter fairways and many more trees. The straight-growing trees on both courses are signs of exceptional year-round golf weather, generally free from blustery winds.

Makena

South of Wailea, the road continues to Makena. In the days when Ulupalakua Ranch was planted with sugarcane, the area contained Maui's second-ranking port. Makena now has the luxurious Maui Prince Hotel, an oceanside complex of low rise condominiums, and an 18-hole golf course.

Five beaches accessible by regular car are, north to south: Poolenalena, Maluaka, Oneuli, Puuolai, and Oneloa. All are swimmable, but safest are Poolenalena, Maluaka, and Puuolai. (Kahoolawe, an uninhabited island that for years has been used as a military bombing target, looms large offshore. Fronting it is tiny Molokini, whose exceptional snorkeling waters can be visited in half-day boat excursions.)

In a 4-wheel-drive vehicle, you can continue on a rocky, rutty road down the coast to La Perouse Bay, named for the French explorer who anchored here in 1786 and then sailed away to mysteriously disappear at sea.

Ahihi-Kinau Natural Area Reserve encompasses the south end of Ahihi Bay and Cape Kinau. This ecologically important area has been set aside by the state to protect and preserve its unique natural resources. The lava flows forming Cape Kinau resulted from Maui's last volcanic activity, estimated to have occurred in 1790. Unusual species of marine life thrive in the reserve's tidal pools and offshore waters. Ninety species of larval fishes have been collected around the cape—more than four times the average number of species found elsewhere in Hawaii—and at least 23 species of stony corals have been found in the southern end of the bay. The ruins of Moanakala, a small fishing village also located in the reserve, is a focus for anthropological research.

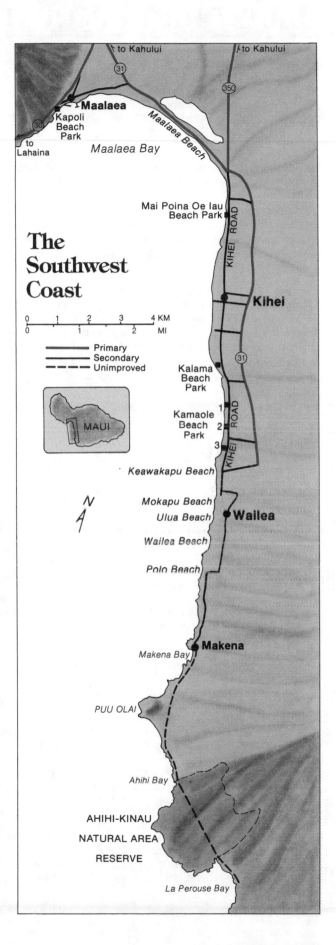

The Southwest Coast

MAUI's QUIET UPCOUNTRY

When you head up the slopes of Haleakala from Kahului, you move into a different Hawaii. Though a favorite of islanders, this part of Maui is, unfortunately, overlooked by many visitors. The weather is cooler here than at sea level—a desirable trait to some island residents.

Upcountry gardens are usually ablaze with colorful, temperate-zone flowers. Cattle graze in lush pastureland, and farmers grow many kinds of vegetables—including cucumbers, tomatoes, most of the state's cabbage crop, and sweet Kula onions (perhaps the pride of the region). Groves of eucalyptus dot the green hillsides, soft clouds drift in and out of valleys and swirl over the higher slopes, and the views down over the isthmus and out to the coast are magnificent. In spring, jacaranda trees along the roadside are strung with purple blossoms.

You can sample upcountry Maui on the drive to Haleakala National Park along highways 37, 377, and 378. To see the heart of the big Kula district, continue on Highway 37 to Kula Hospital and Ulupalakua Ranch. But the best way to explore the upcountry is to drive some of the side roads. Maui maps don't always show them, but almost any road will carry you through a refreshingly rural countryside where the pace is slow, the people friendly, and the scenery restful. The road from Keokea to Kula Hospital has some exceptionally beautiful plantings just before you reach the hospital buildings.

Many of Hawaii's best-known families have year-round or part-time homes upcountry, especially in the southern region generally referred to as Kula. Early settlers, mostly farmers and plantation workers, came from China, Japan, and the Portuguese islands of Madeira and the Azores.

Kula's treasure, the octagonal Church of the Holy Ghost, reflects this heritage: the original parishioners of this 1897 Catholic church were mostly Portuguese. Perched on the hillside above the highway near Waiakoa, the church and its delicate steeple can be seen from many directions. If it's open, go inside to admire the gilded wooden bas-reliefs, Portuguese inscriptions, and the large, Austrian-made altar shipped in sections around Cape Horn.

Another example of the area's multiethnic heritage is St. John's Episcopal Church in Keokea, once a thriving Chinese community. The church was founded by a Chinese

DRIVING TIPS

Driving in a car in Hawaii can be a very pleasurable experience. It helps, though, to understand some of the important features of driving in the islands *before* you slide behind the wheel and head for the open road.

• Most of Hawaii's highways are narrow, two-lane roads. It's advisable—if you have a choice—to rent a compact rather than a full-size car.

• Never go faster than the posted speed limit and, equally important, don't drive too slowly: this invites impatient drivers behind you to pass, risking head-ons.

• If cars press you from behind, pull over at a safe place and let them go by.

• Look out for passing cars coming toward you. The road between Maalaea and Lahaina can be particularly dangerous.

• Go easy on the horn. Hawaii's people don't take kindly to honking, considering it a breach of the aloha spirit.

• Obey yield signs; if you don't, you can find yourself in trouble, particularly on the road to Hana with its many narrow bridges.

• Make sure the blades in your windshield wipers are in good shape; rains can be heavy, and frequent.

• If you drive up to the high country and have trouble restarting your car after a short stop (a variety of reasons can cause this), wait a few minutes, then try the starter again before looking under the hood or calling a garage—chances are good that the car will start.

• Don't drive on unimproved roads unless you have a 4-wheel-drive vehicle; if your car gets stuck, it's expensive to get it pulled out.

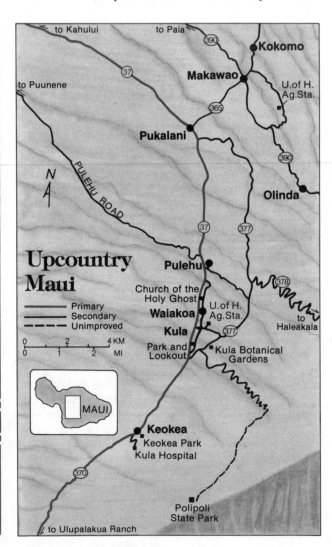

Upcountry Maui

Primary
Secondary
Unimproved

ULUPALAKUA —
PANIOLOS & HAWAIIAN CHAMPAGNE

Historic Ulupalakua Ranch, on Haleakala's southwest slope, encompasses 18,000 acres of the most scenic and pastoral country you are likely to see anywhere. Back in the 1850s and 1860s, James Makee (the erstwhile captain of a whaling ship) grew sugarcane here; he probably never dreamed that Ulupalakua would one day become one of the largest working cattle ranches on the island. And—though upcountry Maui turned out small quantities of wine for Hawaiian royalty even in the last century—Makee never could have envisioned Ulupalakua's producing Hawaii's first commercial grape wine with possibilities for eventual world-wide distribution.

A Lengthy but Scenic Drive

Ulupalakua (accent the first and last "u") is reached via Highway 37, east of Kahului. The drive takes a while; if you are coming from western Maui or Kihei/Wailea, plan on 1½ to 2 hours each way.

More than compensating for the length of the trip is the ever-changing scenery of oceanscapes, cane fields, the West Maui Mountains, Haleakala, colorful flower gardens, picturesque small farms and ranches, and—when you get to the Kula region—sweeping views of the southwest coast and the impressive (if forlorn) bulk of the uninhabited island of Kahoolawe.

Short minutes after you proceed southwest from Keokea, Ulupalakua's verdant grazing lands come into view up the slope of Haleakala to your left. This was once exclusively cattle land, but, in very recent years sheep (grown for meat, rather than wool) have been added to the scene. They, like the vineyards soon visible on your right, indicate that diversification has become not only advisable but essential to the area's cattle ranches.

Though the ranchlands continue up to about 6,500 feet, most of Ulupalakua's acreage extends down the southwest slope to sea level. As altitude decreases, rains become less frequent; grassy meadows and lush plantings gradually give way to scrubby growth, *kiawe* trees, and even cactus.

Paniolos—Old Maui on Horseback

If you keep an alert eye while driving through the cattle country, you may be treated to the sight of *paniolos* (Hawaiian cowboys) at work on the range. No place in upcountry Maui, or perhaps anywhere else, does the cowboy have a more distinguished tradition than at Ulupalakua.

More than 150 years ago, three Spanish-Mexican cowboys arrived in Hawaii, brought over from California by King Kamehameha III to control foraging cattle and begin raising them for beef. Islanders called them paniolos, the Hawaiian equivalent of *Españoles*. The Hawaiians themselves soon became paniolos, learning from the three "originals." Today, there are still a few paniolos working Ulupalakua whose fathers, grandfathers, and great-grandfathers rode the range many years before them.

Hawaii's "Napa Valley"?

The idea of a commercial vineyard at Ulupalakua was the concurrent dream of not one person but two: C. Pardee Erdman, owner of the ranch, and Emil Tedeschi, a young man who learned first hand about wine making while growing up in California's famed Napa Valley and was convinced that the climate and rich volcanic soil of upcountry Maui were exceptionally well suited to wine grapes. (To quote Tedeschi: "Napa Valley may be God's Country, but upcountry Maui is surely His vacation spot.")

In 1973, the two men went into partnership and began a venture that was to result, 10 years later, in 2,000 cases of Hawaii's first home-grown commercial wine. Four years of experimentation with 140 varieties of grapes were necessary in order to decide on the one best suited to the 2,000-foot elevation: Carnelian, a deep red hybrid of Cabernet Sauvignon, Grenache, and Carignane grapes.

The First Hawaiian Champagne

Having been advised that Carnelian could make not only red wine but a sparkling white, the partners opted for a champagne as their first commercial product (it has a faint blush of pink). On December 15, 1983, Tedeschi and Erdman hosted a formal celebration at the winery to celebrate Hawaii's entry into the world of grape wine.

Next, from the 1985 harvest, came two wines—Maui Blush and Maui Nouveau. Helping to ease the financial picture somewhat during the winery's struggling early years has been a popular and profitable pineapple wine, Maui Blanc.

In at least one respect, Tedeschi Winery is distinct from wineries on the mainland and elsewhere: It uses an old jail (1856) for a tasting room. Thick lava walls and shade from an ancient camphor tree keep it sufficiently cool for wine storage. (A trap door leads down to the dungeon, which is cooler yet.)

If you don't have a car but would like to visit the winery, check with a travel agency or at a hotel desk; van tours stop at the tasting room en route to Hana.

...Maui's Quiet Upcountry

Lutheran minister who taught Chinese language and culture to the immigrants' children; the name of the church appears in Chinese characters over the doorway. If you bring a picnic, nearby Keokea Park is a pleasant place to stop.

Agricultural Experiment Stations

The University of Hawaii College of Tropical Agriculture operates two experiment stations on Haleakala's slopes: one of 20 acres in Kula and another, 34 acres, near Makawao. To reach the Kula station, turn off Highway 37 on Copp Road, just south of Kula Elementary School, and follow the signs. The terraced plantings include new varieties of bedding plants, All-America award winning roses, and a rare collection of ornamental proteas (see special feature on this page). The Makawao station specializes in macadamias and avocados. Macadamia nut trees, more and more plentiful in parts of the islands, now grow on some of Maui's acreage that formerly was cane fields.

Kula Botanical Garden

If plants and flowers interest you, a visit to Kula Botanical Garden on Highway 377 offers a highly pleasurable experience. There are more than 700 types of plants. Easy paths wind between the beds; a picnic table and various resting places invite you to relax and admire a sweeping view beyond the landscaped slopes. Maui Enchanting Gardens (Highway 37 on the way to Kula Hospital) is a similar garden delight.

THE EXOTIC PROTEA

Since the late 1970s, upcountry Maui, with its rich volcanic soil, has been the locale for one of Hawaii's burgeoning agricultural-floral pursuits—the growing of proteas. These astoundingly diverse South African natives belong to a plant family comprised of about 1,500 varieties—hence the name (say PRO-tee-uh), after the Greek god who was noted for his ability to change shape at will. (Macadamia nuts, another booming crop in Maui, are a protea relative.)

Protea blooms, with many colors to choose from, make superb cut flowers that hold their hue for weeks and retain their shape even after fading. Upcountry growers concentrate on varieties with large and exotic flowers (see the facing page for one example) which shippers then proceed to process and package.

Good places to see the flowers and learn how they are grown are Protea Cooperative of Hawaii near the Kula Post Office, Upcountry Protea Farm on Upper Kimo Drive near Kula Lodge, Sunrise Protea Farm on Highway 378, and Protea Gardens of Maui Flower Shoppe on Highway 377.

Auto Exploring

For the back-country explorer, an unimproved road climbs 10½ miles/17 km from Highway 377 to Polipoli State Park, a recreation area at the edge of a mixed conifer and hardwood forest. A car with 4-wheel drive is best for this trip. You can hike 1,000 feet to the top of Polipoli cinder cone, a Haleakala ridge vantage point from which you can see west Maui and the islands of Kahoolawe and Hawaii. The forest, with hiking trails, contains approximately 35,000 redwoods planted in 1927, some now 4 feet in diameter and 80 feet tall. A low-cost cabin in the recreation area can be reserved through the State Parks office in Wailuku.

Near the end of Highway 37, on a shoulder above the road, you'll find a Hawaiian sacred boulder to which offerings are sometimes still made. According to legend, the boulder is a man turned into lava by Pele, the volcano goddess, whom he had angered.

Highway 37 officially ends at parklike Ulupalakua Ranch (see page 109). If you keep going past Ulupalakua, you'll be on Highway 31 going south and then eastward along the coast as far as Hana. (This route is described on page 119.)

For a pleasant, little-traveled route from Kula back down to the Wailuku-Kahului area, turn west from Highway 37 onto Pulehu Road (about 3 miles/5 km south of Pukalani); it comes out near Puunene Mill. At the upper end of the road, lantana, morning glory, and California poppies bloom alongside grotesquely shaped cactus. Down near the coast, you drive through fields of waving cane.

Makawao. To see another part of Haleakala's slopes, take Highway 365 from Pukalani junction on Highway 37 to Makawao, the spiritual center of Maui cow country. This village once bustled with field hands and upcountry *paniolos* (Hawaiian cowboys), and experienced a boom when nearby Kokomo served as a Marine base during World War II. Although the town is quieter today, it is much more than just boarded-up doorways and dogs snoozing in the sunshine.

Outside of town, subdivisions continue to spring up with the usual, unavoidable subtle changes in the town itself. There is much interest in crafts, now, and in fashions other than "wild west." Along with the venerable, always popular Outdoor Sports (western garb and gear), Komoda Store & Bakery, and Kitada's Kau Kau Korner, newer stores and boutiques line the main street.

A "must," if you are visiting Maui in early July, is Makawao's very popular 4th of July rodeo. Few, anywhere, can match it.

From Makawao, you can drive uphill on Highway 39 to Olinda, past Pookela Church, built of coral by missionaries in 1850, and Seabury Hall, an exclusive college preparatory and boarding school. Going downhill, you reach Paia by continuing down Baldwin Avenue, Makawao's main street, or Haiku by taking the Kokomo and Haiku roads.

Hard-riding paniolos, *born to the saddle and proud of their heritage, are an exhilarating part of the upcountry scene.*

Exotic protea flowers, *available in an astonishing variety of species, colors, and forms, are a Kula specialty (see feature on facing page).*

The quiet, eerie world *inside Haleakala Crater is a once-in-a-lifetime experience, even for seasoned hikers.*

HALEAKALA – HOUSE OF THE SUN

When you reach the overlook atop Haleakala, Maui's 10,023-foot volcano, you will have traveled the only paved road in the world that climbs to that height from sea level in just 40 miles/64 km. The views from the summit are spectacular. Off to the southeast, the tops of Hawaii's Mauna Loa and Mauna Kea float in a sea of clouds. As you turn clockwise, other islands and the rest of Maui come into view—unless clouds below blanket them. The air is bracing at this altitude, probably about 30 degrees cooler than in the valley. In winter you may encounter snow, and temperatures sometimes drop below freezing.

Haleakala National Park includes the summit and astonishing crater of this dormant volcano, which last erupted about 1790. The crater, low down on the southwest flank, is a vast depression carved out of Haleakala's dome by centuries of erosion. Later volcanic activity partially filled the crater with colorful cones and windswept banks of cinders. It measures 7½ miles/12 km long, 2½ miles/4 km wide, 21 miles/34 km around, 3,000 feet deep and covers 19 square miles/49 square km.

According to Hawaiian legend, from the crater rim the demigod Maui, son of Hina, snared the sun. He made it promise to go more slowly across the sky, giving crops more time to grow, fishermen more time to fish, and his mother's tapa cloth more time to dry. Now the sun is careful to travel slowly, and the great mountain is known as Haleakala—"The House of the Sun."

The total area of Haleakala National Park, 28,665 acres, includes an 8-mile/13-km-long strip that extends from the eastern edge of the crater down through Kipahulu Valley to the sea. The lower region of this addition, near the mouth of 'Ohe'o stream, is accessible, but the ecologically fragile virgin forest above 3,100 feet, now a biological preserve, is closed to entry.

The Drive to the Top

Before you start the 1½-hour drive from Kahului to the summit, phone 572-7749 for a taped report on current travel information and weather conditions. The message is updated during the day as conditions change. The crater's coloring shows up best in the afternoon, but clouds often roll in after 10 A.M.

Persons with high blood pressure or a heart condition are advised against driving alone, since the rarefied air can cause dizziness.

You climb first through cane fields and then through pineapple spreads into the Kula upland. From the turnoff onto Highway 378, a serpentine route leads up through pastures—and perhaps through a layer of clouds—into rocky wasteland.

Hosmer Grove. Just past the park entry sign, a paved side road leads in about ½ mile/1 km to Hosmer Grove, a small campground and picnic area ringed with North American pine, cedar, juniper, and spruce trees, deodar from India, cryptomeria from Japan, and eucalyptus from Australia. Trees are labeled along a short, level nature trail, and a sign at the start of the trail identifies birds commonly seen here. Open daily from 7:30 A.M. to 4 P.M., park headquarters lie at 7,030 feet, a mile past the entrance. Here you can pick up a park map-guide and other material and can get help in planning crater trips. An enclosure near the headquarters building permits a closeup look at Hawaii's state bird, the *nene*.

A SUNRISE TO REMEMBER

Few if any places in the world can match the sunrise view from atop Haleakala. Although it requires getting up at a wide-yawning hour (3 A.M. departure for the 2 to 3-hour drive from primary resort areas), the trip is an adventure—almost a pilgrimage—not soon to be forgotten. Recently arrived visitors from the mainland may not mind the early-hour departure too much, considering that Maui time is two or more hours earlier than the time back home.

You'll know that the long, winding drive through the dark was worth it when you look eastward to see the Big Island start to take shape as the murkiness of night gradually gives way to the first faint signs of daylight. When the huge, round, golden star of the show makes its dramatic appearance through the clouds, you will know, far more clearly than those who have missed the experience, what The House of the Sun is all about.

If you decide, before you leave home for Hawaii, that this is a trip you don't want to miss, bring along some winter clothing. The warmth of the resort areas is one thing; the cold, windy, sometimes freezing temperatures of Haleakala's 10,023-foot summit is something else. If you didn't pack warm clothes or can't borrow some, it's best to forgo this trip until another time.

Prefer Sunsets?

If early rising just isn't for you, climbing Haleakala later in the day to view the sunset is a good alternative. The view toward West Maui and Lanai, and the colors of sea and sky, are truly spectacular.

Whether you go for sunrise or sunset, phone 572-7749 for a weather report. Be sure your car has a full tank—no gas (or food) is available in the park.

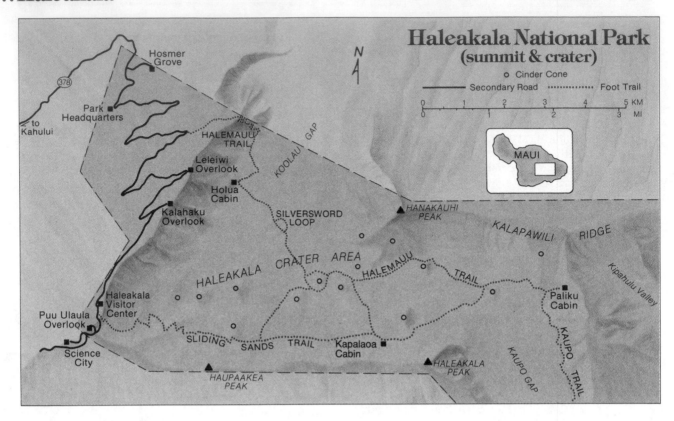

Haleakala National Park
(summit & crater)

Some good view points.

Some good view points. You can stretch your legs at several points along the 10¼ miles/16½ km between park headquarters and the top. At 8,000 feet, walk a mile on Halemauu Trail to the crater rim, where you can look across Koolau Gap, down Keanae Valley, and ahead to the trail zigzagging down the crater wall. There's a similar view at 8,800 feet from Leleiwi Overlook, just a 350-yard walk from the road. Here, in late afternoon, you may see the "Spectre of the Brocken"—your shadow against the clouds, encircled by a rainbow.

Just above, a road goes to Kalahaku Overlook, where you'll find some of Haleakala's famous silverswords and exhibits relating to the crater's cones and lava flows. The silversword, a relative of the sunflower, grows from 4 to 20 years as a rounded mass of stiletto-shaped leaves before sending up a flower stalk as tall as 9 feet with 100 or more purplish blossoms. Blooms develop from May through October. The plant flowers only once and then dies—but not before it sends out seeds to start new silverswords. Except for a few plants on the Big Island, this species of silversword is unique to its isolated habitat on Maui. Another variety grows in very wet areas in the West Maui Mountains.

When You Reach the Summit

Two visitor shelters sit atop the mountain: the Haleakala Visitor Center, on the rim at 9,745 feet, and Puu Ulaula Visitor Center, ½ mile/1 km farther up on Red Hill, the actual summit.

Exhibits at Haleakala Visitor Center explain the crater's features and formation. From here you look down on slopes of cinder blown by the easterly trade winds against the rocks of the original rim. Koolau Gap on the north and Kaupo Gap on the south cut the rim. Beyond Koolau, Hanakauhi's peak often protrudes from a blanket of clouds. On the opposite rim, Haleakala peak stands out like a fortress above Kaupo Gap. Symmetrical cones of varied hues look like small mounds of sand in the crater, but each is several hundred feet high. The largest, Puu o Maui, rises 615 feet from the crater floor. In remarkable contrast to the naked summit slopes are the meadow and stand of trees at the crater's east end, 7½ miles/12 km away, where the annual rainfall is 250 inches.

From Haleakala Visitor Center, a trail climbs 380 yards to White Hill, past ruins of stone wind barriers built by the Hawaiians for sleeping enclosures. The hill is formed of andesite, lighter in color than most Hawaiian lava. Walk a short distance down Sliding Sands Trail to get the feel of the crater; but remember, at this altitude it's an exhausting climb back up.

From Puu Ulaula Visitor Center at the summit, you have a 360-degree panorama of the crater and, on a clear day, of west Maui and the islands of Hawaii, Lanai, Molokai, and Oahu. You can continue for a mile beyond the park, along dead-end Skyline Drive through "Science City," with its domes and antennae for communications and space study. Although the facilities are not open to the public, you'll be rewarded with a precipitous view down to the Lualailua Hills and the south coast desert.

INTO THE CRATER'S DEPTHS

To truly claim you saw Haleakala crater, you should go down inside. The Park Service maintains 30 miles/ 48 km of well-marked trails and three rustic cabins (see below).

Two main trails, Halemauu and Sliding Sands, lead down into and across the crater. They meet near Paliku Cabin at the east end. Sliding Sands Trail takes you about 6 miles/9½ km down along the south face to Kapalaoa Cabin and then northeast 4 miles/6½ km to Paliku Cabin. On Halemauu Trail, you descend the west wall to Holua Cabin, a distance of 4 miles/6½ km, and then go 6 miles/9½ km farther along the center of the sloping crater floor. Short trails connect the two routes.

In half a day, you can make a round trip on Halemauu Trail as far as Holua Cabin. For a long day's hike (12 miles/19 km) or horseback ride, go down Sliding Sands Trail (avoid this steep trail as a way out), cross the floor on Ka Moa O Pele Trail, and climb out on Halemauu Trail—but unless you're willing to hike extra miles up the road, drive two cars to the park and leave one at the start of each trail. For a good overnight trip with no car problem, take Halemauu Trail all the way to Kapalaoa Cabin one day and return the next. You'll cover about 8 miles/13 km each way.

Crater-explorers should carry water for trail use (cabins have a limited water supply), a light raincoat, sun hat, suntan lotion, chapstick, and a light jacket or sweater. Be sure you have a good pair of hiking shoes, well broken in. And—perhaps most important of all— make sure you are in good physical condition for hiking.

Down in the weird environment of the crater, you'll see sandalwood trees; lichen, or Hawaiian Snow, the first plant to appear after a lava flow in higher altitudes; mountain *pili*, distinct from the lowland variety once used for grass houses; and volcanic dikes, remnants of an ancient divide that separated the heads of Keanae and Kaupo valleys.

North of Kapalaoa Cabin is Bubble Cave, formed when molten lava was forced up by gases; the lava stayed in that position until it cooled and later was opened when part of the top collapsed.

At rainy Paliku, large native trees (*ohia lehua, kolea, olapa*), tall grass, and ferns create a haven in the barren waste. Here you occasionally will see the *nene* (Hawaii's state bird).

On Halemauu Trail you pass Bottomless Pit, an old spatter vent, which looks like a 10-foot-wide well. The bottom is 65 feet down—so keep away from the crumbly edges. Nearby are Pele's Paint Pot, a colorful pass between cinder cones, and, on a cross trail, Pele's Pig Pen, a half-buried spatter vent. Near Holua Cabin you'll find the Silversword Loop Trail.

Silversword *plant blooms just once, then dies. The Silversword Loop, southeast of Holua Cabin, leads to a large concentration of them.*

Kapalaoa, Paliku, and Holua cabins. Each cabin accommodates 12 persons. Cabins have bunks, firewood cookstoves, and eating and cooking utensils. Cabin users must bring their own sleeping bags and light source. Reservations for cabins must be made by mail at least 90 days in advance and are limited to three nights per month with only two consecutive nights in any one cabin. Write Haleakala National Park, Box 369, Makawao, HI 96768, giving your social security number, the exact days, the number in your party, and which cabins you wish to use.

Campsites. Holua and Paliku also have camping sites. A permit is required (obtainable at park headquarters); length-of-stay limits are the same as for the cabins. No open fires are allowed, and campers should have a warm sleeping bag and tent with rain fly for cold or wet weather. Camping groups are limited to 15 people.

Guided horseback rides. Trail rides vary from a 2-hour trip to all-day excursions. For information, see page 121.

HANA – A VERY SPECIAL EXPERIENCE

The Maui visitor who leaves without dropping in on "heavenly Hana" misses an opportunity to see old Hawaii at its best. More—much more—than the little settlement usually known as Hana town, the "real" Hana ranges far up Haleakala's lush eastern slopes and stretches for miles along the ocean, roughly from Keanae to Kaupo (the inexactness of its extremities only adds to the Hana mystique).

You can drive the Hana Highway from Kahului to Hana town in about 2½ hours, but you really should allow more time to enjoy the magnificent scenery, perhaps stop for a picnic, swim in a freshwater pool, or just relax awhile in one of the pleasant wayside parks you'll find along the route.

Your trip begins on a fast, broad highway through cane fields. Just before you reach Lower Paia, you'll find H. A. Baldwin Park, a popular camping, swimming, and surfing spot. Next to it, Rin Zai Zen Buddhist Mission is notable for its graveyard with Okinawan-style family mausoleums resembling miniature houses. The old plantation town of Lower Paia has the look of the Old West, with many restored store fronts, restaurants, and shops. Right in town is handsome Manto Kuji Soto Buddhist Temple. The graveyard, above a sandy cove, has markers carved with Japanese characters.

This highway passes Hookipa Beach Park, where swimming is dangerous but surfers brave some fairly large waves. Championship competition in windsurfing, which in recent years has become one of Maui's most popular watersports, is held here annually.

About 20 miles/32 km from Kahului is Twin Falls, an easy-to-reach swimming hole fed by the divided watercourse of a mountain stream. Just follow the sign at the start of a short trail 1¾ miles/3 km beyond Kakipi Gulch.

By now your road hangs on ferny, pandanus-laden cliffs that drop off to the pounding surf. It twists in and out of gulches, many with sparkling waterfalls. The roadsides are a jungle of breadfruit, koa, *kukui*, *'ohi'a*, and paperbark trees, groves of bamboo, tangled *hau* and guava, giant *a'pe* leaves, wild ginger, and even some rubber trees.

The road follows sections of open ditch—part of the system that takes water from these wet slopes to central Maui's farming areas. In this part of the island, people still live off the land and sea and respect the legends breathed by every cliff and hollow. The few villages are merely a sprinkling of houses and a general store; occasionally you'll spot old schools and churches. Just downhill from the highway at Huelo, shortly before you come to Kailua settlement, is Kualauapueo Church, built of stone in 1853.

Since the narrow road bridges streams and waterfalls in almost every gulch, you'll often be tempted to stop and look at roadside plantings or admire a distant view. (In any case, if traffic is stacked up behind you, it's a good idea to find a safe place and pull over until it passes.) It's not always easy, though, to find a safe place to pull off the winding road. But three wayside parks within a few miles of one another are especially inviting:

Kaumahina State Park. About 25 miles/36 km from Kahului, a shady park sits atop a cliff overlooking Honomanu Gulch and the Keanae Peninsula just beyond. Far below you can see Honomanu Bay's black sand beach, where natives fish and swim. Picnic tables and pavilions are spread over the neatly landscaped slopes.

Keanae Valley Lookout. A great two-way view awaits you at the lookout—down over Wailua to the sea, which breaks against Keanae Peninsula in the distance, and up through Keanae Valley to Koolau Gap.

Puaakaa State Park. Between the Wailua and Nahiku turnoffs lies a small park with picnic tables, trails, and a series of fern-banked waterfalls where you can enjoy a refreshing dip. Native plants are marked.

Spur Roads to Keanae, Wailua, Nahiku

From several high points along the road, you look down on small, quiet villages. The little clusters of houses, church steeples, banana groves, and taro patches resemble South Seas scenes.

Keanae. Take the side road down onto Keanae Peninsula, past the pebbly cove where villagers launch their skiffs. You may see someone pounding taro in the yards of the old wooden houses. Keanae's refurbished coral stone church is more than 100 years old. The surf pummels Keanae's lava shore, causing the jagged rocks to glisten from their constant washing. On a clear day, Haleakala looms up to the south.

Keanae Arboretum, above the peninsula, is planted with native Hawaiian and other plants, including 60 vari-

---

HOUSE OF TREASURES

One of Hawaii's newest museums (1983) is Hale Waiwai O'Hana ("House of Treasures of Hana") in the heart of Hana town. A project of the Hana Cultural Center, it was designed by renowned Honolulu architect Vladimir Ossipoff to harmonize with the refurbished, hundred-year-old former courthouse, just a few steps away.

The museum's charm, careful organization, and ease of viewing more than compensate for its small size. Contents include rare photographs of old Hana, quilts, shells, stone implements, idols, and numerous artifacts. Hours are 11 A.M. to 4 P.M. daily except Sunday; there is a small admission charge.

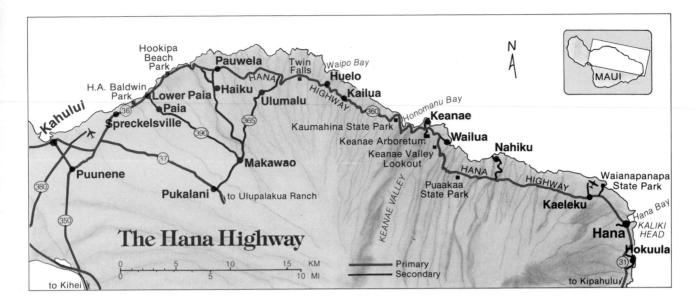

The Hana Highway

eties of wetland taro growing on reconstructed old taro patches.

Wailua. The spur road down to Wailua village passes churches and houses fronted with rows of ti and crotons and ends above a narrow cove at the mouth of the stream. Here villagers put out in fishing boats and children body-surf with homemade boards in the late afternoon while their elders relax on the porches and read—or just sit.

Quaint St. Gabriel's Church, with its painted trim of red hearts, is known as the Miracle Church. It is said that in 1860, when its builders set out to dive for coral and sand, they found these building materials heaped on shore by the waves. Some of the church's graveyard markers have photographs, and most are decorated—usually with artificial flowers in jars of water.

Take the road inland past Wailua's other row of houses for a close look at the taro and bananas grown for Maui and Honolulu markets. The geometrically terraced plots, set in a gently rising valley guarded by mountain walls, are as neat as a memorial park. Irrigation water trickles downhill from one patch to another in the old Hawaiian manner.

Nahiku. A 3-mile/5-km spur road takes you down through Nahiku village, now mostly covered by forest. You pass a few scattered houses, a school, and two churches, ending at the landing used at the turn of the century to unload equipment for building irrigation tunnels through the mountains. Trees here have been left from Nahiku's rubber plantation of more than 75 years ago. You can try out two good swimming holes: one reached by a path from the turn-around at the landing, the other about 400 feet from the wooden bridge and on the right after you pass the churches.

The road from Nahiku to Hana crosses much grazing land. Hana Airport is reached by a turnoff just before you get to the sign directing you to Waianapanapa State Park.

Waianapanapa State Park

Three miles from Hana town, a side road leads to Waianapanapa State Park. Here, a footpath through lush tropical plantings takes you to Waianapanapa and Waiomao caves, two lava tubes near the sea that are filled with water and said to be connected. Waianapanapa Cave has a much-told legend: a Hawaiian princess, escaping from a jealous husband, hid in the underground cavern but, after being discovered by the husband, was slain. The slaying occurred in April, and Hawaiians tell you that the water still runs red with her blood each spring.

Certainly Waianapanapa Cave is an eerie place to swim, but some daring souls take a flashlight and brave the cold water. It's possible to swim underwater, past a point where the roof arches down, into another chamber; there a ledge is said to be the spot where the princess hid.

Out on a point, you'll see a natural rock arch and blowhole; on the grassy ledge where the sea gurgles beneath your feet, three old burial grounds are still in use. Below, Honokalani black sand beach fringes Pailoa Bay. Here you can scout for beach glass or swim when the bay is calm.

The trail to the south of the black sand beach follows the jagged lava coastline to Hana for about 3 miles/5 km. Now used primarily by fishers, the trail, called the King's Highway, was part of the original ancient highway built around east Maui by Chief Piilani before his death about 1527. Smooth steppingstones set into the rough lava and cinders have been washed away in places by high surf. Walking time to Hana town is about 1½ to 2 hours.

The park has inexpensive, furnished cabins available by reservation (see page 121).

Hana Town

Quiet Hana town is inhabited mostly by part Hawaiians, though more and more former mainlanders now make

Keanae Peninsula's *taro fields and quiet way of life represent the Hawaii of bygone years. The area can be explored on a short side trip from Hana Highway.*

their home here. The taro patches, banana clumps, and bits of stone terraces in the nearby gulches provide evidence of the Polynesians who once had a large settlement here. Subsequent sugar, pineapple, and rubber tree plantations were not very successful and finally sold. Since 1944, the fields have been gradually converted to grazing land for several thousand white-faced Hereford beef cattle.

Helani Gardens, a 72-acre commercial nursery, offers five acres of tropical greenery, fishponds, bridges, and a riverside picnic pavilion. Open daily, there is a small admission charge.

Lunch at the quiet and charming Hotel Hana-Maui is a pleasant experience and offers the day-trip visitor a welcome break after the winding drive from Kahului. The hotel, located just up from Hana Bay, has lovely tropical plantings in extensive gardens. Don't plan to stay overnight unless you have advance reservations.

Drive the mile to the top of Lyons Hill (Puu o Kahaula). On this cinder cone above town, a stone cross on a torch-lit platform serves as a memorial to Paul Fagan, who founded the ranch and hotel. There's a nice view down over the rolling hills to Hana Bay.

One of the few modern touches for miles around is Hana's compact shopping center. But still standing is the Hasegawa General Store, subject of the long-popular song of the same name. You can inspect a fascinating Buddhist temple, part missionary and part Oriental in style, and Sunday services are still conducted in both Hawaiian and English at century-old Wananalua Church, built by hand of lava rock (some of which came from a *heiau*, temple) over a 20-year period. The nearby Catholic church is also impressive.

Kauiki Head, a fortresslike cliff, guards Hana Bay. Here armies of Kamehameha and the king of Maui tangled with slingshots. You can walk down the south side of Kauiki Head to an old cemetery and a red cinder beach, popularly known as Red Sands Beach.

At the foot of Keawa Street, on the bay, is a place known locally as Punahoa. Here, many little springs of very cold fresh water gush out of the sand when the tide is low. You can feel them in the water even at high tide if your foot happens to land on one. Old stories tell of Hawaiians diving down with small-necked calabashes and filling them upside-down with fresh water.

From Hana pier, you can walk along the base of the cliff to a plaque that marks the birthplace of Kamehameha's favorite wife, Kaahumanu, in a cave above.

Not to be missed is the Hana Cultural Center's museum (see page 116).

Hana to Kipahulu

Beyond Hana, Highway 31 continues for 10 miles/ 16 km to Kipahulu, in Haleakala National Park. Near Hana, a side road loops down to Hamoa Beach (facilities are for hotel guests only). Currents can be treacherous. At the Hana end of the loop, you pass Pele's Hill (Ka Iwi O Pele), where the fire goddess is said to have left her bones when she assumed a new body to go to the Big Island.

Where the road turns into Wailua Gulch, two impressive waterfalls topple from Haleakala's slopes. The concrete cross standing above the road is a memorial to Helio, a Hawaiian Catholic who converted hundreds to his faith during the 1840s. South of the falls, gnarled *kukui* trees on the mountainside are the remains of a grove. A few more turns bring you to the "Virgin by the Roadside," a shrine containing an Italian marble statue. Every day the statue is draped with leis, and once a year representatives from all of Hana's Catholic churches make a pilgrimage.

At 'Ohe'o Gulch (often called—erroneously—Seven Pools) you're in the national park. Look upstream and downstream from the bridge to see the pools; 24 of them topple into one another and finally flow into the sea. A path descends the south bank to the most accessible swimming and picnicking spots. On the north bank, about 600 yards above the highway is a restored taro farm, funded by the National Park Service and maintained by the Hana Cultural Center. Ranger-led walks and hikes are conducted all year.

The grave of famed aviator Charles A. Lindbergh can be reached by turning left, between two posts, about 350 yards before you would come to the gates of Kipahulu Ranch headquarters. Drive (slowly) along a bumpy gravel road for ¼ mile to Palapala Hoomau Church, where a clifftop graveyard looks down to a magnificent view of the sea.

Driving the Southern Coast

The scenic but sometimes rugged drive beyond Kipahulu should only be attempted in a 4-wheel-drive vehicle. And, even then, it can be a harrowing experience—narrow track, potholes, and lack of guard rails. Most rental car contracts ban travel on the road because of washouts.

Kipahulu to Kaupo. A one-lane gravel road links these two towns; you won't see pavement again for about 8 miles/13 km. The road hugs the edge of rocky cliffs above the water and dips straight into gulches. If you meet a car, one of you may have to back up to find a safe shoulder.

This country is drier than the Hana area, with open pastures divided by lichen-covered stone walls and abundant *hau* and koa trees. The road edges so close to Lelekea Bay that a heavy sea splashes spray right into your car. You'll see a few outrigger canoes on the rocky beach. A switchback trail visible on the hillside just south is the remains of the old King's Highway.

Kaupo's recently restored Huialoha Church (1859) and tidy graveyard perch on a grassy peninsula, an inviting place to picnic or camp. Nearby, ruins of a mission school and a heiau on the hill above the road invite exploration. A larger temple, Loaloa (circa 1730), lies at the start of Kaupo Gap Trail, behind the school off the spur road to Kaupo Ranch headquarters.

Whether or not you need to buy something, a stop at Kaupo Store is rewarding. Notice the hitching rail for horses. The store doubles as a post office—one in which all mail goes into one box and people hunt for their own.

Kaupo to Ulupalakua Ranch. More exciting views of the coastline and distant Hawaii island will greet you as you dip down to the sea at old Nuu Landing, where you'll find village ruins and a salt pond.

The road from here to Ulupalakua is paved and slightly wider. Soon after passing Nuu Landing, you cross a dry river bed, gutted by centuries of flash floods. Walking up to a pool at the head of the gulch, you'll discover caves and petroglyphs.

The gradual climb toward Kanaio carries you through the bizarre landscape of a Hawaiian dryland forest, more pastures, fields of yellow poppies, old lava flows, and cinder cones. About 5 miles/8 km farther stands the old Kahikinui ranch house. Nearby, below the road, you'll see the crumbling stone foundation of Santa Ynez Church, worshipping place of some Hawaiian Catholics whose arrest in the 1830s contributed to the subsequent granting of religious freedom.

The blue sea sparkles below as you drive along at 1,500 feet. Offshore you'll see tiny Molokini Island, to some Hawaiians a still-revered home of ancestral spirits, and Kahoolawe, the uninhabited military target island. Along the road are entries to a few grueling jeep trails; two link up with a footpath along the ocean that takes you west to La Perouse Bay.

Between Kanaio and Ulupalakua you look down on the surprisingly fresh-looking lava from Haleakala's last eruption, some 200 years ago. Puu Olai cinder cone, a Makena landmark, juts into the sea.

Maui's geography and close proximity to neighboring islands make it a land of recreational opportunity: from the undulating coastline to the desolate Haleakala moonscape, the Valley Isle's variety offers the spice of outdoor life. Several miles from its shores lie Molokai, Lanai, Kahoolawe, and exposed Molokini Crater, greatly expanding flightseeing and boating destinations.

For further details on any activity listed below, consult your travel agent, hotel desk, or the Maui Visitors Bureau, 172 Alamaha St., Suite 100, Kahului, HI 96732.

Flightseeing. A great way to gain an overview of the state's second largest island and the world's largest dormant volcano, circle-island tours and charter flights are available through most of the companies listed below.

Plane. Kahului: Kihele Maui Tours, Maui and other island flightseeing including ground tours; Paragon Air, aerial and aerial/ground tours.

Helicopter. Kahului: Alexair, Hawaii Helicopters, Kenai Helicopters, Lei Aloha Helicopters, South Sea Helicopters; Kahului and Kapalua: Papillon Helicopters; Wailea: Maui Helicopters; Kaanapali: Sunshine Helicopters.

Golf. Most of Maui's golf courses flank the western shore, so the Pacific figures prominently as a water hazard, if not scenic distraction, on many holes. All the courses listed below are open to the public. Yardages are from the regular (white) tees.

Public courses. Silversword Golf Course, Kihei, 18 holes, 5,964 yards; Waiehu Municipal Golf Course, Waiehu, 18 holes, 6,367 yards.

Resort/commerical courses. Kapalua Golf Club, Kapalua, 36 holes: Bay Course, 6,111 yards, Village Course, 5,981 yards; Royal Kaanapali Golf Course, Kaanapali, 36 holes: North Course, 6,305 yards, South Course, 6,250 yards; Makena Golf Course, Makena, 18 holes, 6,262 yards; Wailea Golf Club, Wailea, 36 holes: Blue Course, 6,152 yards, Orange Course, 6,063 yards; Pukalani Country Club, Pukalani, 18 holes, 6,570 yards; Maui Country Club, Spreckelsville, 9 holes, 3,247 yards (private course, open to the public on Mondays.)

Tennis. Public and resort or commercial courts are listed below. Many condominiums also have courts for guest use. Check with your travel or rental agent. Most pro shops rent equipment.

Public courts. Wailuku: Wailuku Community Center, 3 courts, and Maui Community College, 4 courts (after school hours); Lahaina: Malu-ulu-olele Park, 4 courts; Kihei: Kalama Park, 2 courts; Hana: Hana Ball Park, 2 regular courts and 3 grass courts.

Resort/commercial courts. Kapalua: Kapalua Tennis Gardens, 10 courts (4 with lights). Napili Bay: Napili Kai, 2 courts, Kaanapali: Hyatt Regency Maui, 5 courts; Kaanapali Alii, 3 courts with lights; Maui Marriott Resort, 5 courts (3 with lights); Royal Lahaina Tennis Ranch, 11 courts (6 with lights); Sheraton Maui, 3 courts with lights; The Whaler, 4 courts. Kihei: Maui Prince, Makena Resort, 6 courts; Wailea Tennis Club, 14 courts (3 with lights, 3 grass courts). Hana: Hotel Hana Maui, 2 courts.

Swimming. You'll find safe swimming at the spots listed below, but always stay alert for such adverse conditions as strong tides or high winter surf. Unlisted beaches may be dangerous; check for posted warnings.

Ocean swimming. Waihee Beach Park, Kapalua Beach, Napili Bay, Keonenui Beach, Kahana Beach, Honokowai Beach Park, Kaanapali Beach, Hanakaoo Beach, Wahikuli State Wayside Park, Puamana Beach Park, Launiupoko State Wayside Park (includes a manmade ocean pool), Kulanaokalai Beach, Awalua Beach, Mai Poina Oe Iau Beach Park, Kalepolepo Beach, Kamaole I, II, III, Keawakapu Beach, Mokapu Beach, Ulua Beach, Poolenalena Beach, Oneuli Beach, Hana Beach Park.

Freshwater swimming. Kipahulu's 'Ohe'o Gulch, Waianapanapa Cave, the mouth of Ulaino Stream, Hinamoo Pool in Nahiku Stream, Puaa Kaa State Park, Keanae Stream, Twin Falls.

Surfing. Check with residents, companies offering surfing instruction or equipment rental (in the Yellow Pages under "Surfboards"), or at your accommodations about water conditions before you paddle out.

Board surfing. Honolua Bay, Napili Bay, Hanakaoo Beach, Lahaina Beach, Puamana Beach Park, Launiupoko State Wayside Park, Awalua Beach, Olowalu Beach, Ukumehame Beach Park, Maalaea Beach, Kalama Beach Park, Mokapu Beach, Popolana Beach, Hookipa Beach Park, Hamakua Poko Papa, Lower Paia Park, H. A. Baldwin Park, Kahului Harbor.

Body surfing. Makuleia Beach, D. T. Fleming Beach Park, Hanakaoo Beach, Kulanaokalai Beach, Kamaole I, II, III, Keawakapu Beach, Mokapu Beach, Ulua Beach, Wailea Beach, Polo Beach, Hamoa Beach.

Beachcombing, tidepooling, and reef walking. An interesting cross section of Maui's underwater environment is yours for the viewing as you stroll through shallow waters. Wear canvas shoes for lava or reef walking; gloves are also a good precaution. Leave rocks as you find them; exposure to light kills some marine life.

Low-tide walking sites. Kahului Bay, Waiehu Beach Park, Waihee Beach Park, Olowalu Beach, Makena Bay, Nuu Bay, Seven Pools Park, Hana Beach Park, H. A. Baldwin Park.

Skin and scuba diving. Bring your certification card for scuba rentals or trips. For any diving (especially scuba excursions), check current water conditions. Also refer to the boating listing for cruises and charters that include diving. For instruction, certification, rentals, and dive trips look in the Yellow Pages under "Divers' Equipment & Supplies," "Skin Diving Instruction," and "Skin Diving Equipment."

Diving spots. Kaehu Beach, Waihee Beach Park, Honolua and Makuleia bays (protected by Marine Life Conservation District status—good diving, but removal of marine organisms is prohibited), Oneloa Beach, Kapalua Beach, Keonenui Beach, Honokowai Beach Park, Hanakaoo Beach, Wahikuli State Wayside Park, Lahaina Beach, Papalaua State Wayside Park, McGregor Point, Ulua Beach, Wailea Beach, Polo Beach, Ahihi-Kinau Natural Area Reserve, Hana Beach Park, Molokini Island.

Boating activities and cruises. Maui's heyday as an international port of call ended more than a century ago, but the Valley Isle still boasts a lot of aquatic adventure. Many combinations of water craft destinations and activities are available, as diverse as windsurfing clinics and inter-island outings on giant trimarans. Larger vessels offer trips ranging from 2 hours to a full day, and include fishing, swimming, skin and scuba diving, and meals. Sunset or dinner cruises, whale watching "in season" (during winter), excursions to neighbor islands, and charters are other options.

The numbers of companies and choices are too vast to cover thoroughly here; specific information can be obtained from hotel activity centers, the Yellow Pages (see "Boating Instruction" and "Boats-Charter"), and local travel publications, particularly near the major harbors of Lahaina, Kaanapali, Maalaea, and Kihei.

Fishing. Contact the Department of Land and Natural Resources (see address in next column) for spearfishing regulations and freshwater licensing and limits; there are no saltwater fishing licenses needed, or limits. For chartered fishing boats, check the Yellow Pages under "Fishing Parties." Based principally at Lahaina and Maalaea, these boats usually make ½-day to full-day trips.

Fishing locations. Channel waters between Maui, Kahoolawe, Lanai, and Molokai are good for trolling or bottom-fishing. Spots along much of Maui's shores provide fine shorefishing; among the most promising sites are Kahului Harbor, Paukukalo Beach, Waiehu Beach Park, Waihee Beach Park, the Kulanaokalai-Launiupoko area, Nuu Bay, Seven Pools Park, Waianapanapa State Park, and Hookipa Beach Park.

For spearing octopuses or small fish, try the waters off Lahaina, Makena, the Waiehu-Waihee area, Spreckelsville, and around Hana. Pier fishing is possible in Kahului, Hana, and Maalaea bays. *Hahalalu* (young bigeye scad) can be caught in late summer from harbor piers and breakwaters.

Cycling. For around-town pedaling, a rental bicycle should suffice; bring your own 5 or 10-speed for cross-country trips; low-geared bikes are not always available at rental outlets. Check with your airline in advance for regulations and costs of transporting a bicycle.

Riding from Kahului Airport to Hana (52 miles/83 km) on Highway 36 uncovers some spectacular scenery. Following a narrow, rough road, you'll climb some fairly steep hills; the trip can be made in a day, but several good campgrounds (no hotels) are along the route.

As bicycle country, the coastline north and south of Lahaina merits the island slogan "no ka oi"—the best. Riding north from Lahaina or Kaanapali, you'll happen upon secluded beaches and lovely panoramas of mountains and ocean. The ride is level and roads are in fairly good condition.

A 2½-mile/4-km bikeway parallels the highway from Lahainaluna Road intersection to Lahaina Civic Center (across the highway from Wahikuli State Wayside Park). This area is limited to day trips, since there are no public campgrounds here; remember to bring water and lunch with you.

Cruiser Bob's Haleakala Downhill, Lahaina; Maui Downhill, Kahului; and Maui Mountain Cruisers, Makawao offer cycling tours down Haleakala Crater Road.

Horseback riding. Rainbow Ranch Riding Stables, near Kapalua, 1, 2, and 6-hour rides, beach rides, riding lessons in Western or English styles; Kaanapali Kau Lio Riding Stables, Kaanapali, 2, 3-hour trail rides along the West Maui Mountains; Thompson Ranch, Kula, 1, 2-hour, day rides through Kula, Haleakala Crater; Pony Express Tours, Haleakala summit, ½-day, day tours in Haleakala; Charley's Trail Rides and Pack Trips, Kaupo, trail rides and overnight rides through Haleakala Crater with cabin or tent lodging; Hotel Hana Maui, Hana, horse rentals by the hour, regularly scheduled rides including breakfast, cookout, beach, sunrise, and full-moon trips; Makena Stables, Kihei, Ulupalakua ranchland rides, hourly rentals; Mo'omuku Stables, Kihei, guided ranchland rides, 2½ hour morning rides, 5½ hour winery rides, and sunset rides.

Hiking, camping, mountain tours. For maps, guides, and other information, contact Hawaiian Geographic Society, P.O. Box 1698, Honolulu, HI 96806; Hawaii Trail and Mountain Club, Box 2238, Honolulu, HI 96814; Hawaii Sierra Club, Box 11070, Honolulu, HI 96828; Department of Land and Natural Resources, Division of Forestry and Wildlife, 54 South High Street, Wailuku, HI 96793.

Camping information. For campsite specifics and permits, including the Polipoli Spring State Recreation Area and Waianapanapa State Park, contact the State Parks Division, Box 1049, Wailuku, Maui, HI 96793. For information on Haleakala National Park, write to Box 537, Makawao, Maui, HI 96768. A private camp with six cabins on a beach south of Lahaina is operated by Camp PECUSA (Protestant Episcopalian Camps, USA). For details, write to Holy Innocents Church, Box 606, Lahaina, Maui, HI 96761.

Mountain touring. Holo Holo Tours, Lahaina, takes to dirt roads in vans to show off Maui's upcountry—'Ohe'o Gulch, Hana, Kipahulu, Kaupo, and Ulupalakua. No Ka Oi Tours, Kahului, travels the Hana coastline for viewing tropical gardens and waterfalls and swimming in mountain pools.

MOLOKAI

• TOURISM IS ASTIR IN OLD HAWAII'S SLEEPY OUTPOST •

Though sleepy little Molokai (population about 6,500) has long been a popular weekend destination for residents of Honolulu (only 26 miles/42 km away), not until recent years have other travelers been going out of their way to visit this lovely place, proudly referred to by its people as the "Friendly Isle."

Hawaii's fifth largest island, Molokai (pronounced moh-loh-kah-ee) is shoe-shaped, long (37 miles/59 km), and narrow (10 miles/16 km). It was formed by two major volcanic domes. The western end of the island, first to emerge, is now a rolling tableland that rises to only 1,381 feet. The jagged mountains of the northeast, topped by 4,970-foot Kamakou, were formed later by the East Molokai volcano. Kalaupapa, the little tongue of land that juts out from the north coast almost like an afterthought, was created by Kauhako volcano.

New Tourism, New Agriculture

The opening of Molokai's first large, master-planned resort area on the island's west shore in 1977 signaled to the world of tourism that Molokai was going to be heard from—as indeed it has. Adjacent to an 18-hole golf course that stacks up with Hawaii's best are the Kaluakoi Hotel and two condominium complexes.

Many of the island's people, with their agricultural heritage and slow-moving way of life, are still unaccustomed to modern-day tourism. But their once-thriving pineapple operations have dwindled, due largely to changing worldwide economic conditions, so it appears that Molokai's future will be tied to some kind of balance between diversified agriculture and a gradual growth in tourism.

Getting the Most from Your Visit

Unlike the large tourist meccas, Molokai won't "come to you"—you'll have to meet it on its own terms. You can bustle about or just do nothing; the mood and attitude are most decidedly "no push."

Spectacular scenery and fascinating historic sites are everywhere and within short driving distances. The south shore east of Kaunakakai, only a few hours driving on good roads from the airport or your hotel base, offers an excellent introduction to the feel of the island, as do western Molokai and the hill country northwest of Kaunakakai. The trip to Kalaupapa, possible by air, on foot, or by mule (see page 124), is an experience not to be missed.

The *pali*—the northern coast from Kalaupapa eastward to the Halawa Valley—has no roads, but you can charter a helicopter (from Honolulu or Maui), a small plane, or a boat to see this spectacular region of cliffs, waterfalls, and valleys.

Despite all its beauty and charm—and Molokai takes a back seat to none of the other islands in these and other natural attributes—Molokai is nonetheless not for everybody. If you thrive on a whirl of activities, and prefer restaurant-hopping and night life to sitting around quietly in the evenings, one of the bigger islands might be more to your liking.

But if you appreciate a quiet place, find fascination in history and old legends, don't mind roughing it a bit on occasion, and (most of all) can understand and identify with people who still value their generations-old way of life above all else—then, Molokai offers an experience you will never forget.

Kalaupapa peninsula

THE ESSENTIALS

Hawaiian Airlines, Air Molokai-Tropic Airlines, and Princeville Airways have flights daily from Honolulu and Maui to Hoolehua, the island's main airport. Hawaiian also flies from Hawaii, and Princeville connects the island with Hawaii and Kauai. The *Maui Princess*, a high-speed boat, also journeys between Maui and Molokai.

Getting Around

You can capture the flavor of Molokai in one day if you are content just to visit the most celebrated places—Halawa Valley and the lookouts over Kalaupapa. But to explore and "get away from it all," the best reason for going to Molokai, you'll want more time.

Molokai's main highways are few but excellent. A regular compact or intermediate-size car is all you'll need to drive the south shore to Halawa Valley, west from the airport through Molokai Ranch land to the Kaluakoi Resort, and in Upper Molokai through to Hoolehua Homesteads, and to Palaau State Park overlooking Kalaupapa.

Car rental. Rental cars are available from several agencies located just adjacent to the main airport at Hoolehua. It's important to make advance reservations.

Special tours. If reservations are made ahead of time, group tours of some of the island's highlights can be arranged with Gray Line and Robert's Hawaii tours. Several island operators take visitors to Kalaupapa.

Where to Stay

Molokai has three hotels: the Kaluakoi Hotel & Golf Club on the western end of the island at Kepuhi Beach, Pau Hana Inn on the south coast at Kaunakakai, and Hotel Molokai, 2 miles/3 km east of town. Condominiums include Paniolo Hale and Ke Nani Kai (both near the Kaluakoi Hotel & Golf Club), Molokai Shores near Kaunakakai, and Wavecrest Resort on the southeast shore.

See page 129 for a guide to Molokai's recreational facilities.

KALAUPAPA: WHERE FATHER DAMIEN BROUGHT HOPE

For almost a century, Kalaupapa, the tiny peninsula that juts out from the north coast's fortresslike cliffs, was the place of banishment and isolation for sufferers of leprosy. The once-dread disease has now been brought almost completely under control, and no new patients are admitted. Those who remain have arrested cases. Though free to leave, they prefer to live out their lives here in the place they consider their home.

The peninsula is also Kalaupapa National Historical Park and the park service staff is working with the state and with residents to preserve and restore historic buildings and interpret sites to bring to life the stories of the settlement's heroes. Father Damien, the colony's first white resident, devoted himself to relieving the victims' suffering from 1873 until he died in 1889 after contracting the disease. Though his body was sent to his native Belgium in 1936, a monument to this martyr (who has been proposed for sainthood) stands in the graveyard of St. Philomena, the church he built (see photograph, page 16).

The settlement welcomes visitors, and there is no health hazard if you follow the rules. You must have a permit from the State Department of Health to visit; but your airline or tour operator will get it for you. Minimum age for visitors is 16.

No roads lead to Kalaupapa; the only ways in or out are by air, or by riding a mule down the 3 mile/5km zigzag trail along its abrupt and confining mountain wall. On the peninsula you must sightsee with a guide from Ike's Scenic Tours or Damien Tours. Take a picnic lunch; Kalaupapa has no restaurant.

You can fly directly to Kalaupapa Airport from Honolulu or Maui or shuttle from Molokai Airport. See the list of carriers above, and ask your Kalaupapa tour company for help with arrangements. Rare Adventures, Ltd. (Box 200, Kualapuu, Hawaii 96757) operates the mule ride and its trip includes the tour of the peninsula by van and a picnic lunch. The mule ride—from the stables at Kalae to the settlement—takes a little more than an hour each way. With sheer lava cliffs falling off at the edge of your path, this ride is not for the faint-hearted. It is safe (even for inexperienced riders) and is a unique way to see some of Molokai's most majestic scenery.

Kalaupapa. Kalaupapa has several churches (St. Francis and Kanaana Hou are particularly charming), a community hall, general store, bar (beer and wine only), and wharf where barges come in twice each year to deliver vehicles and some other provisions. Three-fourths of the patients live in trim cottages, have gardens and television, and do their own cooking.

Kalawao. The easternmost district, Kalawao, lies 2½ miles/4 km across the peninsula. The colony was started here, but the settlement gradually moved to the Kalaupapa side, which is drier and less windy.

Kalawao has two historic churches: Protestant Siloama, set before a backdrop of mist-shrouded peaks; and St. Philomena, Father Damien's church.

Lawrence McCully Judd Park is a magnificent spot where you can picnic on a grassy bluff and watch the surf pound the green cliffs of the Pali Coast.

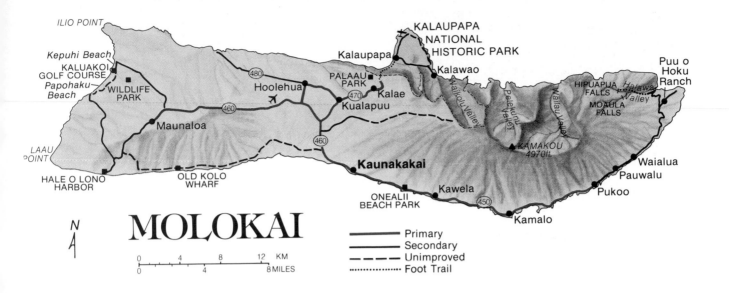

MOLOKAI

Scale: 0 4 8 12 KM / 0 4 8 MILES

Primary
Secondary
Unimproved
Foot Trail

Kaunakakai and the South Shore

Small Kaunakakai, 8 miles/13 km from the airport, is a lively place. At least once a week, people come from all over the island to shop and swap small talk. The bread at venerable Kanemitsu Bakery is famous all over the state. The Mid-Nite Inn got its name from a bygone era when it served saimin to travelers waiting for a midnight-departing interisland steamer; now it closes at 9 P.M. Saturday, the most popular market day, usually winds to a close with dancing and partying at the few night spots.

Barges load and unload their cargoes at Kaunakakai's big, busy wharf; fishing boats add to the activity. The foundation of the home of Kamehameha V lies next to the wharf.

Visitors can hire the sailboat *Rodonis* or the fishing boat *Noio* by advance reservation at Molokai Ranch office. *Rodonis* sails to Lanai and Maui; overnight trips are available.

Kaunakakai to Halawa. It's less than 30 miles/48 km from Kaunakakai to Halawa, but you should figure on at least 3 hours to allow time for sightseeing. Highway 450 (Kamehameha Highway) is easy driving as far as Pukoo; after that, the road becomes rough, narrow, and winding—but the views provide ample compensation. You gaze across the narrow channels to Lanai and Maui, while inland rise steep green mountain slopes, topped by 4,970-foot Kamakou.

Along this coast lies the only remaining concentration of offshore fishponds, built hundreds of years ago on all the major islands to stock and fatten fish for the tables of Hawaii's kings and chiefs (see page 128).

Onealii Park, just east of Kaunakakai, makes a pleasant picnic spot. It has a pavilion, rest rooms, drinking water, and a wading pool. Adjacent is a park for Kawela Plantation, a 6,000-acre agricultural/residential subdivision extending from the ocean to 4,000 feet elevation.

Kawela, a couple of miles beyond Onealii Park, was the site of a famous battle in the mid-1700s. Here the Molokai chiefs with their allies from Hawaii defeated attacking warriors from Oahu.

Forty-acre Kakahaia Pond, about 5 miles/8 km east of Kaunakakai, is a federal wildlife reserve and a refuge for the endangered Hawaiian coot and Hawaiian stilt.

Tiny Kamalo, a heavily populated area many years ago, has a small boat harbor and a wharf built sometime between 1850 and 1875. A sugar mill once stood just west of the present stream bed.

Stop at Kamalo's tiny St. Joseph's Church, a classic frame chapel with tall steeple and fine old glass windows. Built in 1876 and restored in 1971, it's the second of two churches founded on this side of the island by the famous Belgian priest, Father Damien (see page 124), who devoted his life to helping leprosy victims at Kalaupapa.

A mile beyond St. Joseph's Church, a monument marks the spot where, in 1927, Ernest Smith and Emory Bronte safely crash-landed their plane, ending the first civilian trans-Pacific flight after 25 hours and 2 minutes. The fliers, who took off from California, had hoped to reach Honolulu but ran out of gas.

Farther on, a Hawaii Visitors Bureau marker points to two *heiau* (temples) up on the ridge; though important ones, they are scarcely discernible.

Next comes long-abandoned Ah Ping's store; the only Chinese graveyard on the island (there are other gravesites) is located behind it.

Kaluaaha Church, a short distance past Ah Ping's, was built by the first missionaries and is Molokai's earliest church still standing. Its 3-foot-thick walls of plastered stone went up in 1844; the buttresses, iron roof, and faded red steeple (now fallen in) came later. The church is in disrepair now and the congregation meets elsewhere. Be very careful if you go inside—the roof is gradually collapsing.

(Continued on page 127)

Creamy waves *of Halawa Bay lap gently at Molokai's eastern shore, where Halawa Valley meets the sea.*

"High-rise" *on a low-rise island, giraffe is one of many African animals roaming in Molokai Ranch Wildlife Park.*

Father Damien's Our Lady of Sorrows Church, built two years before St. Joseph's Church and also recently restored, is just down the road in a palm grove. Anyone can attend the services, conducted only on special occasions. In a nearby pavilion stands a statue of the good father carved by a local artist.

Be content just to read about most marked places of historic interest from here on—often they're on private land and hard or impossible to see. Observe instead how the people live today. At scattered houses, you'll see nets drying and laundry flapping in the breeze. Families usually spend weekends out swimming, fishing, cooking, and camping.

Iliiliopae Heiau in Mapulehu Valley, now on the National Register of Historic Places, is one of the largest and most fascinating in Hawaii. For many years it could not be visited, but today, by phoning the Petro family (558-8113), you can receive clearance and directions. A visit is like going back many hundreds of years in time. A particularly awesome sight is the football-field-size top platform. If you visit the heiau, wear shoes that grip well and be prepared for some tricky walking as you ascend and descend the three platforms.

Between Pukoo and Waialua, you pass the site of a royal taro patch and the stack of a sugar mill that burned down about a hundred years ago.

Soon you are climbing through Puu O Hoku Ranch. Off the eastern tip of Molokai lies the islet of Mokuhooniki, used for bombing practice in World War II. There is a fine view of western Maui, with Haleakala looming shadowlike behind. Beyond the ranch buildings, between the road and sea, you'll spot a dense stand of trees: a sacred *kukui* grove that is the burial place of Lanikaula, a famous Molokai prophet for whom the grove is named.

Halawa Valley. Finally, the rough road zigzags down the ridge into Halawa Valley, guarded to the north by mighty Lamaloa Head. Here, in reach of an ordinary car, you'll find Hawaii's version of the South Seas of stories and paintings. Broad, deep, and green carpeted, the valley is backed by cliffs; two high falls plummet to a stream that meanders out to the sea.

Hundreds of people once lived in Halawa, considered one of the earliest settlements in the islands (about A.D. 500). Even a few decades ago, taro farmers and fishermen were active. Though a few houses still stand, the jungle has gradually encroached on the geometric taro layout.

At the foot of the ridge, the road forks. One leg (paved) runs down to the shore, where you can swim in the bay if it's calm or at the mouth of the stream. The other road (dirt) heads into the valley a little way, past some old houses almost hidden in the lush foliage, a wooden church (still in use), and ruins of a mid-19th century stone church. The wooden church resembles a dollhouse.

Halawa's *pièce de résistance* is Moaula Falls, a pleasant hour's hike—but take along mosquito lotion and be wary of going too soon after a rain. The lower part of the main trail up the far side of the valley is overgrown now. To reach it, you have to ford the wide part of the stream, since a locked gate on the ranch jeep trail bars access to the bridge.

For an easier route, walk up the road to the last house and then follow a trail of sorts alongside a water pipe. You'll cross a couple of irrigation ditches and a narrow part of the stream where rocks serve as steppingstones. Don't lose sight of the pipe. When you come to a water tank, pick up the main trail; the pipeline continues alongside. As you walk through the tangle of *hau, kukui,* mangoes, Surinam cherries, *liliko'i,* and ginger, you'll spot the old stone terraces of many abandoned taro patches.

The falls drop from a towering cliff with such force that the surface of the pool below is a mass of bubbles. According to legend, you should swim only if the *mo'o* (lizard) is happy. To find out his mood, toss in a ti leaf—if it floats, all is well. Even if the leaf sinks, the mountain-cold water is too good to miss.

Upper Molokai

Heading west from Kaunakakai on Highway 460, you pass Kiowea Park. A coconut grove here was planted for King Kamehameha V in the 1860s. Across the highway and well worth a look is charming "church row."

Soon the road climbs 11 miles/17½ km from Kaunakakai on highways 460 and 470 to the crest of the island, high above Kalaupapa. At Kualapuu, Highway 480 branches toward Hoolehua Homesteads (homes are spread over many miles) and the airport and offers a view over the gigantic Kualapuu Reservoir. Water from wet, uninhabited Waikolu Valley is carried through the mountain to the reservoir through a 5-mile/8-km tunnel.

Kualapuu remains a pretty little plantation town despite the decline of pineapple growing in recent years. About 2 miles/3 km northwest of town at Hoolehua is a landmark, Puukapeelua or "Hill of the Caterpillar God"; its name springs from a legend in which a Molokai girl's lover turned out to be a giant caterpillar. When the people tried to burn the caterpillar, it released millions of tiny caterpillars that swarmed over the island.

Kamehameha the Great camped for a year at Kauluwai to get his troops conditioned and provisioned before attacking Oahu, which is visible from this high ground on clear days.

At Kalae, the R. W. Meyer Sugar Mill, built in 1878 and still under family ownership, is gradually being restored. It's included in the National Register of Historic Places. The lovely old Meyer home is next door.

Palaau Park. The road ends on a 1,600-foot cliff where a steep foot trail zigzags down to Kalaupapa, the only access by land to the settlement. The topside view of the cliffs stretching to the east is as awesome as the sight of the little peninsula laid upon the sea like a carpet, but a better vantage point is the lookout in Palaau Park. The park road, near the end of Highway 470, travels through a beautiful wilderness of koa, paperbark, ironwood, and cypress trees. After passing a small arboretum, which has 40 species of trees labeled, it ends at a campground.

Here you have a choice of two short trails. A footpath, arched with ironwoods that create a cathedral quality, leads to the Kalaupapa overlook. You can make out the wharf, churches, lighthouse, landing field, crater, and other features of the peninsula. The history of Kalaupapa is inscribed on a plaque at the viewing point.

The other walk follows a truck trail carpeted with ironwood needles for about 200 yards, and then turns right into a narrow footpath that climbs about 50 yards to a 6-foot-high phallic rock.

Waikolu Lookout and Kamakou Preserve. This remote area in central Molokai provides spectacular scenery and an opportunity to see some of Molokai as it existed a century ago. However, you must drive a gravel-and-dirt road (a turnoff from Highway 460) to reach it; drive this road only in dry periods and when the sky is clear over the mountains.

The drive takes you through a forest, planted since 1900 as watershed, that is resplendent with pines, cedar, eucalyptus, 'ohi'a, ferns, and clumps of ginger. After 9½ miles/15 km, you come to the Sandalwood Boat, a large depression in the ground the size and shape of a ship's hold, dug more than a century ago to measure the amount of sandalwood a ship could carry. Hawaiian chiefs bartered the wood for trinkets, whiskey, and finery from white traders who, in turn, sold it at great profit, especially in China where it was highly prized.

At Waikolu Valley Lookout, you step to the edge for a magnificent view of a deep, narrow gorge laced with high waterfalls.

Just beyond is a sign-in box at the entrance to the 2,774-acre Kamakou Preserve established to protect a precious high elevation rain forest with 250 kinds of Hawaiian plants and rare native forest birds. (See hiking information, page 129.)

West Molokai

Highway 460 heads west from the airport through Molokai Ranch lands. It's 8 miles/13 km to the turnoff to Kepuhi Beach and the Kaluakoi Hotel & Golf Club, 10 miles/16 km to the end of the road at Maunaloa, a company town for Dole's pineapple workers until Dole phased out its Molokai operations in 1975. Hilly, picturesque, and graced with many Norfolk Island pines, Maunaloa still is home to some workers who bought their houses and stayed on. A few former mainlanders live here also. The shops and market are patronized not only by residents but by vacationers staying at nearby condominiums.

After the hotel turnoff, another 5 miles/8 km brings you to the hotel at Kepuhi Beach. From this western coast, you can see Oahu across the channel. On moonless nights, Honolulu gleams in a luminous mist on the horizon.

Here, in the Kaluakoi Resort area, tourism has been on the rise since the late 1970s. The Kaluakoi Hotel & Golf Club, low (2-story cottages), sprawling, and quietly luxurious, is currently western Molokai's only hotel, though an additional hotel has been proposed for the Kaluakoi property. Two condominium complexes, Paniolo Hale and Ke Nani Kai, now exist, with more planned for the late 1980s. The 18-hole oceanside golf course, designed by Ted Robinson, adds to the resort's appeal.

Near the Kaluakoi Hotel & Golf Club, the Molokai Ranch Wildlife Park (a 2,000-acre, privately owned preserve) contains small herds of animals, mostly African, from the same latitude as the island. Such animals as eland, oryx, Indian black buck, and giraffes roam freely in a habitat like that of their homeland. Though the preserve's primary purpose is to sell surplus animals to zoos as the herds expand, visitors can see and photograph the animals on the preserve during guided safari van tours. Check at the hotel for information.

The Pali Coast

The coastline from Kalaupapa to Halawa is one of the most spectacular in Hawaii. From its towering green cliffs, waterfalls plunge hundreds of feet into the ocean or disappear halfway down as winds blow them into a mist. The cliffs are honeycombed with caves. One at sea level is navigable to some 200 feet inside the island. Several beautiful valleys break the 2,000-foot pali.

Only from a boat or plane can you see it all. Airplane flightseeing tours take you by, as do regular interisland flights traveling the north route between Oahu and Maui. For a closer and longer look, you can hire a boat at Kaunakakai or charter a small plane.

FISHPONDS IN THE OCEAN

At least as long ago as the 15th century, ponds were built along shallow coasts and shores on all the major islands. A tasty assortment of fish was stocked and fattened in them to satisfy the appetites of Hawaii's kings and chiefs. Most ponds are now in ruins, but a few on Molokai are still in commercial use; you can see most of these as you drive eastward from Kaunakakai on Highway 450. Ponds were enclosed by thick walls of coral or basalt. Each had one or more breaks covered by grates with openings wide enough to let young fish in but too narrow to permit fattened fish to leave. The water had to be shallow—no more than 3 feet deep—so sunshine could penetrate it and promote growth of microscopic food on the bottom. Alii Pond, just east of One Alii Beach Park, has a 2,700-foot-long wall, recently restored. Two others of note are Niaupala (33½ acres) at Kaluaaha, and Kupeke (30 acres), just east of Pukoo.

MOLOKAI RECREATION GUIDE

 A glimpse of Molokai's uncomplicated yesteryears more than compensates for a lack of commercial recreation. On the Friendly Isle, fewer manmade attractions mean fewer distractions, so you can better appreciate the coexistence of residents and their surroundings.

Golf. All courses listed are open to the public. Yardages are from the regular (white) tees.

Kaluakoi Golf Course, Kepuhi Beach, 18 holes, 6,618 yards; Maunaloa Golf Course, Maunaloa, 9 holes, 2,910 yards (contact Molokai Ranch Office in Kaunakakai for permission); Ironwood Hills Golf Course, Kualapuu, 9 holes, 2,799 yards.

Tennis. Several courts are open to the public: Kaunakakai Community Center, Kaunakakai, 2 public courts; Kaluakoi Hotel & Golf Club, Kepuhi Beach, 4 resort courts; Ke Nani Kai, Maunaloa, 2 resort courts; Wavecrest, Kaunakakai, 2 resort courts.

Swimming. The waters along Molokai's accessible southeast shore are mostly too shallow or silty for swimming, but they are ideal for windsurfing. Frequent rough water limits swimming at the west end's beautiful beaches —long expanses of white sand interrupted by lava outcroppings—and also along western Molokai's north shore; the best beach here is Moomomi, at the end of Highway 480. Even on calm days swimmers should be alert to possible dangerous currents.

Farther east on the pali shore, you find safe water at the entrances to Pelekunu, Wailau, and Halawa valleys in calm water conditions (there is road access at Halawa). Streams running through these valleys to the bays are also nice for a dip. Coves with sandy beaches characterize the shoreline near Waialua, southwest of Halawa, though none are exceptional swimming beaches.

Surfing. Halawa Bay is one of Molokai's best beaches for both board and body surfing. Good surfing is also found at Rock Point, between Honouli Maloo and Honouli Wai on the southeast shore and at Kepuhi Beach on the west end.

Beachcombing, reef walking, skin/scuba diving. Mudflats constitute the majority of Molokai's southern shoreline, limiting shallow-water activities. The island's west end and Halawa Bay on the east end, though, are good for diving. Moanui Beach near Halawa Valley offers good reef walking on a fringing reef that borders much of Molokai's southern shore.

Boating and fishing. Though many boating companies, especially from Maui, consider the Friendly Isle a notable spot to drop anchor, only a few make Molokai their home port. The sailboat *Rodonis* makes half-day and full-day cruises to Lanai for snorkeling and whale-watching (in season), and overnight trips to Lanai or Maui can be arranged. Hokupaa Ocean Adventures offers north shore cruises from Halawa Valley, Box 141, Kualapuu. Visitors can hire the fishing boat *Noio* by making reservations with the Molokai Ranch office in Kaunakakai.

Cycling. The western side of the island, near the Sheraton Molokai, includes the safest cycling on Molokai. Another two-wheel option follows the 28-mile/45-km coast route (Highway 450) running eastward from Kaunakakai. This route provides good biking until the last few miles through Puu O Hoku Ranch and into Halawa Valley.

Horseback and mule riding. Equestrians can schedule rides through the Kaluakoi Hotel & Golf Club, Hotel Molokai, or at Kahanui Stables. Hawaiian Horsemanship Unlimited offers guided tours for experienced riders (telephone 567-6635).

For a less conventional ride, consider the Molokai Mule Ride, an excursion down a cliffside trail, to Kalaupapa and back (see page 124).

Hiking—easy or difficult trails. A switchback trail connects upper Molokai to Kalaupapa. From Kalaupapa's Lawrence McCully Judd Park, you can walk a mile along the shore to Waikolu Valley. Off the Waikolu Valley Lookout road, a number of jeep or foot trails go for a mile or two to the edge of the forest; a few longer ones lead to spectacular view points.

In Halawa Valley, an easy hour-long walk leads to Moaula Falls (be wary after recent rains). A more difficult route, scrambling over rocks, takes you up to Hipuapua Falls. A jeep trail heads up the north wall of the valley, past Papa Heiau to the top of Lamaloa Head, continuing through forest and grasslands to the top of Papalaua Canyon's 1,000-foot waterfall.

At Kamakou Preserve (see page 128), a 45-minute hike leads to a redwood boardwalk that takes you through the Pepeopae Bog, a break in the forest canopy resplendent with dwarf *'ohi'a*. Keep an eye out for rare native forest birds, including the red *'apapane* and the green *amakihi*.

Camping. The forested mountain area overlooking Kalaupapa Peninsula includes camping facilities in Palaau State Park, as does Onealii Beach on the coast just east of Kaunakakai. Another fine spot for mountain camping is a meadow with a stream a few hundred yards east of Waikolu Valley Lookout (get permission to camp from the Division of Forestry, Kaunakakai).

The north shores of Halawa and Wailau valleys offer camping, too. The beach on the south side of Halawa is a county park with pavilion, rest rooms, and grills. To camp, you need a permit from the county office in Kaunakakai. At times (usually in the summer), Wailau Valley is accessible by boat.

Palaau and Onealii parks are especially inviting picnic spots. Lawrence McCully Judd Park on Kalaupapa Peninsula and Kiowea Beach Park near Kaunakakai also afford pleasant picnicking.

LANAI

• PINEAPPLES, WIDE-OPEN SPACES, AND SOME OF THE ISLANDS' FINEST BEACHES •

Long known for delicious pineapples rather than for tourism, Lanai has only recently begun to develop facilities for visitors. The island has long produced lots of pineapple—more than 12,000 acres. But it also retains 78,000 additional acres of wide-open space. Two luxury hotels and golf courses, one outside Lanai City and one at Hulopoe Bay, will soon be available. For now, the island's limited accommodations make it an exclusive hideaway only a half hour by air from Honolulu.

Excellent swimming and snorkeling, miles of coast made to order for beachcombers, good hunting and fishing all await you on Lanai. You can drive or hike to lookouts above deeply eroded gulches or search for—and find—many remains of old Hawaii. Most of Lanai's 2,100 people live in Lanai City, where an impressive number (65 percent) own their homes. Some 445 work for the pineapple company.

Sixth in the island group in size—just 17 miles/27 km long and 13 miles/21 km wide—Lanai is actually an extinct volcano with a single crater, Palawai. Some say "Lanai" means a swelling or hump. If you look at the island from Maui, you will see that the name fits the contour of the land: a smooth, curved ridge rises from the southern base to an altitude of more than 3,000 feet and then slopes down again to the northern tip. Deep gulches cut into the ridge on the east side above a half-mile-wide coastal plain. On the west side, the ridge drops down to a plateau at 1,500 to 2,000-foot elevation, ending in cliffs above the sea. Vegetation on the plateau is scrubby, but gulches and hillsides on the windward side boast luxuriant growth. Rainfall in high areas averages 42 inches a year; in lower areas, 12 inches.

Ghostly Beginnings

One of Lanai's legends claims that the island was inhabited only by ghosts or evil spirits for a thousand years after the Polynesians had settled the other islands. Then Kaululaau, nephew of Maui's king, was banished to Lanai as punishment for one of his mischievous acts. Though he was not expected to survive, Kaululaau won out by driving all the ghosts from the island, making it safe for humans.

Protestant missionaries arrived on Lanai in 1835. Twenty years later, a Mormon colony was started in Palawai Basin. The colony later dissolved in a dispute between the church and the leader, Walter Murray Gibson, who refused to turn over his land acquisitions. His extensive holdings eventually passed on to sugar interests and then cattle ranchers; by 1910, most of the island had been bought up by a single ranching company.

"Fruit Basket" with a Future

After the land was purchased by the Dole Company in 1922, the semiwasteland became an exotic fruit basket. Dole still owns all but a few parcels that include house lots sold to employees. (Today, Dole is part of Castle & Cooke Foods, a division of Castle & Cooke, Inc.)

The island's lands are managed by the Koele Company, also a Castle & Cooke subsidiary. Koele is designing a long-term master plan for the entire island, calling for low-density development of homes and hotels on a portion of the open space, coupled with detailed management and improvement of the island's natural resources.

Tiny Manele harbor, a drop-off point for day-trippers

THE ESSENTIALS

Hawaiian Airlines, Air Molokai, and Princeville Airways provide daily service into Lanai Airport (a short drive southwest from Lanai City) from Honolulu, Maui, Molokai, and Hawaii. Several nonscheduled air taxis also serve the island. You can see easy-to-reach sights between a morning arrival and afternoon takeoff. Excursions from Maui sail to Lanai for the day or longer.

Getting Around

The only major paved roads radiate out from Lanai City— to Kaumalapau, to the northeast coast, and to the Hulopoe and Manele bay areas. You can rent a 4-wheel-drive vehicle (which you need to really explore the island) from Oshiro Service & U-Drive, 850 Fraser Ave., Lanai City, HI 96763. Oshiro also offers charter tours of the island.

Dirt roads that crisscross the pineapple sections are generally good. Others are often in too poor condition for passenger cars; during rainy weather, they may be impassable even in a jeep. Before starting out for off-beat areas, let someone know where you are going and get good directions.

The Koele Company, P.O. Box L, Lanai City, HI 96763, can help you plan hiking, hunting, and pack trips.

Where to Stay

The island's pioneer Hotel Lanai, a comfortable white frame, former plantation building with a veranda sits on a pine-covered hillside in Lanai. It has 11 rooms, all with bath, a dining room, and a bar. It will soon be joined by Koele Lodge outside town and Manele Bay Hotel at secluded Hulopoe Bay.

See page 137 for a guide to Lanai's recreational facilities.

PINEAPPLE —
TO LANAI BY WAY OF HARVARD

No one is certain just how or when the pineapple first came to Hawaii. It was not brought by the early Polynesians. The first mention of it appears in the diary of Don Francisco de Paula y Marin, a counselor to King Kamehameha I, who wrote on January 21, 1813, "This day I planted pineapples and an orange tree." Commercial production began on Oahu in 1882 when Captain John Kidwell, an English horticulturist, brought from Florida a shipment of the Smooth Cayenne variety grown almost exclusively in Hawaii today.

The pineapple is a true fruit, but it grows on a low plant, not on a tree where many visitors expect to find it. New plants are started by planting the crown, taken from the top of the fruit. After the fields are prepared, machines lay long rows of plastic mulch strips, simultaneously fumigating the soil beneath. The strips conserve moisture, increase soil temperature, and discourage weeds. New plants (around 20,000 per acre) are inserted in holes poked through the strips at regular intervals.

It takes from 18 to 22 months from the planting to the harvesting of a pineapple. In the first crop, each plant bears one 4 to 5-pound fruit; a ratoon (second or third) crop may have one or two smaller pineapples.

Harvesting is done by hand because pineapples must be picked when they are fully ripened. Workers move through the field, picking the ripe fruits and placing them on long-armed harvest machine conveyors. Sometimes crews work around the clock. The pineapples move by conveyor belt into bins on waiting trucks.

Most pineapple goes to canneries, but a growing proportion of fresh fruit is airlifted directly to mainland market areas.

James D. Dole—Pineapple Pioneer

Lanai underwent many years of decline during the late 19th and early 20th centuries. Attempts to make the island agriculturally productive didn't succeed; within a few years after experiments with sugarcane failed in 1901, the island's population—once well over a thousand—dwindled to less than two hundred.

All this changed when, in 1922, James D. Dole's Hawaiian Pineapple Company acquired control of the island and began growing pineapple. Kaumalapau, on Lanai's southwestern shore, was developed into the harbor necessary for shipping pineapples to the company's cannery in Honolulu.

Dole came to Hawaii in 1899 after graduating from Harvard. (Sanford B. Dole, president of the Republic of Hawaii at that time, was his first cousin once removed.) He soon began experimenting with pineapple plantings on 60 acres of homestead land at Wahiawa, in central Oahu. From these humble beginnings the pineapple industry expanded dramatically until, 25 years later, it became vital to the economy of all of Hawaii's islands.

Thrive though it did for many years, Hawaiian Pineapple Company was hard hit by the Great Depression of the early 1930s; controlling interests were acquired at that time by Castle & Cooke, Inc.

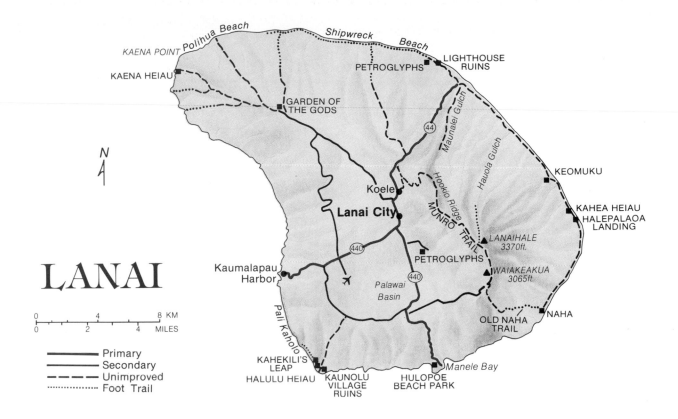

LANAI

0 — 4 — 8 KM
0 — 2 — 4 MILES

———— Primary
———— Secondary
- - - - Unimproved
········· Foot Trail

Lanai City

No place else in the islands is quite like Lanai City. Situated at 1,600 feet, just below the mountains, its climate resembles a California mountain town in summer—comfortably cool days, crisp nights. Immediately noticeable as you enter town is the stately presence of hundreds of towering Norfolk Island and Cook Island pine trees, planted by the pineapple company. The village is very still at night—until a whistle breaks the early morning calm, reminding workers there's work to be done that day. If the fields are too wet, the whistle doesn't blow.

Lanai City has plantation offices, school, hospital, several churches, post office, golf course (just barely), bank, two service stations, cafe, a bakery that also serves breakfast and lunch, courthouse, and jail. Only a few stores dot the streets. There's no such thing as a traffic jam and nary a stoplight to be seen—here or anywhere else on the island.

Lanai City, the island's one and only residential area, houses virtually the entire citizenry, the great majority of whom are Filipino. The modest homes cover a number of blocks outside the business section with their metal roofs and seemingly endless variety of colors and add-ons. Home gardens feature giant mango trees and a variety of tropical plants, but many azaleas, camellias, lilies, and other colorful temperate-zone flowers also thrive at this elevation.

Kaumalapau Harbor

Highway 440 from Lanai City to the harbor at Kaumalapau passes through acres of pineapple for 6 miles/9½ km, the fields broken only by red dirt roads that crisscross them. You may see irrigating and harvesting machines; the latter load fruit onto trucks at the rate of 10,000 pineapples per hour. But planting and picking are done by hand. During the harvesting peak in summer, you see scores of pickers, many with their heads all but covered by scarves, big hats, and goggles.

The road descends in curves to the harbor, which is backed by steep bluffs. The company-built harbor accommodates the barges that carry pineapples to the cannery in Honolulu; it always has a few fishing boats as well. At the 400-foot dock, cranes transfer the pineapples from trucks to barges.

North of Kaumalapau, the plateau ends in a bluff above the sea. To the south, jagged cliffs rise as high as 1,000 feet out of the water.

Hulopoe Beach and Manele Bay

Another pineapple-lined trip from Lanai City is the 8-mile/13-km drive to Manele Bay on a different section of Highway 440. Along the way you can detour to the Luahiwa petroglyphs, located near the base of the steep slopes around Palawai Basin, but you'll need a guide or

Waves lap *at sandy shore of Hulopoe Bay, which has a good swimming beach and picnic area.*

Machine conveyors *and trucks are important to pineapple harvesting— but most important are the people who hand-pick the ripened fruit.*

good directions to find them. You take a dirt road off the highway, then scramble up grassy banks to boulders that have one of Hawaii's most concentrated and best preserved collections of ancient rock carvings.

Manele Bay has a small boat harbor with a breakwater and berths for pleasure craft. Just beyond the breakwater, anchored in a cliff, is an old wooden chute; many years ago it was used to load cattle onto ships. Low lava stone walls and platforms on the hill above are remains of early native houses.

To the west is Hulopoe Bay, with a beautiful tree-fringed swimming beach (best on the island, but with an abrupt offshore dropoff) and an adjacent rock-rimmed pool for children. The park here contains the island's only improved picnic site, with tables, barbecues, showers, and restrooms. Bluffs along this coast were once submerged, and marine fossils have been found as high as 1,200 feet.

It's only a short walk or drive to the southeast end of the Hulopoe shore, and well worth the time for the view of Pu'u Pehe, an impressive sea stack known as "Sweetheart Rock." The story has been passed down through the years of a young Lanai warrior whose wife, captured from a Maui chieftain, died in a storm. After burying her atop the rock, the grief-stricken husband took his own life by flinging himself down into the churning sea.

Both Manele and Hulopoe are part of a marine life conservation district. Be sure to heed the restrictions posted throughout the region.

Kaunolu Village

Probably the most extensive and best preserved ruins in the islands are those of Kaunolu Village at the end of a rutty, rocky 3-mile/5-km jeep trail through grasslands south of the pineapple fields. Remains of 86 houses, 35 stone shelters, and various grave markings and garden sites are scattered across a point above the sea.

(Continued on next page)

WHAT'S IN A NAME?

No sooner do arriving passengers deplane in Hawaii than they become aware of the sight and sound of the islands' colorful place names. Unfortunately, most visitors depart knowing little more about the significance of these names than they knew upon arrival; they've missed an opportunity to share something special with the people of Hawaii.

Below you'll find a small sampler of meanings of some of Hawaii's better-known cities and towns, streets, and landmarks. Certain prominent names about which you might be curious aren't included because researchers and historians disagree on their translation—the words "Oahu," "Kauai," and "Hawaii" itself, for example. But you can read about these three and thousands of other Hawaiian names in the excellent book, *Place Names of Hawaii*, published by the University of Hawaii Press and available in many bookstores. Organized alphabetically for ready reference, it contains not only meanings but also pertinent background information on each place listed.

Ala Moana . . . . ocean street	Kaunakakai . . . . beach landing	Makawao . . . . forest beginning
Haena . . . . red hot	Kaupo . . . . landing of canoes at night	Makena . . . . abundance
Haiku . . . . speak abruptly		Manele . . . . sedan chair
Haleakala . . . . . . house of the sun	Kealakekua . . . . pathway of the god	Maui . . . . the demigod Maui
Halekulani . . . . . . house befitting royalty	Keanae . . . . the mullet	Mauna Kea . . . . . . white mountain
Hanalei . . . . crescent bay	Keauhou . . . . the new era	Mauna Loa . . . . long mountain
Hanapepe . . . . crushed bay (due to landslides)	Kihei . . . . cloak	Napili . . . . *pili* grass
Honolulu . . . . protected bay	Kokee . . . . to bend	Nawiliwili . . . . . . the *wiliwili* trees (Hawaiian natives)
Iao . . . . cloud supreme	Koko . . . . red earth	Paia . . . . noisy
Ilikai . . . . surface of the sea	Kona . . . . leeward	Poipu . . . . crashing (as waves)
Kaahumanu . . . bird feather cloak	Koolau . . . . windward	Punahou . . . . new spring
Kahala . . . . amberjack fish	Kula . . . . plain	Ulupalakua . . . . .ripening breadfruit
Kahului . . . . the winning		Waianapanapa . . .glistening water
Kalaupapa . . . . .the flat plain	Lahaina . . . . cruel sun	Waikiki . . . . spouting water
Kamehameha . . . . . the lonely one	Lanai . . . . day of conquest	Wailea . . . . water of Lea (canoe makers' goddess)
Kapalua . . . . two borders	Lihue . . . . cold chill	
Kapiolani . . . . arch of heaven (rainbow)	Lunalilo . . . . very high (of royalty)	Wailua . . . . two waters
Kailua . . . . two seas	Makaha . . . . fierce	Wailuku . . . . . water of destruction
	Makapuu . . . . bulging eye	Waimea . . . . reddish water

Now a national historic landmark, Kaunolu was once an active fishing community and a favorite recreation spot of Kamehameha the Great after he conquered all the islands. His house, on the edge of the eastern bluff above a usually dry stream bed, overlooked the bay, the village, and Halulu Heiau on the west bank.

Today you can see remains of this *heiau* (temple) and, spread along the east bank, parts of rock platforms where grass houses once stood enclosed by sections of stone walls. Many boulders have petroglyphs, a few with bird-like figures peculiar to Lanai.

From Kahekili's Jump, a break in a cliff above the sea, fleeing warriors are said to have leaped into the 12 feet of water 62 feet below. Their survival depended on clearing the ledge of rock that protrudes 15 feet into the sea at the base of the drop.

From Kaunolu you can walk about 2 miles/3 km along cliff tops to Pali Kaholo, at 1,083 feet the highest point in Lanai's coastline. You can also go from Kaunolu to Manele along the shore, but this difficult and rocky walk takes most of a day.

Garden of the Gods

You'll find the Garden of the Gods about 7 miles/11 km along a dirt road out of Lanai City; ask for good directions. The road passes first through pineapple fields and then through an area of lantana, *poha*, Norfolk Island pine, ironwood, and eucalyptus.

The garden is a varicolored canyon of windswept sand with fantastic lava formations standing all around, weird survivors of the decomposition and coloring wrought upon the less durable substances by wind, rain, and sun.

Dirt roads and jeep trails traverse the arid, uncultivated plateau that is northwestern Lanai. One road goes all the way to the white sands of Polihua Beach. Here surf casting is rewarding, but the strong current makes swimming dangerous and the windblown sand is often intolerable.

The Munro Trail

Lanai has beautiful forests, deep in gulches and high on mountain ridges. Munro Trail (also called Lanaihale Road), a dirt road best driven in a 4-wheel-drive vehicle, takes you to Lanaihale at the top of the island. On a clear day, you can see all of the major islands except Kauai from this 3,370-foot elevation.

The 7-mile/11-km route extends from the southeast hills near Waiakeakua to Koele's rolling grasslands. Near the top of the ridge, it cuts through a heavy rain forest of tree ferns and other exotic tropicals, most of them planted years ago by Hawaii's late naturalist, George C. Munro. Stands of Norfolk Island pines, in particular, were planted to increase the island's ground water, tapped for irrigation. Weather studies show that the trees collect moisture from the hill-hugging clouds.

A trail leads off to a lookout over 2,000-foot Hauola Gulch, Lanai's deepest ravine. From the road, you can see man-made notches in Hookio Ridge at the head of Maunalei Gulch. Warriors used these for protection and as bases for attack in 1778 during a battle in which the king of Hawaii massacred many Lanai natives.

The road overlooks the pumping station down in Maunalei Gulch, the island's watershed, which has tumbling waterfalls, a *kukui* grove, and lush valley plants.

The Windward Coast

About 3 miles/5 km from Lanai City, the narrow, paved road (Highway 44) that runs northeast to the windward coast passes a particularly pretty picnic area: rolling green hills and grassy knolls, shaded by a few *lama* and *olopua* trees that were once part of an extensive forest. There's a fine view over the 7-mile/11-km-wide channel between Lanai and Molokai. Then the road cuts a corkscrew course down to the shore.

Shipwreck Beach. At pavement's end, you can drive or walk (at low tide only) northwest on a dirt road to an old lighthouse foundation and along part of Shipwreck Beach—a stretch of 4 miles/6 km or more where a few hulks of old ships lie rotting and rusting on the reef. The shore (part sand, part black lava, part tidal flats) is littered with timbers and other remnants of once-proud vessels. Beachcomber shacks near the lighthouse ruin are built mostly of lumber from outmoded steamers purposely abandoned in this shallow reef graveyard.

From road's end, walk about 100 yards west along a marked trail to Kukui Point, where a score of petroglyph-covered boulders feature the carved figures of strange "birdmen" like those at Kaunolu.

The road to Naha. From the end of Highway 44, a jeep road of dirt and hard-packed sand follows the coastline south for about 15 miles/24 km to Naha, an old village site. A parallel road of sand and silt hugs the shore for part of the way. Spots become flooded during high tide, but beachcombers can cross over to it on one of many connecting spurs. Clumps of *kiawe* trees here are so wind-bent they look like banks of tall wild grass. *Kiawes* along the somewhat protected inland route have old, gnarled trunks and branches that reach over the road in places to provide a lacy green canopy.

Keomuku, an abandoned village on the coast road, consists of a few old houses and a picturesque, weathered church (built in 1903), nestled in an oasis of palm trees. Just beyond, you can walk inland to see the remains of Kahea Heiau on the bluff above. At the foot of the bank is a boulder covered with weathered petroglyphs. Stones from the heiau were used for the Maunalei Sugar Company's plantation railroad bed.

The road ends at Naha. Off its narrow sand beach are good grounds for spearfishing, casting, and squidding. You can hike uphill for a mile or so along an old trail.

LANAI RECREATION GUIDE

 Though smallest of the visitable islands, Lanai offers a number of outdoor attractions. With the islands' second lowest population density, and continuing to be almost undiscovered by visitors, Lanai has a lot of uncrowded terrain to explore.

Golf. Cavendish Golf Course, Lanai City, 9 holes, 3,100 yards, is open to the public.

Tennis. There are two public courts in Lanai City at the Lanai Elementary and High School. On school days, students have priority until 2:30 P.M.

Swimming. You'll find Lanai's best swimming on the southern shore. Coconut-fringed white sand beaches highlight neighboring Hulopoe and Manele bays; both feature public facilities (picnic sites, barbecues, showers, restrooms), the only ones on the island. Hulopoe also has a rock-rimmed pool for children's swimming.

Beachcombing. Shipwreck Beach on the north shore consists of more than 4 miles/6 km of white and black sand and tidal flats. The lucky beachcomber's booty from this marine graveyard may include glass fishing net floats or the rare paper nautilus shell. On the southeast coast, the shore-hugging unpaved road to Naha provides access to sand and silt exploring grounds.

Skin and scuba diving. Hulopoe and Manele bays are both underwater conservation districts; though diving is excellent, removing any marine life from these areas is prohibited.

Fishing. On the northwestern cape, you might be tempted to swim at Polihua Beach's white-sand shore—don't, for the strong current is dangerous. Instead, try your luck at surfcasting here. The waters off Naha provide opportunities for spear fishing, casting, and squidding. Both shore and deep-sea fishing lure anglers to the water off the coast between Naha and Hulopoe. You can also shore fish at Kaumalapau Harbor.

Boating. For charters to Maui or Molokai or along the Lanai coast, contact Hornblower Sailing Charters, Lanai City.

Hiking, camping, and mountain touring. The cool, forested areas at the island's higher elevations offer the most pleasant hikes, but you can follow a 2 mile/3 km route between Kaunolu and Pali Kaholo, the highest point of Lanai's coast (1,083 feet). You can also walk along the shore east to Manele Bay; this is a rocky, more difficult hike.

Inland, you can hike up to Lanaihale (3,370 feet above sea level), the island's highest peak. One route, about 4½ miles/7 km long, starts near Koele, catches the Munro Trail, and passes through a rain forest on the way to the summit. The Koele Company, Lanai City, can help plan hiking and hunting trips.

Camping. Limited facilities are available at Hulopoe Beach by reservation; contact the Koele Company for details.

Off-road driving. Kaunolu Village, a national historic landmark, is considered the most extensive and best preserved set of ruins in the state. Reached by a rutted, rocky 3-mile/5-km jeep trail, remains of the former fishing settlement include 86 house sites, 35 stone shelters, gardens, and gravesites.

Oshiro Service and U-Drive in Lanai City rents 4-wheel-drive vehicles.

PETROGLYPHS — FRAGILE MEMENTOS

Petroglyphs, ancient rock carvings found on all the islands and mentioned frequently in this book, offer a fascinating glimpse of the Hawaiians of earlier times—how they perceived their world and what they considered to be important.

Some of the finest (and best preserved) examples are in caves, where people could patiently scratch and chip at the rock walls while taking shelter from heavy rains and storms. Petroglyphs are also found along old trails, where travelers stopped to rest.

Earliest carved figures were composed of straight lines, looking a little like bent matches or "stickman" drawings. Later came triangular forms, distinctively Hawaiian; and, lastly, more fully shaped and rounded forms.

Tragically, vandals have defaced many of Hawaii's finest petroglyphs. Those who view them should remember that these historical carvings—though chiseled in rock—are both fragile and irreplaceable and should be treated accordingly.

HAWAII

Hawaii, youngest and southernmost island in the Hawaiian chain, is almost twice as large as all the other islands combined; hence its most common nickname, the "Big Island." Because it's also one place in the United States where you are likely to see volcanic action and is world-famous for its orchids, it has two other nicknames—the "Volcano Island" and the "Orchid Isle."

Dominated by Giants

In spite of its Big Island title and its area of 4,050 square miles/10,492 square km, Hawaii is a small piece of land indeed to contain two single mountains that are probably the tallest and bulkiest on earth. Mauna Kea and Mauna Loa rise 30,000 feet from the ocean floor. Mauna Kea, a dormant volcano, peaks at 13,796 feet above sea level; Mauna Loa reaches 13,677 feet.

Of the five volcanoes that formed the Big Island, only Mauna Loa and Kilauea (on Mauna Loa's southeast slope) are active. Although Mauna Loa has erupted only twice since 1950 (for a few hours on July 5, 1975 and, more recently, on March 25, 1984), Kilauea has spouted off dozens of times in the last decade. Volcanism has ceased in the north corner of the island, and the old Kohala Mountains (5,480 feet) have been eroded into cliffs and canyons where they face the northeast trades.

A Vast Land of Variety

Much of the Big Island is lava wasteland, but there is an amazing variety of terrain, climate, scenery, and things to do. In 40 miles/64 km you can travel from tropical beaches into fields of waving cane, up through rain forest or grassy pasture, and over lava slopes with snow banks and below-freezing temperatures. This southernmost piece of the United States has the nation's only coffee industry and is the state's biggest producer of sugar, papayas, avocados, macadamia nuts, anthuriums, vegetables, beef, and Christmas trees—but grows none of its pineapple.

More and more of the 111,000 Big Island residents are turning to the care and feeding of visitors. Resort complexes are continuous from Kawaihae to Anaehoomalu Bay, and from Kailua to Keauhou Bay.

Outdoor experiences on this island range from swimming to skiing. Because Hawaii is not as well endowed with beaches as the other islands, resorts provide their own, trucking in sand to lay over the lava base. Swimming pools often nudge the ocean's edge. If you like to hike, hunt, ride, or camp, Hawaii presents territory unsurpassed. A special sport is 4-wheel-drive exploring through rough and primitive country, much of it high and cool.

Peering Into the Past

Hawaii was the first to have Western ways implanted. It boasts Hawaii's most famous historic and legendary personalities: Kamehameha the Great, born in Kohala about 1753, ruled his kingdom from Kailua, where he died in 1819; Captain James Cook, who put the islands on the world map, was killed at Kealakekua Bay in 1779; the first company of missionaries landed at Kailua in 1820; and the state's most fascinating lady, the volcano goddess Pele, still lives on Hawaii in Halemaumau, Kilauea's firepit.

Molten lava ignites palms during former Puna eruption

Hawaii, the Big Island, lies 200 miles/320 km southeast of Oahu. It's one of four islands that has direct air service from the west coast of the mainland. This makes it possible to arrive at Honolulu, visit other islands (either by regularly scheduled flights or on special tours), and leave for the mainland from Kona on United Airlines. Or you can reverse the trip, going into Hawaii and out through Honolulu.

Aloha Airlines and Hawaiian Airlines connect Hilo and Kona with Honolulu and other island cities. There's commuter service between Hilo and Kona. Princeville Airways flies to Kamuela Airport (Waimea). Big Island Air provides charter service from Kona's Keahole Airport.

Travelers whose schedules prohibit a more lengthy stay can visit Hawaii's major attractions on one-day flightseeing tours from Honolulu.

Getting Around

Most all-island tours stop for one or two nights on the Big Island and take you over part of it quickly in a bus or "stretchout" limousine. To visit all districts on your own, plan on at least four days. You can loop around the island (216 miles/346 km) on good paved roads from Hilo, through the national park, up the Kona Coast, across the top of the island through Waimea and Honokaa, and back down the coast to Hilo (or make a reverse loop). Each half of the trip between Hilo and the Kona Coast can easily take a day to drive. You'll need at least a half-day more if you plan to explore the Kona or Kohala areas.

The Puna District south of Hilo is a separate side trip. You'll probably want most of a day if you plan to poke around this area.

The Saddle Road across the northcentral part of the island provides access to rugged roads that climb Mauna Loa and Mauna Kea. It's an alternate, but slower, route between Kohala and Hilo.

Cars, campers, and 4-wheel-drive vehicles. All major car rental agencies have vehicles at General Lyman Field (Hilo) and Keahole Airport (Kona). In addition, you'll find some island-only companies at the airports, in Hilo, and Kailua. Several companies offer campers with airport pickup. It's wise to reserve transportation in advance; you may also qualify for discounted rates.

Bus and shuttle services. Rural buses run between Hilo and Puna, Ka'u, Hamakua, and Kona (via Honokaa and Waimea) on at least two round trips a day. Shuttle buses run between Kailua, Keauhou Bay, and Kona mountainside towns. The free, double-decker London bus (9 A.M. to 5 P.M.) operates between Kailua village and the Kona Surf. Hilo has a city bus service and a shuttle bus that operates Monday through Saturday between the hotels, the main shopping areas, and various visitor attractions.

Big Island Limousine Service operates from the Keahole Airport on the Kona Coast.

Where To Stay

You can explore sections of this large island during a brief stopover, but, to see all of its widely scattered places of interest, plan to stay in at least two spots. The main hotel bases are Hilo and the Kohala-Kona Coast. Each area offers a range of accommodations—from expensive oceanfront hotels to more modest condominiums.

Most of Hilo's hotel rooms are along the shore of Waiakea Peninsula on Banyan Drive (Aston Naniloa Island Resort, Hilo Bay, Hilo Hawaiian, Hilo Hukilau).

Kona's hotels stretch from Kailua south to Keauhou Bay. Among the largest are the King Kamehameha (beach and shops), Kona Hilton, Keauhou Beach, Kona Lagoon, and Kona Surf (golf courses). You'll also find condominiums in all shapes and sizes. North of Kailua lie Kona Village, Royal Waikoloa, Hyatt Regency Waikoloa, Mauna Lani, and Westin Mauna Kea.

Outside these large hotel centers, look for the Parker Ranch Lodge up in cool Waimea, historic Volcano House on the edge of Kilauea Crater in Hawaii Volcanoes National Park, Kilauea Lodge in Volcano near the park's entrance, and Sea Mountain at Punaluu. Military families can stay at Kilauea Military Camp, a recreation center a mile away from Volcano House. Inexpensive cabins are located in the national park and in Mauna Kea and Hapuna state parks; see page 173 for information on reservations.

Touring the Island

Tour companies schedule trips to Hawaii's main attractions. Tours can be booked through travel desks of major hotels or directly with tour operators and travel agents. Several activities centers in Kona arrange fishing charters, dive tours, luaus, and other events.

For a fast look at all or part of the island, Big Island Air, Kenai Helicopters and Kona Helicopters run flightseeing tours from Keahole, and Papillon Helicopters flies from Waikoloa Heliport. Panorama Air Tours offers 1-day sightseeing excursions from Honolulu.

The Shopping Experience

Only a few of the Big Island hotels contain extensive shopping arcades; the King Kamehameha (Kailua) and luxury resorts to the north are among the best. But half the fun of shopping on this island is discovering the small specialty shops: Kamaaina Woods in Honokaa (koa, monkeypod, other wooden objects); Kamaaina Crafts in Hilo (handicrafts); Hale Manu Crafts outside Hilo (lauhala products woven from pandanus leaves); nurseries around Hilo (anthuriums and orchids); Volcano Art Center in the original Volcano House (painting, sculpture, prints); macadamia nuts and coffee (Kona); Little Grass Shack in Kealakekua (handicrafts); Kailua Candy Company in Kailua (chocolate-drenched macadamia nuts); Kona Arts Center in Holualoa (paintings, ceramics). Your best swimwear and tee shirts will be located in Kona Coast stores.

Dining and Entertainment

Hawaii offers every type of entrée from seafood (Kona) to Parker Ranch steak (Waimea). You'll also find good Japanese dishes around Hilo, Honokaa, and in the Puna District. Dinner at the Volcano House is a treat. Regularly scheduled luaus are held at the King Kamehameha, Kona Hilton, Kona Village Resort, Westin Mauna Kea, Royal Waikoloa, and Mauna Lani. Reservations must be made well in advance. The Westin Mauna Kea's buffet lunch is also popular.

On pages 172–173, we've included a guide to the island's recreational facilities. For information and addresses of specific accommodations, excursions, and attractions, contact the Hawaii Visitors Bureau, 75-5719 W. Alii Drive, Kailua-Kona, HI 96740 or 180 Kinoole Street, Hilo, HI 96720.

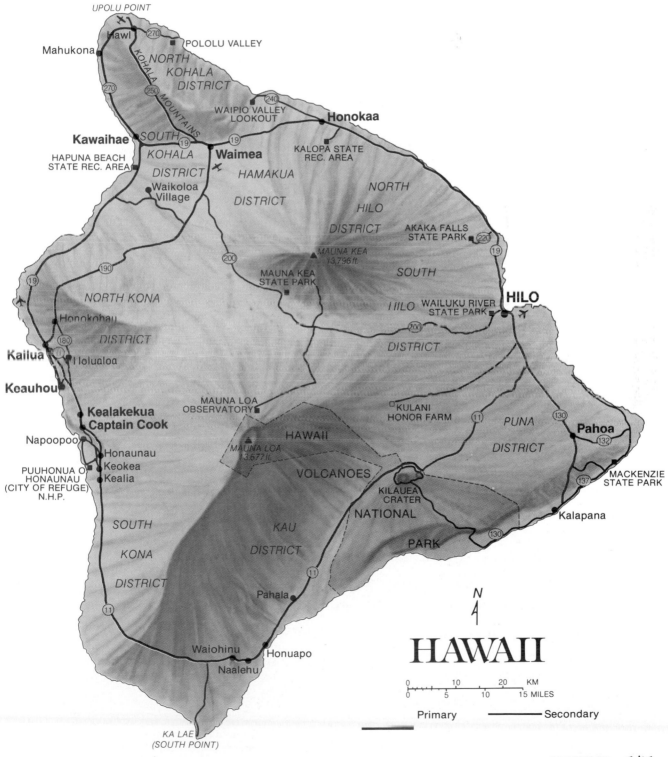

Backdropped *by snow-topped Mauna Kea, Hilo sprawls along magnificent crescent-shaped bay.*

HILO – THE BIG ISLAND'S "BIG CITY"

H ilo is a cane field town now grown up to be the fourth largest "city" in the state, though its population is only 42,000. It sprawls along the crescent-shaped edge of Hilo Bay; Mauna Loa and Mauna Kea are backdrops on clear days.

Hilo has some big hotels, restaurants, night life, and shopping areas. But the town is unpretentious, busy with its flower industry, sugar shipping, and with its role as the Hawaii county seat and home of the University of Hawaii at Hilo. Its architecture combines old wood buildings with metal roofs and contemporary, lava-walled offices. Store owners still have time to talk with you as they ring up your purchases.

Hilo invites leisurely exploration, whether by foot, by car, or by the Hele-On Banyan Shuttle bus that runs round-trip from Banyan Drive to Hilo's major attractions.

Along the Waterfront

Hilo's waterfront is a greenbelt sculptured into a handsome park. Following a disastrous tsunami (seismic wave) that destroyed the bayfront in 1960—including homes and businesses that had been rebuilt after an even more destructive tsunami in 1946—the spunky little town was rebuilt again, this time on higher ground. The waterfront, now lined with paths and gardens, is exceptionally lush and green because Hilo receives almost 140 inches of rain a year (most of it at night and in the early morning).

Banyan Drive, a tree-shaded parkway, rounds Waiakea Peninsula past most of Hilo's hotels. Each banyan along the drive bears a plaque with the name of the celebrity who planted it.

Coconut Island, the palm-fringed islet in Hilo Bay, was once a Hawaiian sanctuary with birth and healing stones. Now it is a pleasant picnic spot reached by a bridge from Waiakea Peninsula.

Liliuokalani Gardens spreads over almost 30 acres of Waiakea Peninsula, with stone lanterns, pagodas, curved bridges, and plants and trees representative of both Japan and Hawaii.

Suisan Fish Market, 85 Lihiwai Street, bustles with activity around 7:30 A.M. Monday through Friday. That's when the fish are auctioned off in two or three languages, including "pidgin"—an exotic island blend of Hawaiian, English, and Japanese. You can look and listen, but only licensed fish dealers can bid. At Sampan Harbor, the "sampans" unload their catch around 5:30 A.M. and 4 P.M.

Wailoa River State Park includes the area around the Wailoa River, Waiakea Pond, and the Waiolama Canal. The Wailoa River has the distinction of being the state's shortest river; it flows less than half a mile. The park's picnic area can be reached from the end of Piilani Street or by crossing footbridges near the Wailoa Visitor Center.

Wailoa Cultural and Visitors Center has changing exhibits on the Big Island's culture, history, and scenery and an information counter. The center is open Monday through Saturday 8 A.M. to 4:30 P.M.

Downtown Hilo

Inquire at the Hawaii Visitors Bureau (180 Kinoole Street) for the self-guided tour booklet put together by the American Association of University Women, or explore downtown Hilo on your own.

Central Christian Church, corner of Haili and Kilauea streets, was originally known as the Portuguese Church. This wooden Victorian was built in 1892 by immigrants who became Protestants to have services in their native tongue rather than the Latin required in Catholic churches.

Haili Church, 404 Haili Street, was built by Protestant missionaries. This yellow frame, New England style church, recently renovated following a 1979 fire, has services in Hawaiian and English. The choir is justifiably famous.

St. Joseph's Catholic Church, corner of Haili and Kapiolani streets, is Hilo's largest church. Complete with cracked bell, it resembles an early Spanish mission.

Lyman Missionary House and Museum, 276 Haili Street (Monday through Saturday 9 A.M. to 4 P.M.), returns the visitor to 19th century Hilo. Hand-hewn timbers from local forests and stones mortared with coral were used in the construction of this 1839 home built by the Rev. and Mrs. David Belden Lyman, missionaries who arrived in the islands in 1832. The house is furnished with antiques and curios from the missionary period; each year a traditional New England Christmas is reenacted. The Lyman Museum next door opened in 1973. In the Island Heritage Gallery, exhibits focus on the belongings of the early Hawaiians and the various ethnic groups who immigrated to the Big Island. Man's Heritage Gallery contains artifacts fashioned of glass, wood, crystal, and jade. The Earth's Heritage Gallery displays large collections of both lava formations and minerals from around the world. The museum admission fee covers the entrance charge for both buildings.

The Naha and Pinao Stones are museum pieces in front of the Hawaii County Library on Waianuenue Avenue. In ancient days, the huge, rectangular Naha Stone stood before the temple of Pinao, near the present library site, while the Pinao Stone was the temple's entrance pillar. The Hawaiians used the Naha Stone to determine the legitimacy of claimants to the Naha royal bloodline. One who could move the stone would become king of the island; one who overturned it would conquer all the islands. It's said the prophecy was fulfilled when Kamehameha the Great overturned the stone while still a young boy—even though he was not of Naha blood.

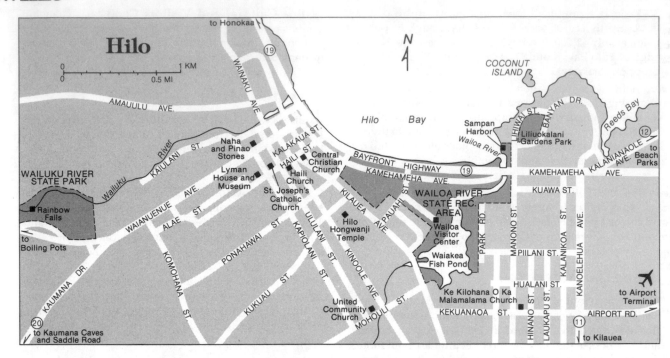

East Hawaii Cultural Center, 141 Kalakaua Street, includes galleries, workshops, studios, and a gift shop. The 1932 building, listed on the National Register of Historic Places, once housed the county's police station and the district courthouse. Its architecture combines traditional Hawaiian style and art deco design.

In and around Hilo

Visit temples and churches, learn about the art of growing orchids and anthuriums, try a taste of macadamia nuts, or relax at one of the beaches along Highway 12 (see the next page).

Hilo Hongwanji Temple, 398 Kilauea Avenue, was built in 1925 for the oldest Japanese Buddhist mission in the state, founded in 1889.

United Community Church, on the corner of Kinoole and Mohouli streets, resembles an oriental temple. Built in 1937 as the Hilo Chinese Christian Church, it now has a "melting pot" membershp and English services.

Ke Kilohana O Ka Malamalama Church, 588 Manono Street, serves about 200 members of a small Protestant sect, Hoomana Naauao O Hawaii. The church has Hawaiian-English services, two choirs, and Hawaiian language classes.

Wailuku River State Park lies along the banks of the Wailuku River, which empties into Hilo Bay. The state's second longest river, the Wailuku flows 32 miles/51 km from its source high on the slopes of Mauna Kea.

Rainbow Falls. The rainbow that gives the falls its name is visible many mornings in the spray and mist. A short trail to a secluded picnic spot starts near the lookout.

Boiling Pots. This site is a mile farther inland at the end of a foot trail from the corner of Wailuku and Peepee Falls drives. The "pots" are a series of deep, round pools, 20 to 50 feet across, cut in the lava stream bed and linked by falls and rapids. Turbulent water flows beneath the lava and bubbles up as if boiling. The pools are inviting, but the currents can be treacherous—check conditions before entering the water.

Kaumana Caves are on Kaumana Drive about 5 miles/ 8 km from downtown. From the picnic ground, a stairway descends to a fern grotto between two large lava tubes. The two tubes and their many branching caverns were formed during Mauna Loa's 1881 flow, which lasted for 9 months. The cave leading toward Hilo can be explored (wear old clothes and take a flashlight); it's been followed for more than half a mile. The other is dangerous and should not be entered.

Gardens and nurseries flourish in Hilo's rainy climate. The Big Island is famous for its anthuriums and orchids, many of which are grown around Hilo. The Hawaii Visitors Bureau (180 Kinoole Street) can provide information on the gardens and nurseries open to the public; some of the larger ones are listed below. The greatest concentrations are along Highway 11 and around Pahoa. Many nurseries also offer plants for sale (make sure purchases are properly packaged and certified for export to the mainland) or they will arrange to ship plants back to you or to friends on your gift list.

Akatsuka Orchid Gardens, on Highway 11 at 22-mile marker between Hilo and Volcano (daily 8:30 A.M. to 5 P.M.), is a fully covered display garden of orchids and other island plants. Both flowers and plants are for sale.

Hilo Tropical Gardens, 1477 Kalanianaole Avenue (daily 9 A.M. to 5 P.M.), is a 2-acre garden of orchids, tropical flowers, shrubs, trees, and natural tidal pools. The gift shop has a fine selection of Hawaiian handicrafts.

Hilo Orchidarium, 524 Manono Street (daily 9 A.M. to 5 P.M.; donation requested), is the headquarters for the annual orchid show. Only orchids are displayed in its landscaped garden.

Hirose Nurseries, 2212 Kanoelehua Avenue (daily 7:30 A.M. to 5 P.M.), has a variety of tropical plants and flowers and a large gift shop.

Nani Mau Gardens, 421 Makalika Street off Highway 11 (daily 8 A.M. to 5 P.M.; admission fee), a 20-acre collection of plants, contains more than 100 varieties of tropical fruit trees and over 2,000 varieties of orchids, red ginger, and anthuriums, all lovingly tended. Visitors can wander through the grounds, which include a Japanese garden, waterfall, and miniature lake, either alone or with a guide. The herb garden features medicinal plants.

Kualoa Farms, on the corner of Mamaki and Kealakai streets off Highway 11 (Daily 8 A.M. to 4 P.M., tour fee), is a leading exporter, with more than 20 of its 62 acres devoted exclusively to anthuriums. Guides take you through the orchards and gardens, explaining the cultivation of the plants. A highlight of the tour is the collection of rare palms.

Mauna Loa Macadamia Nut Mill and Visitor Center, 4 miles/6½ km from Hilo on Highway 11 (daily 9 A.M. to 5 P.M.), offers self-guided tours through a visitor center, orchard, and mill illustrating how macadamia nuts are grown and processed. Don't leave before sampling their wares. The gift shop sells nut products.

Hale Manu Crafts, off Highway 11 near the Panaewa Rainforest Zoo, specializes in weaving with *lauhala,* the leaf of the pandanus tree. Available for sale are hats, purses, mats, and baskets all woven of lauhala, along with other gift items.

Panaewa Rainforest Zoo, Stainback Highway (daily 9 A.M. to 4:30 P.M.), is Hilo's charming zoo. Situated in the Panaewa Rainforest south of Hilo, the zoo is designed around the theme of animals and plants found in the world's tropical rain forests.

Onekahakaha Beach Park, 3 miles/5 km from Hilo on Highway 12 (Kalanianaole Avenue), is Hilo's largest developed beach park. You'll find a strip of white sandy beach, a tidal pool perfect for children's wading, plus picnic pavilions and firepits.

James Kealoha Beach Park, a mile farther along Highway 12, also has picnic tables and a strip of sandy beach.

Leleiwi Beach Park, five miles/8 km from Hilo on Highway 12, offers sheltered coves, a lava-rock beach, and cooler swimming because of some freshwater inflows.

WHAT DO THEY CALL THAT FISH?

Whether you plan to catch them, look at them, or just eat them, chances are that you'll encounter fish of some kind during your Hawaiian vacation.

The names of many of the fish on the menu or in fish markets may be unfamiliar to you. To aid in identification, we've put together a listing.

'ahi	yellowfin tuna
aholehole	mountain bass
aku	skipjack tuna
akule	bigeye scad
'ama'ama	mullet
a'u	marlin, swordfish
awa	milkfish
'aweoweo	red bigeye
hahalalu	young bigeye scad
hihiwai	freshwater limpet
humuhumu	triggerfish
kaku	barracuda
kalikali	pink snapper
kamanu	Hawaiian salmon
kawakawa	little tuna
mahimahi	dolphin fish

moi	threadfin
'oama	young goat fish
'o'io	bonefish
ono	wahoo
'o'opu	goby
'opae	freshwater shrimp
'opakapaka	pink snapper
'opelu	mackerel scad
'opihi	saltwater limpet
puhi	eel
uhu	parrot fish
uku	gray snapper
'ula'ula	red snapper
ulua	jack crevalle
u'u	squirrel fish
weke	goat fish

Palm-fringed *Black Sands Beach at Kaimu attracts sightseers, beachcombers, anglers—and photographers. But don't swim here; currents are treacherous.*

Bright anthuriums *thrive in the shade of giant tree ferns near Pahoa. The long-lasting blooms are a favorite tourist buy.*

THE PUNA DISTRICT

The triangle-shaped Puna District reflects the Big Island's geological youth. Fresh lava flows and the pounding sea combine in an ever-changing landscape and seacoast—a living museum showing how the Hawaiian Islands were formed.

This diamond-shaped district also forms the easternmost tip of the Big Island—and of the state. The district is dominated by Hawaii Volcanoes National Park to the southwest and ruled by Pele, who doesn't hesitate to let her influence be known. The region's bucolic tranquility contrasts with upheaval—freakish evidences of Kilauea's fiery behavior in 1955 and 1960. Lava from recent volcanic activity has made its way to the sea covering forests, housing subdivisions, and roads en route. But with the rich soil and rainy climate, desolation is eventually replaced by new plant life.

The Puna coast is lined with Hawaii's famous black sand beaches, formed when lava hits the ocean, explodes into bits, and is ground fine by the waves. But these beaches also change and eventually disappear as the sea washes away the lava bits, reclaiming its lost territory.

An agricultural area, the Puna District was once known for its cane fields; it's now a major producer of papayas and anthuriums. Anthuriums bloom in the shade of beautiful palm and citrus trees in the front yards of many roadside homes.

This is a region of contrasts, from subdivisions to small settlements, from tropical forests to areas laid bare by lava from the rugged coastline to the shoulders of a very active volcano.

Highways through Puna

Prior to recent eruptions, you could make a loop trip of Hawaii Volcanoes National Park and Puna from Hilo. Highway 11 takes you through the park and on around the island. In the park it intersects with Chain of Craters Road (see page 152), which then meets Highway 130 at the park entrance. (Currently, lava flows cover the highway near the Wahaula Visitor Center at the Kalapana park entrance.) Highways 130 and 11 part ways at Keaau south of Hilo; Highway 130 then cuts through the Puna District to the coast near Kalapana. Highway 137 stretches along the coast from near Kapaahu to Honolulu Landing. Highway 132 connects Pahoa and Cape Kumukahi.

When Highway 130 is open you can make a long day trip from Hilo along Highway 11 through the park, down Chain of Craters Road to the sea, and then back to Hilo via Highway 130 or with a detour along highways 137 and 132.

The park, though, deserves a longer visit. Even without the closed road, it's best to break the excursion into at least two days. For a shorter triangle through the Puna District, follow Highway 130 to Kalapana, come back along the coast on Highway 137, and return to Highway 130 and Hilo along Highway 132 or on one of the subdivision roads.

Highway 11 to Hawaii Volcanoes National Park

Highway 11 is also known as the Hawaii Belt Road or the Mamalahoa Highway. This is the circle-island route that provides access to nearly all of the Big Island. South of Hilo, Highway 11 skirts the western edge of the Puna District while climbing to the rim of Kilauea's caldera (see page 150). Along the way you'll pass fields of anthuriums and scattered towns.

Mountain View. Mountain View is the center of anthurium nurseries along Highway 11. In the town itself, St. Theresa's Church was built and decorated by Father Evarist, who was also the artist for the Star of the Sea Painted Church (see page 148). He finished in 1936; the paintings in the church show fine baroque detail. Opposite the church is a Japanese shrine. Try the stone cookies at the Mountain View Bakery before leaving town.

Gardens and nurseries. Many nurseries in the area are open to the public; look for a "Visitors Welcome" sign outside. Among the larger ones are Anthuriums of Hawaii and Hawaiian Flower Gardens in Mountain View, and Hawaiian Tropical Orchids near Volcano.

Along Highway 130

At Keaau is the junction of highways 11 and 130. Highway 130 continues through the heart of the Puna District. South of Pahoa, the road cuts through tropical forests and an old lava flow before reaching the sea near Kalapana. Near Kaimu Black Sand Beach, a spur road connects the highway with a section of Highway 137, which runs along the coast. At the park entrance, Highway 130 becomes Chain of Craters Road. (It is here the road is currently closed due to lava flows.)

Keaau. This old plantation town is growing. Plantation quarters in the town have been restored and converted to shops for local artisans. Across the street, the Christmas Store has a variety of Hawaiian Christmas ornaments and other items. Also note the town's fine Hongwanji Buddhist Temple.

Pahoa. A town of false-front buildings and some wooden sidewalks, Pahoa is the home of the school that has several times been converted to eruption headquarters for volcanologists, evacuees, reporters, and spectators. Note the attractive Sacred Hearts Church.

Gardens and nurseries. Anthuriums abound in this area; you'll see these colorful flowers growing in lava-encrusted yards under orange and tangerine trees. Some of the major nurseries in the area include Hawaiian Greenhouses, Anthuriums of Pahoa, Taira's Big Isle Anthuriums, and Puna Flowers & Foliage. Check locally for gardens and nurseries open to the public.

...The Puna District

Lava flows. As you're Kalapana-bound on Highway 130, park at the marked turnout about 4 miles/6 km out of Pahoa and have a look below at the impressive remains of the 1955 eruption. But watch out for obscured holes and cracks. You can climb a 20-foot cone and peer into its still steamy interior. Note the deep cracks in the old, now partly brush-covered roadway that was cut off by the eruption. From here, scientists actually watched an eruption start: a fissure opened, the road split, and small explosive fountains shot up through a bulge of lava. "Pele's Kitchen" contains old tree molds, yellowish from sulphur and other gases that steamed out of them after this eruption.

The highway crosses two 1955 lava flows that reached the sea. You can see the cones from which they came outlined against the sky.

The 1986 lava flows that reached the sea near the Hawaii Volcanoes National Park's Wahaula Visitor Center covered the famed Queen's Bath. This delightful natural swimming hole, about 10 feet by 100 feet, was a favorite gathering place for youngsters, who dove from its rocky banks.

Kalapana to Honolulu Landing

Turning back towards Hilo, Highway 137 follows the coast through jungle growth, providing stunning views to the ocean. A spur road at Kaimu Black Sand Beach connects this road with Highway 130. In addition to the beaches noted below, the road takes you past three other black sand beaches; a trail leads over the sun-baked roads to the

largest. The beaches along this section of Hawaii's coast are ideal for picnicking or exploring, but currents make swimming dangerous.

Houses closer together than others in the region identify two old villages—Opihikao and Pohoiki. As you approach Opihikao, watch for concrete tombs atop old lava. The settlement's wooden church, on a side road *mauka*, is more than 100 years old. Country lanes heading inland from the two villages pass small farms, houses, and sources of 1955 lava, emerging onto the main roads below Pahoa.

Up the coast from Pohoiki lie some startling contrasts: a vast wasteland of recent origin and fields of orchids and papayas thriving in crushed old lava.

In 1960 Pele went on a month-long rampage in this region, destroying two villages, 1,500 acres of cane and other farm crops, a photogenic natural pool, inshore waters rich in mullet, and beach lots so desirable they're in use again. Lava fingers buried a dozen homes, but others have gone up to take advantage of the newly formed black sand beaches. Near the junction of highways 137 and 132, you'll pass a few things miraculously spared.

Along the entire route from the park back to Honolulu Landing, you'll find a mixture of old and new Hawaii, with both natural and manmade attractions.

Harry K. Brown Beach Park. Near Kalapana, Harry K. Brown Beach Park contains legendary boulders (some arranged as picnic furniture under umbrellas of palms and pandanus) and the remains of Kekaloa Heiau. According to legend, a wizard built this heiau. He proved his powers by eating the pulp of bananas and hanging the skins, which developed new pulp. You can splash about in Waiakolea Pond and swim in the sea, when it's calm, or in a saltwater swimming pool built in the gray sand dunes.

Star of the Sea Painted Church. Nearby is a tiny treasurehouse of painting. Finished in 1929, the art is by Belgian Father Evarist Gielen, who studied briefly in Europe with Father John, the artist of the famous Kona "Painted Church" (see page 161). Two barrel-vaulted ceilings, one over the altar recess, appear to be supported by columns that are only painted on. Six pictures with large designs and soft colors float on painted ceiling ribs; windows have painted canopies. A large nativity scene over the door is Florentine in tone. The church itself was recently repainted. To the Hawaiians, accustomed to worshipping outdoors, the paintings provided a compromise between their old religion and new. Another example of Father Evarist's work can be found in Mountain View.

On the shore behind the church is an ancient canoe ramp. Villagers still use the huge rock slabs to launch their outriggers swiftly, between wave breaks. A plaque explains the technique.

Kaimu Black Sand Beach. A few road curves east of Kalapana lies the spectacular black sand beach of Kaimu, where waves lap the trunks of coconut palms growing almost at the water's edge. Picnic here, walk the long crescent, watch the expert surfers, but don't swim—there are hazardous currents.

Kalani Honua. This retreat between Kalapana and Kapoho is an artistic, cultural, and recreational center. The emphasis is on Hawaiiana, with performing and visual arts, seminars, and camps. Individuals or groups are housed in cedar lodges.

MacKenzie State Park. The park campground sits in a shady grove of ironwoods along the coast just past Opihikao. The shore fishing is good, and a portion of an ancient Hawaiian foot trail runs through part of the park. The currents are dangerous—don't swim here.

Isaac Hale Beach Park. On Pohoiki Bay, this was once Puna's shipping port. Now it's a launching place for small boats. There is good fishing and hiking, but no swimming.

Kapoho Cone. You can get a good look at this green-cloaked prominence from an old eruption. Drive up a grassy road to the cone's low rim, then walk down inside to jungle-shrouded "green lake" of perhaps 10 acres. Its green color is caused by the great quantity of algae.

Cape Kumukahi Lighthouse. The lucky lighthouse stands on the shore at the end of Highway 132, near where it crosses Highway 137. The river of lava from Pele's 1960 flow crushed the station's cottages and then stopped, split, and continued to the sea on either side of the lighthouse. Local residents claim Pele spared the fishermen's beacon and consider the spot a special place. The lighthouse tower, now automated, stands on the state's easternmost point which, during the lava flow, was extended about 500 feet closer to California. There's an ancient Hawaiian graveyard atop the mile-wide flow about 100 yards north of the road.

Koae. Highway 137 continues north to Koae through a blanket of cinders that are alive now with orchid fields. A cream-colored church punctuates the blackness around this settlement. Koae was virtually abandoned when its houses buckled under a heavy cinder shower. Fishermen's trails lead to more black sand beaches.

Honolulu Landing. Passenger cars can travel as far as Honolulu Landing. Through a grove of ironwoods, you'll see 1840 cinder cones hard enough to drive on. The beach at Honolulu Landing washes away each winter—proof of the ocean's force in changing the coastline. Do not swim here—the currents are dangerous.

Cape Kumukahi to Pahoa

Highway 132 completes the triangle of roads through the Puna District, connecting the coast with Pahoa. Off the road, you'll see a few things miraculously spared during the 1960 lava flow. Left on the side of an old cinder cone are 16 gravestones, usually flower-decked. The molten river temporarily forked and went around them. The road also cuts through a cone formed by the 1955 eruption's largest vent, which produced 800-foot fountains. Lesser cones, turned yellow, red, and burnt orange by gases, are also visible.

Kapoho. On Highway 132 you pass right over the buried village of Kapoho. To the north is the 420-foot black cone built up on the eruption site. Most of Kapoho's 250 people moved to Pahoa and now grow their anthuriums there, but their new orchid fields lie above the old town site in a graben that has ideal growing conditions. The Kapoho region's newest crop is Norfolk Island pines for Christmas trees, many of which are shipped to the mainland's west coast.

Lava Tree State Park. Hidden in a tropical forest are the "petrified Hawaiians"—weird, lava-encrusted tree trunks. Two centuries ago this was a grove of large ohia trees; then came the 1790 eruption from Kilauea. A flow of hot lava poured through the forest and around the trees. The tops were burnt off by the heat. Moisture in the tree trunks chilled and hardened the lava, forming a shell around each tree. After the molten lava drained away, the lava trees were left. A deep fracture runs through the park and there are other dangerous cracks throughout it—these may be siphons that drained vast quantities of lava back into the earth. The eerie lava tree shells combine with the peaceful new growth covering the landscape to provide a memorable stopping point.

TIPS ON GETTING AROUND

Points of interest on all the islands are identified by red-and-yellow warrior markers placed by the Hawaii Visitors Bureau. Note the total absence of billboards and the restrained use of advertising signs.

Though the Islands use official highway numbers, many of the roads are not really worthy of the description "highway," and islanders still call them by name or nickname. On all islands, dirt roads crisscross plantation lands. It's unwise to attempt these without getting permission and directions. It's easy to get stuck or lost on them, and you might meet a mammoth, fast-moving hauling truck.

You may be confused by names you hear or see on maps that are not towns or even settlements. Generally these are the *ahupua'a* names—names given to a land division or historic district in old Hawaii. An *ahupua'a* usually extended in a wedge shape from the mountain slopes to the sea.

HAWAII VOLCANOES NATIONAL PARK

The best known and most popular of the Big Island's many attractions is Hawaii Volcanoes National Park. Each year a large number of visitors journey to this park in hopes of witnessing the fire goddess, Pele, in one of her tempestuous moods. She's unpredictable, though; Pele does perform often, but she may not be at her fiery best during your visit.

Even without flashy shows of molten lava rivers and mountains spewing fire, Hawaii Volcanoes National Park is a fascinating place to explore. Within its 344 square miles/894 square km are two live volcanoes, Mauna Loa and Kilauea; a bizarre volcanic landscape abounding with fantastic features; rain forest; and rare plants and birds. Established in 1916, the park encompasses the summit caldera and upper northeast flank of Mauna Loa, Kilauea's caldera and southern and eastern flanks, and a stretch of Puna's coast at Kalapana.

The park, 30 miles/48 km southwest of Hilo, has two entrances and can usually be reached by two routes (unless closed by lava flows, see page 147). Highway 11 takes you directly into the main part of the park. Highway 130 heads south to Puna's coast, connects with the Chain of Craters Road for a tour through the park's Kalapana section, and ends at the main part of the park. When the roads are open, you can make the 90-mile/144-km loop trip from Hilo or visit the Kalapana section separately.

Both park entrances have visitor centers stocked with map-guides and booklets on volcanoes, plants, and wildlife. At Kilauea Visitor Center (daily 8 A.M. to 5 P.M.), comprehensive museum exhibits explain volcanic action. A film of recent eruptions is shown hourly from 9 A.M. to 4 P.M. Displays at Kalapana's Wahaula Visitor Center depict early Hawaiian life.

Getting to Know the Volcanoes

Mauna Loa's summit is 13,677 feet; Kilauea's is 4,090 feet. In contrast to the explosive behavior of many steep-sided volcanoes in other parts of the world, these gently sloping volcanoes erupt relatively quietly with spectacular fire fountains and fluid lava flows that form lakes, rivers, and falls. Often, crowds of people can get close enough to have good views of the eruption. In fact, Kilauea is called the "drive-in volcano" because of its easy visitor accessibility.

Mauna Loa. At times erupting lava from this volcano has stayed within its summit caldera, Mokuaweoweo. Still other times, the lava has spilled over and down the slopes or issued from rifts in the mountainside far below. Mauna Loa's flows have covered half the island and even journeyed as far as the sea. During the volcano's March, 1984 eruption, lava emerged from a vent in the northeast rift near Red Hill and flowed to within a few miles of Hilo. That period of activity, lasting 22 days, was the longest on the northeast rift in 103 years. It was also the first time that Mauna Loa and Kilauea had erupted simultaneously in 116 years.

Kilauea. This volcano's huge crater—2½ miles/4 km long, 2 miles/3 km wide, 400 feet deep—contains Halemaumau, the crater within a crater that is said to be the firepit which Pele, the volcano goddess, now calls home. This main vent is less than a mile in diameter. Its depth changes with each refilling or collapse of its bottom. For more than a century, Halemaumau was a bubbling, sometimes overflowing lava lake. The almost continuous activity ended with steam explosions in 1924. Since this vent is connected with a reservoir of molten magma deep beneath the earth, lava lake activity continues sporadically, marked by the rise and fall of the crater floor.

Kilauea's outbreaks in the last two decades—so many it's hard to keep count—have also included fireworks in its satellite craters and flank eruptions some miles from the summit along both east and southwest rift zones. A five-year period of intermittent activity began in February, 1969, in and about several pit craters along the Chain of Craters Road. Lava traveled both by surface streams that covered the road and through underground lava tubes. Since 1969, flowing lava has repeatedly reached the sea to form a couple hundred acres of new land.

Fountains played along a stretch of Ka'u Desert near Mauna Iki in September, 1971, the first activity along Kilauea's southwest rift zone since 1920. Kilauea's joint eruption with Mauna Loa in March, 1984, was part of a series of eruptions along the eastern rift that began in January, 1983, and is still continuing. The 1983 lava flows destroyed homes in a hillside housing tract outside the park's eastern boundary. The 1986 lava flows destroyed homes in Kapaahu and Kalapana closing Highway 130.

Crater Rim Drive

The 11-mile/18-km Crater Rim Drive takes you from Kilauea Visitor Center around and into the summit caldera, across both rift zones, and over bleak desert. En route you'll see two types of lava flows, *pahoehoe* and *aa*. The smooth-looking, ropey lava is *pahoehoe* and the blocky, jagged lava is aa. The chemical composition of both types of flow is the same. Usually a flow begins as pahoehoe and becomes aa somewhere down the slope.

Volcano House. Before you begin your trip along Crater Rim Drive, stop at the Volcano House, located across the street from the visitor center. Styled like a hunting lodge, the hotel has 37 rooms and a rim-side view of Kilauea Crater; Halemaumau smokes in the distance. The Volcano House makes a good base for park explorations; note the continuously burning fire in the lobby. Lunch is crowded; dinner is more relaxed.

The 3-mile/5-km, self-guiding Halemaumau Trail starts near Volcano House and crosses the scorched and scarred floor of Kilauea caldera to the rim of Halemaumau. This is the park's most popular hike. If you take it, start early before the sun bakes the crater floor. Arrange a ride back from Halemaumau Overlook, or walk out of the crater and back 3½ miles/5½ km on Byron Ledge Trail.

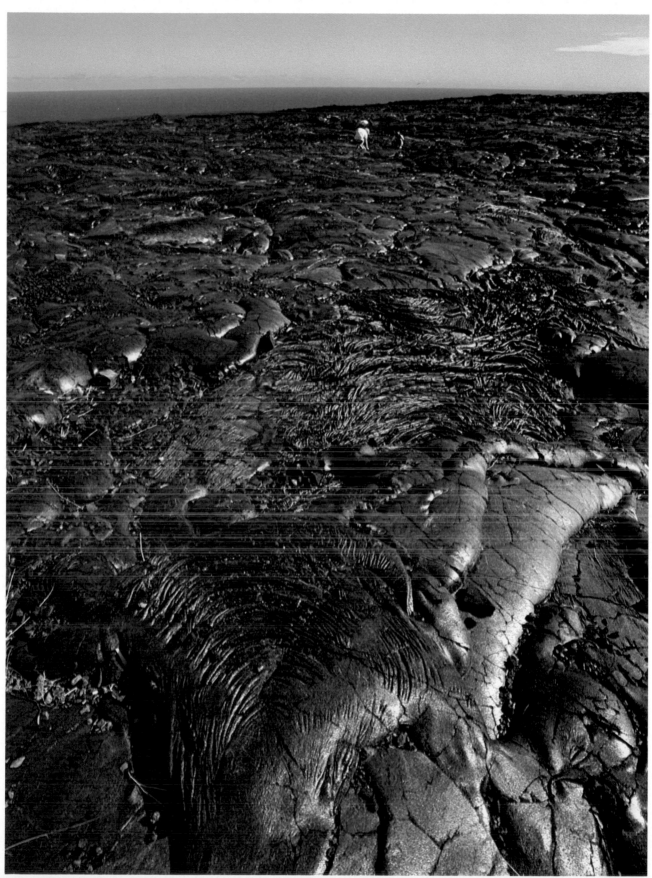

A sea of lava *dwarfs visitors in Hawaii Volcanoes National Park. This ropy lava is called* pahoehoe; *rough, cindery type is* aa.

...Hawaii Volcanoes National Park

Volcano Art Center. The current Volcano House was built in 1941. Part of the original 1877 structure was moved across the street adjacent to the visitor center and now houses the Volcano Art Center. This first-class gallery features local artists' work. Exhibits include paintings, photos, and sculptures—all inspired by the volcanoes.

Sulphur Banks. Heading west on Crater Rim Drive, you come first to the Sulphur Banks, where volcanic fumaroles emit gases and vapors that cool when they reach the surface, leaving colorful mineral deposits. Along Steaming Bluff, you can be engulfed by steam from hot water released through deep ground cracks.

Mauna Loa Strip Road. This side route takes you up the mountain to a shelter and overlook at 6,662 feet, the start of an 18-mile/29-km trail to Mokuaweoweo caldera. Along the road's lower reaches are tree molds as large as 5 feet across, formed when liquid lava cooled around tree trunks, crusting on the outside but burning out the inside.

The road passes Kipuka Puaulu (Bird Park), an oasis (*kipuka*) created when a Mauna Loa flow divided. It left intact 100 vegetated acres with unusual native plants, including some edible berries and a few plant varieties found nowhere else. Here are picnic grounds, an exhibit describing the plants and native birds, and a pamphlet to guide you on an easy, mile-long nature trail. From Bird Park, the Mauna Loa Strip Road continues up over 10 paved but narrow miles (16 km). You're rewarded with a panoramic view on clear days.

Thomas A. Jaggar Museum. Continuing counterclockwise on the Rim Drive, you come to Kilauea Overlook, a picnic spot on the edge of the vast, lava-streaked depression. Half a mile farther is the Thomas A. Jaggar Museum, housed in the former Hawaiian Volcano Observatory building. Exhibits, video monitors, and seismographs tell the story of Hawaiian volcanoes both past and present. Brightly colored murals by Herb Kane illustrate Hawaiian volcano legends, including the story of Pele, goddess of the volcano. Just beyond the museum's wall of windows is Kilauea Caldera.

Next door is the Hawaiian Volcano Observatory. Located on the high point of the caldera's west wall, this facility's research program is geared toward gaining a better understanding of volcanic behavior and improving methods of predicting volcanic activity. It is closed to the public.

Halemaumau Overlook. From the halfway point on the drive, walk the short trail to the overlook on the east edge of Halemaumau, right along its cracked and crumbly—but safe—brink. Depth and coloring of the firepit depend upon Pele's current mood; the temperamental lady just may send up sulphurous smoke to irritate your eyes and throat.

Devastation Trail. Park at Devastation Trail, a half-mile of boardwalk atop cinders that takes you through a skeleton forest wrought by the violence in Kilauea Iki (Little Kilauea) Crater in 1959. Note how the ohia trees are once more coming to life with new foliage. The walk ends at Kilauea Iki Overlook (also accessible from the rim drive).

Kilauea Iki. Straddling Kilauea Iki's rim is Puu Puai, the 400-foot cone of pumice and ash formed during the 1959 eruption when dazzling fountains of lava shot as high as 1,900 feet. It rears up 150 feet from the old, now-buried roadbed. The Kilauea Iki trail takes you across the floor of the chasm. As on the Devastation Trail, plant life is once more taking root. You'll see ohia and fern seedlings growing in the crater's cracks.

Thurston Lava Tube. This easternmost point on the drive is in the famous Fern Jungle, a moist tangle of giant tree ferns and several varieties of smaller ferns growing in the shade of weathered ohia trees. You can walk on a ¼-mile loop trail through forest to a 450-foot tunnel, 10 or more feet high. This ancient tunnel was created during an eruption when the outer crust of a lava flow hardened while the molten river within continued to travel. When the supply of lava stopped, the tube drained out and left a tunnel. Lava tubes or tunnels are common in Hawaii.

Chain of Craters Road

You'll need to backtrack from the Thurston Lava Tube in order to take the turnoff for the Chain of Craters Road. It's a 27-mile/43-km drive from Kilauea Caldera, at the 4,000-foot mark, to the coast.

You'll drive by three active fault escarpments, edges of the east rift zone, and approach the smoldering base of Mauna Ulu (growing mountain)—a 385-foot-high vol-

Kipuka Puaulu
Bird Park
Golf Club
MAUNA LOA STRIP ROAD
Tree Molds
Sulphur Banks
11
Kilauea Visitor Center
Steaming Bluff
Volcano House
Volcano
to Hilo
Kilauea Overlook
to Kona
Observatory
HALEMAUMAU TRAIL
KILAUEA CALDERA
Byron Ledge
Thurston Lava Tube
KILAUEA IKI CRATER
Devastation Trail
Halemaumau Crater
CRATER RIM DRIVE
Keanakakoi Crater
Fern Jungle
N
CRATER RIM TRAIL
Lua Manu Crater
Puhimau Crater
CHAIN OF CRATERS ROAD
Kilauea Caldera
0   1   2 KM
0   1 MI
HAWAII
Kokoolau Crater
—— Primary
—— Secondary
····· Foot Trail
to Kalapana

152 HAWAII

cano built up by the eruptions. From the vents of Mauna Ulu came the lava and cinders that blanketed the old road; from its depths, lava flowed through tubes to the ocean. The best view of Mauna Ulu is from the top of Puu Huluhulu, an older crater lightly forested with ohia trees.

Exposed remnants of an old highway can be seen from the pullout at Alanui Kahiko. Look up to the cliffs over which the billowing pahoehoe spilled. The flow of lava buried much of Naulu Forest.

The Park's Kalapana Section

Near the coast, make a stop at the trailhead at Puu Loa. Walk the old Puna-Ka'u Trail for ½ mile east over pahoehoe fields to mounds etched with petroglyphs.

Chain of Craters Road winds westward along the Puna coast. As you drive through this section of the park, you'll follow a road atop 60-foot cliffs with views inland over the undulating pahoehoe lava. Kilauea's current activity centers above this area in the East Rift Zone just east of the park's boundary.

Kamoamoa. The coastal Kamoamoa campground and picnic area overlook an arch created when wave action eroded a 100-foot lava tube. On its south side, back of a canoe landing, are long, narrow enclosures that were canoe sheds. The rock walls you see in all directions formerly outlined village compounds. One long wall, from sea to pali, is of turn-of-the-century construction and now separates the campground from the partially repaired ruins of Moa Heiau.

Wahaula Heiau. Next to the Wahaula Visitor Center at the park's Kalapana entrance are the ruins of the Wahaula Heiau, one of the islands' oldest heiau. The temple was built in approximately A.D. 1250 by the Tahitian priest Paao, who introduced the severe system of taboos and sacrifices practiced in Hawaii until 1819.

A coastal trail from the heiau leads to a lookout point where you can view clouds of steam created by lava flowing into the sea through lava tubes. Nature is creating a black sand beach along this stretch of coast.

The Road Westward from the Park

From Kilauea's summit, Highway 11 swoops down the volcano's southwest slope—the Ka'u Desert, barren and bleak except when winter and spring rains make it bloom with native yellow *mamani* and white *alahee* (a coffee relative with a carnation scent). Highway 11 then circles westward toward the Kona Coast.

Just inside the park boundary, less than a mile walk on the Mauna Iki (Footprints) Trail will lead you to a spot where, in 1790, warriors battling Kamehameha the Great for control of this island were asphyxiated by fumes and dust while fleeing boulders and mud balls belched from Halemaumau. (Hawaiians believed that Pele interceded to help Kamehameha.) Most of the footprints left in the hardening ash have eroded, but one set is protected under glass. The trail continues a mile to a dome that fired in 1920 at the head of the Great Crack, a huge fissure that extends to the sea. In this area, lava fountains broke out again in 1971.

CONDOMINIUMS: HOMES AWAY FROM HOME?

If you're planning a family vacation and feel that daily dining out palls when small children run rampant, or if there are more than two of you and you're planning a visit of a week or longer, staying in a condominium can save you money and provide more space than a hotel room.

Where are condominiums located? Condos have sprouted up on all of the major islands. Some are indistinguishable from neighboring resort hotels; many offer similar recreational facilities (restaurants, pools, tennis courts, bike rentals, and preferred tee times at nearby golf courses).

You'll discover large condominium communities in the following resort areas: Maui's west coast, Hawaii's Kona coast, Kauai's Princeville and Poipu regions, and Oahu's Waikiki district.

Is daily service a must? Not all condominiums offer daily (or even weekly) maid service. If your family needs someone to tidy up regularly, or if you like fresh towels and clean beds every day, ask whether such amenities can be included. You'll also want to know the location of the closest laundry facility.

Do you need a kitchen? Supermarket shopping for breakfast supplies, picnic lunches, and snacks cuts costs, allowing you to splurge on dining out in the evening. It's also convenient. No matter when hunger pangs strike, you can whip up a meal or create *pupus* (appetizers) to savor while watching the setting sun. Be sure there is a market nearby.

The drawbacks: You have to shop, prepare the food, and clean the kitchen. To many people this may not resemble a vacation.

How can you rent a condominium? Check with your travel agent for tour packages that include condos and car rentals.

For additional information and condo listings, write the Hawaii Visitors Bureau, Suite 801, 2270 Kalakaua Avenue, Honolulu, HI 96815 or the Hawaii Visitors Bureau office on the islands you plan to visit. Addresses are listed in each chapter.

Drier in climate than other island areas, Ka'u is farm country, rich in macadamia nuts, sugarcane, and cattle-feeding grasses. The cane grows at higher elevations here than anywhere else in the country, some at 3,300 feet. You'll sample the district when you drive the 50-mile/80-km stretch of highway between Hawaii Volcanoes National Park and the Kona Coast. If you have time, you can explore side roads and visit the southernmost point in the United States.

From the Park to Punaluu

Between the boundaries of the park and Waiohinu, the road travels through mixed grasslands ribboned with windbreak trees that run up onto Mauna Loa's steeper flanks. The cane fields in the area take more than three (rather than the usual two) years to mature because of their elevation.

Pahala. From pretty little Pahala village, drive the cane haul road uphill several miles to luxuriant Wood

Fierce wooden replicas *of ancient gods guard Puuhonua O Honaunau National Historical Park.*

Valley. In 1868, the mightiest cataclysm in Hawaii's history smothered a village here with an avalanche of mud set loose by an earthquake. The quake also triggered simultaneous eruptions of Mauna Loa and Kilauea and lethal seismic waves that swamped Puna and Ka'u villages, depressing the southern coastline about 7 feet.

In town, you'll notice the colorful Wood Valley Temple. Winding southward back to the highway on a parallel strip of the old Belt Road, you'll pass weathered houses, eucalyptus and African tulip trees entwined with bougainvillea, and part of a large orchard of macadamia nut trees. Navel oranges, grapefruit, mangoes, guavas, and avocados also sprout in Ka'u pastures, along with scattered remnants of old sisal.

Punaluu. Drive south to the black sand beach at Punaluu. A visitor center and museum show exhibits from the area. The ruins of Kaneeleele Heiau lie about 500 feet east of the beach. A 404-acre resort complex here, Sea Mountain at Punaluu, includes condominiums, an 18-hole golf course, a restaurant, and a center for the Aspen Institute for Humanistic Studies.

A tiny church on the hill above Punaluu guards the settlement. In its graveyard is a shrine to Henry Opukahaia, a Punaluu boy who sailed to New York in 1809, became a Christian, and died in New England—but not before he had influenced missionaries to come to Hawaii to teach his people.

The road south from Punaluu continues in a loop back to the main highway. At Ninole Cove, fresh water bubbles up through lava at the ocean's edge. There's a pebbly beach with "stones that give birth" (stones with holes that contain baby stones said to multiply). On the hill above the golf course clubhouse, ruins of two ancient temples are accessible to walkers.

Punaluu to South Point Turnoff

Honuapo sits where the main highway meets the shore. A spur road opposite a former sugar mill (now used as a community center) leads into Whittington Beach Park and to a decaying old sugar-shipping wharf.

Naalehu, 3 miles/5km beyond, and Waiohinu, a little farther, are the last places at which to buy gasoline for South Point exploring or, if you are Kona-bound, for the next 50 miles/80 km. Naalehu has a shopping center, several small restaurants and grocery stores, and an old grandstand and community center in the main park.

Jungled Waiohinu village is distinguished by having the Mark Twain Monkeypod Tree, a new tree growing from the roots of one planted by Mark Twain in 1866 and felled by a storm in 1957. It also possesses the island's most elegantly trimmed frame church, Kauahaao, built in 1842 and set beside a tidy old cemetery. The Shirakawa Hotel resembles an oversized house with its parklike gardens of hibiscus and orchids. The hotel offers *furo* (and conventional baths). Locals from the Kona area make the trek for dinner in the hotel's dining room.

The Nation's Southernmost Tip

Ka Lae, or South Point, is the most southerly piece of ground in the United States. A ruggedly beautiful, wind-swept cape, it contains remnants of one of the oldest known Hawaii settlements (A.D. 750).

To explore this area, take the marked turnoff from Highway 11 about 3½ miles/6 km west of Waiohinu. Drive downhill for about 10 miles/16 km through pasture that is sometimes parched, sometimes verdant and abloom with lantana and native wildflowers. Along the way you'll see some of the large windmills designed to generate power for the area. Any people you see will likely be fishermen; the currents that meet off the treeless point create outstanding fishing.

Salt pans (lava boulders with depressions in which sea water was allowed to evaporate) are scattered on the grounds of an automated light tower where the pavement stops. Here, too, are the remains of Kalalea Heiau, a fishermen's shrine and part of a complex of ruins designated a national historic landmark. Fishers still bring offerings of food and drink to the *mana* (spirits) in the shrine.

On the point where the lava slope dribbles away, look for rings (more than 80 of them) chipped in leeward edges; the early Hawaiians secured their canoes by running bowlines through these rings. The moorage of today's anglers is just up the west side beneath a 50-foot cliff that has hoists and ladders welded to its face. Just inland, you'll spot a turbulent, rock-bound pool—a lava tube formed when a hot spot in the cooling flow collapsed into the ocean. A bit farther north, a spur road goes out to the edge of the shore, where along the rising bluff you'll get a fine view of black rock to Mauna Loa.

On the windward side of the cape, breakers pound dunes of yellowish ash and patches of green sand. Bishop Museum archeologists, excavating a habitation site dating from A.D. 1000 1 mile/1 km east of the canoe mooring holes, turned up a fish hook "factory." Just inland is Palahemo, the early settlers' well—a tidal waterhole on which fresh water floats. On its rim are petroglyphs.

Along a spur road of sorts that connects Kaulana Bay with the main road lies Makalei Cave, where ancients slept on stone platforms.

South Point to Kona

West of the South Point turnoff, Highway 11 crosses miles of old Mauna Loa lava flows. Because of rainfall differences, some more recent flows have forest cover; other, older ones remain barren and black. Though the land here is harsh, it does have a delightful oasis—Manuka State Park, a wayside picnic ground and arboretum of native and imported plants.

Milolii, at the south end of Kona, is a tiny Hawaiian-Filipino fishing community about 2,000 feet below the highway. It's reached by a winding, bumpy side road of

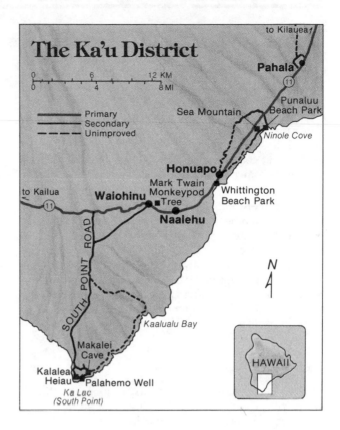

The Ka'u District

0   6   12 KM
0   4   8 MI

— Primary
— Secondary
--- Unimproved

about 6 miles/10 km. Even though the village is strung out on lava rubble that supports only *kiawe* and palms, villagers grow anthuriums and ferns on hauled-in soil. Anglers return to the village in the afternoon with their catch, which they truck to Hilo's fish auctions.

Houses are of old lumber and corrugated iron. You'll see goats tied up outside and pigs nosing about for food. Most families have kerosene or gas stoves and refrigerators and generator-powered lights, television, and telephone. The store has canned and packaged goods and cold drinks—honk your horn out front to have it opened.

Services are conducted at the century-old Hauoli Kamanao Church (there's a Catholic church, too). Children go *mauka* to school; the older ones board during the week.

South of town, roads fit only for 4-wheel-drive vehicles lead to petroglyphs, lava tubes, caves, coconut groves, and Ahole Heiau.

A Kona Stopover

If you're driving from the national park, you won't have much time for exploring between Milolii and your next stopover (probably in the Keauhou Bay to Kailua resort area). So Puuhonua O Honaunau and other places of interest in the southern Kona region are covered in the following pages as excursions from there.

THE KONA COAST

You'll often hear and read references to "Kona" and "the Kona Coast." These vague designations refer to about 60 miles/96 km of Mauna Loa's and Hualalai's western slopes that are part of the two big districts of North Kona and South Kona. This sun-soaked region of Hawaii is marked by jagged fields of lava for much of its length. Offshore, beautiful tropical waters teeming with fish provide a playground for snorkelers and deep-sea fishermen alike. With the advent of direct air service from the mainland's west coast to the Kona Coast's Keahole Airport, the area becomes an important gateway to the Big Island.

At the heart of the Kona Coast lies its major resort town, Kailua-Kona. The town's real name is Kailua; since there are two other Kailuas in Hawaii (one on Oahu and one on Maui), the U.S. Postal Service designated it Kailua-Kona. Many locals just call it Kona. To make matters even more confusing, the Hawaii State Board on Geographic Names has now decided it should be called simply Kailua. Kailua-Kona by any of its names encompasses both the town and the area stretching south 5 miles/8 km to Keauhou.

Exploring Kailua-Kona

Kailua-Kona may be the Kona Coast's major resort town, but it still possesses the atmosphere of a small village. Easily explored on foot, the town offers a wonderful array of things to see and do.

The main part of town runs along Alii Drive between the Hotel King Kamehameha and Kona Hilton. Strolling this banyan-shaded stretch of road bordering Kailua Bay, you'll discover open-air restaurants, snack bars, shop-filled arcades, tiny boutiques, and several historical treasures. At the north end of the strip, you can sit on the seawall and people-watch or view the bay. The Kona Coast is famed for its fantastic, golden sunsets.

The royal compound. King Kamehameha the Great spent his final ruling years in the Kailua-Kona area. You'll find his royal palace grounds north of the seawall on a tiny peninsula of land adjacent to the Hotel King Kamehameha. These few acres, known as Kamakahonu, were the center of governmental activities from 1813 until King Kamehameha's death in 1819. Here, also, King Kamehameha II held a feast marking the overthrow of the religious *kapu* system (see page 160).

The restored royal compound (a national historic landmark) includes Ahuena Heiau, an imposing lava rock platform complete with thatched buildings and fierce-looking wooden gods. Artifacts and illustrations depicting early Hawaiian life are on display in the Hotel King Kamehameha's lobby and adjoining shopping arcade.

Free, guided historical tours of these displays and the royal grounds are offered by the hotel Saturday through Thursday at 1:30 P.M. and Friday at 3 P.M. In addition, the hotel provides a hula exhibit with demonstrations of the traditional hula Monday and Wednesday at 10 A.M. An ethnobotanical tour highlighting plants used by early

Hawaiians for food, medicine, clothing, and housing is conducted at 10 A.M. on Tuesday, Thursday, and Sunday. To participate in any of the events, meet in the Hotel King Kamehameha's lobby at the appropriate time.

Kailua Pier. Across the cove from Kamakahonu is Kailua-Kona's busy wharf area, embarkation point for charter fishing trips, scuba and snorkeling excursions, and various boat cruises. Captain Beans' unusual double-hulled vessel with its bright red sails, a familiar sight in the bay and along the coast, provides daytime glass-bottom boat rides as well as evening dinner cruises.

Walk out on the pier in late afternoon to welcome back the charter fishing boats. You may even see a lucky angler proudly posing with a record catch. The waters off Kailua-Kona are world-renowned as excellent deep-sea fishing grounds for Pacific blue marlin, *ahi* (yellowfin tuna), *ono* (wahoo), *ulua* (jack crevalle), mahi mahi, and swordfish. Annual fishing tournaments boast cash prizes rivaling those of some golf and tennis tournaments.

For more information on fishing charters and boat excursions, see page 173.

Hulihee Palace. In the middle of town stands this gracious, two-storied building with verandas overlooking the bay. It was built in 1837–38 by Kuakini, brother of Kamehameha's favorite wife and governor of the island in 1820. In the 1880s the handsome building served as King David Kalakaua's summer palace. This fine home, now a museum, has been restored to the elegance of the Kalakaua period. Featured are 19th century furnishings made from native woods as well as fascinating Hawaiian artifacts.

The palace is open daily from 9 A.M. to 4 P.M., with the last guided tour at 3:30 P.M. There is an admission fee.

Mokuaikaua. Directly across Alii Drive from Hulihee Palace stands the oldest church in the islands, Mokuaikaua. Completed in 1837 by the first company of missionaries, the church has rock walls mortared with coral, and hand-hewn ohia wood beams more than 50 feet long joined by ohia pins. The white, New England style steeple is a Kailua-Kona landmark. You enter the grounds through a 1910 missionary memorial arch.

St. Michael's Church. Two spreading monkeypod trees frame this church on Alii Drive at the south end of town. St. Michael's was finished in 1848 at the site of the first Catholic mission established on the Neighbor Islands. It has a quaint, coral grotto shrine. Hale Halawai, Kailua-Kona's open-sided community hall, is in a coconut grove opposite the church.

Kailua Candy Company. Two of Hawaii's most famous products, Kona coffee and macadamia nuts, star in the homemade candies produced by this candy manufacturer. A Hawaiian warrior marker pinpoints the location of the factory/store located on Kaiwi Street, a short drive north of the town center. Guided back-of-the-house tours, conducted Monday through Friday between 9 A.M. and 3 P.M., include some tasting. Candies produced by the Kailua Candy Company include mouth-watering morsels like Kona coffee swirls, chocolate macadamia nut fudge, and macadamia nut brittle. The store is open weekdays from 9 A.M. to 5 P.M., and 9 A.M. to noon on Saturday.

South to Keauhou

South of the Kona Hilton, Alii Drive winds along the coast for about 5 miles/8 km to its end at the posh resort community of Keauhou. On this stretch of road, lined with beach houses and an increasing number of condominiums, you still pass tangles of gnarled *kiawe*, views of the ocean pounding against lava shoreline, and occasional brilliant accents of bougainvillea. You'll also pass White Sands Beach, sometimes called Disappearing Sands Beach because the waves and currents that challenge expert body surfers occasionally carry away the sand and expose its lava base.

Historic sights. The coastal area between Kahuluu Bay and the Kona Country Club, once a playground for Hawaiian royalty, is dotted with a number of historical sights, including a half-dozen heiau.

At Kahaluu Bay, take a peek at blue-and-white St. Peter's Catholic Church. Scarcely larger than a playhouse, it was built on the site of a heiau to surmount superstition. Just north of the church is Kuemanu Heiau, a well-preserved temple dedicated to surfing.

You can see several heiau and petroglyphs on the grounds of neighboring Keauhou Beach Hotel and Kona Lagoon Hotel. The spring-fed Po'o Hawaii Pond, a king's bathing pool, sits in a lush coconut grove at the Keauhou Beach Hotel. Adjacent to the pond is a reconstruction of King Kalakaua's beach house, a frame structure originally built a century ago. It's now being furnished as a museum.

Kona Gardens. You'll discover still more heiau and petroglyphs along with ancient home sites, burial platforms, and a section of an ancient wall in the Kona Gardens. This botanical and cultural park is located across the street from the Keauhou Beach Hotel. You'll find vendors selling Hawaiian flowers, fruit, and vegetables along the roadside in front of the park.

Kahaluu Beach Park. A tiny beach park spreads over the bay's south shore. An ancient stone breakwater, believed to be built by the *menehune* (legendary race of dwarfs), once protected the bay from treacherous currents. Storms and heavy surf have taken their toll, though, and the wall is crumbling, making the bay a less safe place to swim and snorkel.

Keauhou resort area. Though it's now the site of the Kona Coast's premier planned resort development, Keauhou Bay was previously an anchorage and canoe landing for Kona's resident fishermen. A monument just south of the pier marks the birthplace of Kamehameha III.

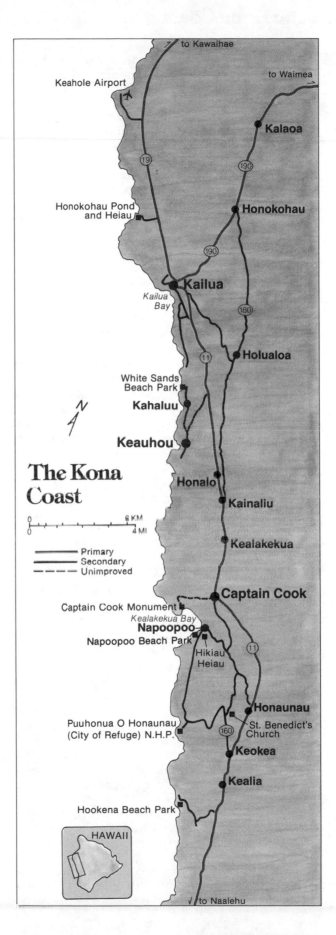

The Kona Coast

...The Kona Coast

Looking across the undulating fairways to Keauhou's championship golf course, it's difficult to believe that this area of luxury hotels and condominiums was once nothing more than a bed of bleak, black lava.

Royal slide. High on a hill above Keauhou Bay lies part of the ancient royal *holua* (slide). The hand-laid rock course originally extended about a mile to the sea. Kings and chiefs covered the 50-foot-wide channel with *pili* grass and ti and banana leaves and rode down it on wooden sleds. Replicas of these sleds can be viewed at the Bishop Museum in Honolulu. From Alii Drive, the slide is accessible by foot from a spot opposite the Kona Country Club's entrance.

A Drive Through Coffee Country

Between 800 and 2,000 feet, Kona is coffee country—cool and green, with dependable afternoon cloud cover. Here grows the only coffee commercially produced in the United States.

The coffee belt extends from Honokohau in the north to Kealia in the south. It's bisected by Highway 11 and, above Kailua-Kona, by Highway 180 (which eventually joins 11 near Honalo). You can reach the area on Highway 11 from Kailua-Kona or, from Keauhou, by taking Kamehameha III Road uphill from Alii Drive. Highway 182 (Hualalai Road) out of Kailua-Kona also intersects with Highway 180 just south of Holualoa.

As you drive the narrow roads through coffee country, you'll see grove after grove of the bushy, glossy-leafed trees whose product has made this area famous worldwide. About March each year, the trees turn snowy with fragrant white blossoms. In fall, the berries from these blossoms turn bright red and are ready to harvest.

In spite of Kona coffee's popularity as a gourmet brew, the industry has been waning. Statistics show a fall in production and a decline in coffee acreage, partly due to the scarcity and high cost of labor. Many farmers now grow macadamia nuts for diversity. Production has begun to pick up slowly in the last few years, however, perhaps indicating a reversal.

Much of the coffee country's charm comes from its string of towns cluttered with old wooden buildings, country stores interspersed with modern ones, and little box houses perched precariously on the hillsides. Roads wind under spreading trees and past colorful garden plantings: white and yellow ginger in summer; gold Timor shower trees and wild sunflowers in November; red and white poinsettias in winter; jacaranda, coral shower, and silver oak trees in spring.

Kona Arts Center. This colorful art gallery and workshop is housed in two restored historic structures in Holualoa on Highway 180. The old Holualoa Congregational Church building now holds the center's Little Gallery, which features displays of art center members' work as well as traveling exhibits. Weaving and Hawaiian craft

workshops are held in the Little Gallery as are concerts and other performing arts.

Still other art and craft classes in painting, drawing, and batik are given in the Coffee Mill Workshop, located across the road from the Little Gallery in a renovated coffee mill. Stop in for a warm greeting and to see people of all ages busily engaged in art and craft projects.

Along Highway 11. In Honalo, near the junction of highways 180 and 11, you can visit the lovely Daifukuji Buddhist Temple and charming St. Paul's Catholic Church, built in 1864.

Rural Kealakekua, the business and banking center of the Kona area, has a Hongwanji Buddhist Temple and three fine mission churches: Central Kona Union Church, built in 1859 of rocks mortared with coral plaster; diminutive Lanakila, a wooden chapel that has stood since 1868; and Christ Church, the island's oldest Episcopal sanctuary (1868–74).

While in Kealakekua, you can also tour and taste at Mrs. Fields Macadamia Nut Factory. Free tours every half-hour include a first-hand look at the preparation of fresh-roasted macadamia nuts, along with some sample nuts to enjoy. The factory is open daily from 8:30 A.M. to 5:30 P.M. The factory store sells nuts, candies, and cookies.

Also in the area is Kona's first historical museum. The exhibits, housed in the old Greenwell Store in Kalukalu Ahupua'a, include artifacts, photographs, and memorabilia of Kona's colorful past. Built around 1867 of native stone and burned coral lime, the Greenwell Store was restored to its original condition by the Kona Historical Society in 1979.

Royal Kona Coffee Mill and Museum. Near the town of Captain Cook, where the district's civic buildings are located, a side road winds down through the coffee trees to the ocean. Along this route you'll find the Royal Kona Coffee Mill and Museum. If the mill is in operation, you can watch the sorting, bagging, and drying of local coffee beans.

In the museum and store, enjoy a free cup of coffee and browse through the gallery of photographs illustrating the area's coffee industry from infancy through modern times. A display of equipment with large signs tells the story of the roasting, cooling, and grinding process that has been going on at this mill for over a century. It's open daily from 8 A.M. to 4:30 P.M.

Kealakekua Bay Area

Continuing along Napoopoo Road, you'll journey through groves of coffee, mango, and avocado trees before you reach beautiful Kealakekua Bay.

Napoopoo. On the shore of Kealakekua Bay is the village of Napoopoo, where typical houses are engulfed in foliage and set behind low stone walls. Townsfolk market

158 HAWAII

Murals and frescoes *adorn interior of St. Benedict's, one of the island's two "painted churches."*

Alii Drive, *the Kona Coast connection between Kailua and Keauhou, passes shops, hotels, and fine spots to watch the surf meet the lava shoreline.*

leis and bracelets of seeds and shells at the road turn-around by the bay.

At Napoopoo County Park the beach is pebbly, but you can swim in remarkably clear ocean waters laced with cool springs in a bend of the bay. This body of water is so rich in sea life that it has been made a marine preserve. Kealakekua Underwater State Park offers snorkelers and divers 100 feet of visibility with a myriad of tropical fish and spectacular coral growths.

Captain Cook Memorial. Tranquil Kealakekua Bay was once the scene of violence that resulted in the death of Captain James Cook, famous explorer and the island's European discoverer. He was killed in 1779 while trying to end a melee between his men and the natives. Only a month before, on his first landing, the Hawaiians had mistaken Cook for their god Lono and led him into Hikiau Heiau, where he was honored in a special ceremony.

In the same heiau on the shore of Kealakekua Bay, Cook read the islands' first Christian burial service over one of his men. At the foot of the stone path leading up to the sun-scorched temple platform, you'll see plaques commemorating both this ceremony and Henry Opuka-haia, the Hawaiian boy who was instrumental in bringing the first missionaries to the islands.

From the heiau or Napoopoo's shore, look across the vast bay to the wooded spit of land on its north side. Midway along this spit stands a 27-foot white obelisk erected in 1874 near the spot where Captain Cook died. The monument is isolated by soaring bluffs riddled with ancient burial caves. Though a rough jeep road links the town of Captain Cook with the obelisk, the best way to see the monument up close is on one of the tour boats that cruise down from Kailua-Kona or Keauhou Bay (see page 173).

Ancient battleground. A narrow, 3-mile/5-km coastal road takes you from Napoopoo to Honaunau Bay and Puuhonua O Honaunau. En route you cross the barren Keei plain, a stretch of lava rock and wispy grass. This was the site of a battle in the early 1780s between Kamehameha's forces and those of Kiwalao, the rightful heir to the neighboring districts. Kiwalao was defeated and killed.

On the hill above Keei, notice the handsome stone church. It's old Kahikolu, completed in 1841 and then rebuilt in 1853. The church, with its interesting graveyard, has been restored. A road leads to it through the brush about ½ mile up Napoopoo Road, on the way to the Royal Kona Coffee Mill and Museum.

Puuhonua O Honaunau

In Hawaii's pre-Christian era, a *puuhonua*, or "place of refuge," was a haven for the lawbreaker and war-vanquished. Though there were similar refuges on the Big Island and other islands in the chain, the one on the shore of Honaunau Bay—associated with the Kamehameha dynasty—is historically the most important.

For perhaps 400 years, people scurried by trail from the south or swam Honaunau Bay from the north to reach this sacred place ahead of their pursuers. After they were purified, they were free to leave and return home, protected by the amnesty bestowed upon them by the priests.

Kapus. Hawaii's people were governed by *kapu* (sacred rules of life). These kapu included laws forbidding commoners to go near a chief, touch his possessions, walk in his footsteps, or even let their shadows fall on royal grounds. Women weren't allowed to eat with men. Fishing and hunting times were governed by kapu.

If a kapu was broken, it was feared that the gods would become angry and create a lava flow, tidal wave, or some other form of devastation in retaliation. The penalty for breaking a kapu was death; escape to a place of refuge was the only salvation.

A puuhonua also protected noncombatants during battles as well as defeated warriors.

History of Honaunau. Wooden figures facing out to sea guarded this place of refuge from waterborne assault; on the landward side, it was secured by a wall more than 1,000 feet long, about 12 feet high, and 17 feet thick—and hand laid without mortar. About 1650, Hale-o-Keawe Heiau was built to honor the reigning king of Kona. When Keawe died, his bones were placed in the temple. Between then and 1818, the bones of 22 other ruling chiefs were also interred in the temple. It was believed that the royal line of high chiefs had a special power or *mana* that remained with them even after they died; this power protected the puuhonua.

In 1829, the refuge temple was razed by the Hawaiians, who by that time had rejected the old religion and system of laws. This historic site was set aside in 1961 as a national historical park with the goal of restoring the area to its late-1700s appearance. Today you can see the wall, another temple platform built around 1550, and the reconstructed Hale-o-Keawe Heiau, rebuilt from sketches and descriptions made by early European visitors. Replicas of the wooden gods were carved from giant ohia logs and once again face menacingly seaward.

The shady coconut grove outside the wall was formerly the palace grounds for the ruling chief. Here you'll see some reconstructions of early thatched houses, the royal canoe landing, a few Hawaiian canoes built in the traditional manner, and the royal fishpond.

The park is open daily from 7:30 A.M. to 5:30 P.M. You can guide yourself about with a map-folder that describes the grounds. At the visitor center, tile murals and taped messages tell the story of ancient Hawaii. Rangers give talks in the amphitheater, and techniques of canoe carving, thatching, weaving, and other early Hawaiian crafts are demonstrated around the grounds.

For more information on the heiau around the islands, see page 169. If you're planning a circle-island tour, two good stops are at the Wahaula Heiau (see page 153) and at Mookini Heiau in North Kohala.

Highway 16 Offerings

As you head back up Highway 16 toward Highway 11, you can make two stops, one at Barry's Nut Farm and one at St. Benedict's Church—Kona's famous "Painted Church."

Barry's Nut Farm. Considered one of the world's most beautiful macadamia nut orchards, Barry's Nut Farm boasts a thriving botanical garden of more than a thousand varieties of plants in addition to the macadamia trees. The Big Island's first public bonsai collection, Fuku-Bonsai, is also on display here. It features a wide variety of plants and stylings and an educational exhibit explaining bonsai creation.

You can tour the nut farm daily from 9 A.M. to 5 P.M.; there's no admission fee. The farm's gift shop sells Hawaiian handicraft items.

St. Benedict's Painted Church. Not far from Barry's Nut Farm, a side road leads to St. Benedict's, a charming church tucked amid lush, tropical foliage. In December, the brilliant red poinsettias create a dramatic framing for the tiny white building.

The church's famous interior decoration was applied by Father John Berchmans Velghe, a Belgian priest who wanted to bring to his parishioners the splendor of medieval Europe. He turned his 1902 gable-roofed church into a miniature cathedral (and a folk art masterpiece) by painting its walls, ceiling, and pillars with copies of religious works with Hawaiian motifs. On the wall behind the altar, perspective painting of the light-dome, apse, and transepts of Burgo Cathedral in Spain gives you the illusion that the vaulted nave continues.

Outside, the church has charming carpenter's Gothic details—a frontal lattice and a belfry that resembles a storybook castle. A few of the adjacent fenced gravestones have iron-pipe crosses and markers with photographs. Some inscriptions are in Chinese, some in Hawaiian, and others in Portuguese.

The South End of Kona

Southern Kona contains lava flows from Mauna Loa, new forests and orchards, and a few settlements.

Highway 11 passes below the 100,000-acre Honaunau Forest, where more than 800,000 Australian red cedar and tropical ash trees were planted for harvest at the end of the century. The road crosses all three 1950 Mauna Loa flows, which buried several buildings in their path to the sea. It spans Honomalino farmlands, occupied by a huge macadamia nut orchard and healthy plantings of bananas, avocados, citrus, and vegetables. In the scattered housing tracts, flower gardens provide colorful accents in the rough lava.

Hookena, a couple of miles down a narrow, twisting spur road, is almost a ghost town. You'll find a handful of cottages, a swimming beach, and park pavilion (no drinking water or lights). A few families are still in residence; others come on weekends to camp and fish. Notice the pilings of an old wharf where interisland steamers once loaded coffee, oranges, cattle, lumber, and passengers; it was abandoned in the early 1930s when the road from Hilo finally reached Kona. To the north lie remnants of the main street—a stone wall with gates, shade trees, posts that supported gas lamps, ruined houses, and a Congregational church, built in the mid 1850s, with a still-visible altar inscription in Hawaiian. The cliff above the beach is honeycombed with burial caves.

Milolii settlement, at the southern end of the Kona Coast, is described on page 155.

North Kona to Kohala

Two highways lead from Kailua-Kona through North Kona to the South Kohala district: Palani Road connects with the Hawaii Belt Road (190) that travels a high route for about 40 miles/64 km to Waimea; Queen Kaahumanu Highway (19) follows the coast just above the sea for about 35 miles/56 km to Kawaihae.

The coast road traverses bleak lava wasteland. It passes Honokohau Harbor, which was blasted out of lava and dredged to create a small boat harbor. To see remnants of ancient Honokohau, a national historic landmark, take the paved spur off Queen Kaahumanu Highway at the Honokohau Harbor road sign. At the harbor, a dirt road leads to the area. On the north side of the harbor are two fishponds, still in use. A heiau stands on the south side of the harbor entrance near the head of the channel; on the same side of the harbor, you'll also find a good swimming cove and beach.

Farther north at Keahole, strange circular house platforms and shelter and burial caves have been discovered. Still farther north on the coast is Kona Village Resort, a luxury hideaway featuring Polynesian atmosphere and plush, thatched bungalows. The resort's accommodations and lush gardens nestle between the fingers of a lava flow from now-dormant Hualalai's last sputterings in 1801.

The Hawaii Belt Road, the alternate route north from Kailua, starts out past hillside homes, goes through coffee farms, wilderness, and ranch land, and finally emerges onto the Waimea plateau. It passes through a seemingly endless landscape of dry grass and cactus that stretches from the sea to the domes of the great volcanoes. Cattle graze along the roadside. On a clear day, you can see Haleakala on Maui.

Around Puu Waawaa Ranch, swaths of black lava that once flowed from Hualalai and Mauna Loa cut through the grasslands. You'll see cupcake-shaped Puu Waawaa, the island's largest cinder cone, which furnishes pumice for the manufacture of a lightweight aggregate.

For information on the South Kohala coastal resorts, see page 163. You'll find details of North Kohala on page 164, and a history of cool Waimea and its neighbor, the Parker Ranch, on page 165.

Framed by palms, *a Kohala lifeguard sits atop tower, reaping the day's reward: a sky-painting sunset.*

Manmade greens *and fairways combine with natural black lava obstacles to form Mauna Lani Hotel's oceanside course, one of the state's most beautiful and most challenging.*

THE KOHALAS & WAIMEA

In the Big Island's northwest corner, the two districts of North and South Kohala encompass a vast region of great contrasts. Ranches and truck farms spread over cool, windswept Waimea Plateau. North of the plateau the old Kohala Mountains rise up to 5,000 feet, flatten out into cropland, and then break apart into a series of awesome roadless canyons. South Kohala's sunny coast offers luxury resorts, popular beach parks, and remnants of old Hawaii.

You can make a loop trip along the west coast to the island's northern tip, down the center to Waimea, and return to Kona.

South Kohala

Continuing north from Kona along the Queen Kaahumanu Highway (19) through the South Kohala district, you may well wonder where all the people are. The road traverses miles of black lava fields, their monotony only occasionally broken by a clump of *kiawe* trees.

South Kohala's attractions lie off the main highway along the coast. Here, historic sites help bring Hawaii's past to life, and resorts foretell of this area's future.

Luxury resorts. In spite of the fact that this part of Hawaii contains some of the island's most beautiful beaches, it has remained relatively undeveloped until recent years. The first to claim a beautiful spot along this sun-drenched coast was the Westin Mauna Kea, followed by two more coastal hotels, the Royal Waikoloa and the Mauna Lani. The Royal Waikoloa is part of the planned Waikoloa development, which also includes the Hyatt Regency Waikoloa, Shores at Waikoloa condominiums, and Waikoloa Village in the neighboring highlands. The Mauna Lani Resort area incorporates the Mauna Lani Point, Mauna Lani Terrace condominiums, and the future Ritz-Carlton Hotel. The Mauna Kea Resort region includes The Villas and private homes. This entire area boasts fine championship golf courses.

Royal Waikoloa Hotel lies adjacent to Anaehoomalu Bay's palm-fringed, crescent-shaped beach. In addition to a host of resort amenities, the hotel has several historic attractions. The turquoise waters of ancient, royal fishponds lie between the hotel and beach. Markers indicate the sites of preserved petroglyphs and burial caves on the Waikoloa Beach Golf Club course.

Hyatt Regency Waikoloa, the area's newest, contains 62 oceanfront acres and 1,244 rooms in three separate towers. This megaresort features a manmade sand-edged lagoon filled with tropical fish, a dolphin pool, canal boats and air-conditioned trams to transport you to your room, and a variety of swimming pools and restaurants.

Waikoloa Village's condominiums and golf course sprawl across lava fields 2,500 feet above the coast. At this elevation the air is cool and refreshing. You'll also find a country store with one gas pump and riding stables. The turnoff for the development is a mile north of the Royal Waikaloa Hotel.

Mauna Lani Bay Hotel sits on a lovely stretch of beach a few miles north of the Waikaloa Beach Resort. This luxury hotel, with a five-story atrium and garden of flowering plants and cascading pools, also features historic sights on its spectacular Francis H. I'i Brown Golf Course including ancient housing sites and petroglyphs. The Mauna Lani carefully restored the area's royal fishponds. On the beach at the edge of the fishponds is the Eva Parker Woods Cottage where displays and artifacts embody the spirit of early Hawaiian culture; this section of the Kohala coast was a resort and meeting place for early Hawaii's ruling class.

Westin Mauna Kea, farther north, overlooks still another beautiful crescent beach. This elegant hotel, developed by Laurance Rockefeller, is worth a sightseeing stop. Its open courtyards and walkways are a treasure house of oriental and Pacific area art.

Puako. North of the Mauna Lani Bay Hotel are some of Hawaii's oldest and most sophisticated petroglyphs. Take the paved side road to Puako. En route you'll pass modest vacation homes; restored Holu Loa Church, built in 1858–60; and a Catholic church in the round, with soaring roof and fine use of lava. Near the end of the Puako road, an Hawaii Visitors Bureau warrior marker points out the trail to the petroglyphs. The first big group of carvings is just 600 feet inland, but you can follow the marked trail beyond to two more groups.

Hapuna Beach State Recreation Area. This popular beach is less than a mile south of the entrance to the Westin Mauna Kea. Its 300-acre recreation area includes pavilions, picnic facilities, and a good sand beach. Tent camping is not permitted at Hapuna, but A-frame shelters are available by reservation. Winter waves attract body surfers, but caution is advised in swimming here.

Pu'ukohola and Mailekini heiau. Just south of Kawaihae, on the road to Spencer Beach Park, you can visit two outstanding heiau that are the nucleus of a national historic site. Pu'ukohola Heiau guards the road like a giant fortress. It's even more impressive when you walk closer to its 224 by 100-foot platform composed of lava rocks and boulders carefully fitted together without mortar. Kamehameha built this last sacrificial temple in 1791 for his war god Kukailimoku because a prophet said Kamehameha would then be assured of becoming ruler of all the islands. Keoua Kuahuula, his last rival for control of the island of Hawaii, was slain when he arrived for the heiau's dedication. His body was offered as the principal sacrifice.

Mailekini Heiau, an older temple across the road from Pu'ukohola, was converted into a fort to protect the Kawaihae area during Kamehameha's time.

Spencer Beach Park. Located on Ohaiula Bay, Spencer is one of the island's most popular beach parks. It has a sandy beach, shallow waters for children, a *kiawe*-shaded lawn for picnics, good snorkeling areas, and showers.

... The Kohalas & Waimea

Kawaihae. This tiny community is the site of an important harbor. In early days Kamehameha I sailed from this port to conquer the neighboring islands; in 1820 the first New England missionaries paused here. At one time, Parker Ranch cattle had to swim through the harbor and be hauled aboard steamers bound for Oahu. With the construction of an actual port, cattle can now be loaded directly on board barges. Today, Kawaihae is one of the island's major commercial ports.

North Kohala

Near Kawaihae, Highway 19 turns inland, heading across the island through cattle country and Waimea to Honokaa on the east coast. Highway 270, the road north from Kawaihae, spans a raw coast of black rock under a blanket of *kiawe*, passing a string of coves splendid for snorkeling. The parched country of the west turns green as you move into the normally rainy belt of North Kohala.

Here is the Hawaii of several decades ago, remarkably untouched, somnolent, but with a secure position in history as the birthplace and boyhood home of the first Kamehameha. When Kamehameha was growing up, taro covered the hills and valleys, and the region was the island's most populous. Taro and native villages gave way to sugar plantations, each with mill towns and gracious baronial estates, but now the last sugar mill has been phased out.

Lapakahi State Historical Park. Between Kawaihae and Mahukona stands the partially restored site of a 600-year-old seaside village. Strolling through this former home of Hawaii's working class, you'll see house plots, burial sites, family heiau, fishing shrines, and a garden of sugarcane, sweet potatoes, and gourds. The archeological dig connected with the discovery of Lapakahi has answered many questions as to how average Hawaiians lived down through the centuries. The park is open Monday through Saturday from 8 A.M. to 4 P.M.

At Mahukona, once Kohala's sugar-shipping port and now nearly abandoned, you can swim and fish from the old landing or at the beach park.

Kapaa Beach Park. You reach Kapaa Beach Park, north of Mahukona, on a mile-long paved road that winds downhill from Highway 270. Though there's no sand, snorkeling here is excellent—try the area around the park's old canoe landing. If you walk five minutes north and then around a fence, you'll find the ruins of another village occupied until 1915.

Mookini Heiau. The turnoff to Upolu Airfield takes you to Mookini Heiau, the state's first registered national historic landmark and one of two sacrificial temples of the highest rank built in A.D. 480. An Hawaii Visitors Bureau warrior marker points the way down a dirt road. Much remains of the 250 by 130-foot platform and surrounding walls. Kamehameha I was born just west of the heiau; his birthsite is marked with a plaque.

Hawi. This once-thriving plantation town, 7 miles/11 km from Mahukona, is the best known of a handful of settlements with colorful old houses, stores, churches, and temples along the northern coast. It's also the Big Island's northernmost town.

Kapaau. If you follow Highway 270 east from Hawi, you come upon a gilt-and-bronze figure of Kamehameha in front of the Kapaau Courthouse. Completed in 1880 by an American sculptor working in Italy, it was lost at sea, recovered, and placed here near Kamehameha's birthplace. A replica, the better-known of the two statues, stands across from the Iolani Palace in Honolulu.

Kapaau has a couple of quaint temples: diminutive St. Augustine's Episcopal Church, dedicated in 1884 by a largely British congregation, and the district's prize—Kalahikiola Church. Located ¼ mile up a side road marked by a warrior sign, Kalahikiola Church was designed by missionary Elias Bond, who also started Kohala's first sugar plantation to provide work for the Hawaiians. For six years, until 1855, parishioners hauled stones from ravines for the church's meeting house. To make mortar, they brought sand from the shore, coral from the sea, and wood (for burning the coral) from the mountains.

Beyond the grounds, set off by a stone arch, are the empty frame buildings of the old Kohala Girls' School that Bond started. The road to the church passes macadamia nut groves and the mission homestead—white buildings framing a generous lawn with fruit and shade trees.

About 2 miles/3 km east of the church turnoff, another warrior marker points to Kamehameha Rock, a huge boulder said to have been carried up from the sea to a nearby heiau by Kamehameha.

East to Niulii. In gulches between Kapaau and Niulii, villagers still grow wetland taro and sweet potatoes in the old Hawaiian way by diverting a stream through rock-terraced plots and letting the water dribble down from one to the next (look down Waikane Gulch as you pass to see how it's done).

In the late 1800s, Chinese laborers were hired to build a narrow-gauge railway for the sugar industry in this area. The railway, connecting Niulii and the port of Mahukona, was eventually abandoned and dismantled. The Chinese remained to work in the sugar mills. Among them were Hakka men who founded a Tong Wo Society in Halawa. The society's main building, once the scene of gambling and opium smoking, has been restored. Plaques engraved with proverbs edge the ornate building's doors and windows and scrollwork enhances the beams and posts.

Niulii is a scattering of houses in jungle. A thick pandanus forest now screens the quaint Japanese graveyard from the ocean it once overlooked. Take a side road down to the cove below the Keokea Beach Park, a grassy flat with an old heiau crowned by a jaunty lookout pergola. Another pavilion shelters picnickers from the region's heavy rains. Though the sea may be too wild for swimming, you'll find an inlet protected enough for boats and a stream bed to explore. An adjacent bluff is faced with caves; according to legend, one leads into the heiau that crowns the top.

Pololu Valley lookout. The road ends at a view point about 1½ miles/2½ km beyond Niulii. From here you can look over broad, green-carpeted Pololu Valley and down a coastline of spendid, uninhabited gorges. A trail leads from the parking lot and lookout to a black sand beach; figure about 1½ hours for the round trip.

Waimea—a Ranch Town

From Hawi, Highway 250 winds for 20 miles/32 km back to Waimea along the steep flanks of the Kohala Mountains. The hillsides are covered with sweet grasses, cactus, rocks, wild fennel, and morning glory. Windbreaks of Norfolk Island pines, eucalyptus, and ironwoods border high-country grazing pastures.

About midway, stop at Kahua Ranch picnic shelter for an expansive view of the Kawaihae coast. At 3,564 feet, the road crests above Waimea. Some say Kamehameha planned his island-conquering strategy here, using the plateau to represent the sea and all the visible peaks (the three big volcanoes, Puu Waawaa, and Maui's Haleakala) as the islands.

Parker Ranch. The major portions of this 250,000-acre ranch, one of the largest privately owned ranches in the United States, spread across the slopes of neighboring Mauna Kea and the Kohala Mountains.

In 1809 John Palmer Parker, a 19-year-old seaman, left his ship and went to work for Kamehameha I rounding up cattle that had strayed and gone wild. The cattle had originally been given to Kamehameha by the British Captain George Vancouver. Parker developed a domestic herd from the captured stock and established his ranch around 1815. He also married Kamehameha's granddaughter. Now the ranch has about 50,000 head of cattle. A few of the cowboys (*paniolos*) who work on the ranch today are descendants of the first ranch hands.

At the Parker Ranch Visitor Center and Museum, located in Waimea's Parker Ranch Shopping Center, artifacts, photographs and a 15-minute multimedia show tell the history of the ranch and the Parker family. In a smaller section of the museum, you'll see a collection of memorabilia relating to Duke Kahanamoku, the famous Hawaiian Olympic swimmer and surfing champion. The center is open Monday through Saturday from 9:30 A.M. to 3:30 P.M.; there is an admission fee.

On Highway 190 just south of Waimea lie the historic Parker Ranch Homes. The century-old home of current ranch owner Richard Smart contains his extensive art and antique collection. The other house, the 140-year-old koa wood home of ranch founder John Palmer Parker I, was relocated here. Both homes are open 10 A.M. to 3 P.M. Monday, Friday, and Saturday.

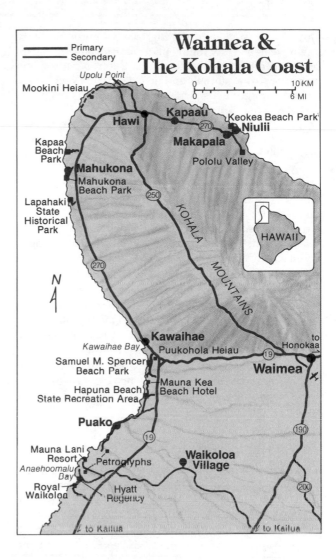

Waimea town. Cool and pastoral Waimea faces out over the tableland to Mauna Kea. The town's post office carries the name Kamuela, and the town itself is sometimes referred to by that name.

It's a village of gingerbread houses, flower gardens, picket fences, and carpenter's Gothic buildings. Notice the ornate bandstand, Lanakila Park pavilion, and Parker Ranch headquarters. Newer buildings contain shops, markets, a theater, and restaurants. This is one of the islands' best places for a steak dinner.

On the east side of town, several churches and temples surround an open green. Visit well-preserved Imiola Church, built in 1857 by Waimea's missionary, Lorenzo Lyons, who composed Hawaiian hymns that are still sung. Sporting a New England style spire, the church has interior walls paneled in koa and chandeliers that are koa bowls.

On the western edge of town at the junction of highways 250 and 19, private Kamuela Museum has a collection of artifacts dating back to days of the monarchy. The museum is usually open from 8 A.M. to 5 P.M.; you'll pay an admission fee.

A bird's-eye view of the Big Island's northeast coast reveals a gently rolling plateau carpeted with sugarcane and dotted with tiny towns. Subtropical canyons complete with waterfalls and lush vegetation veer inland from the rugged cliffs. Though you won't find resorts in this area, you can wander down side roads to jungled gorges, ponds, rocky points, and quiet villages on portions of the old highway now replaced by a straighter, wider Belt Road, Highway 19.

The drive from Waimea to Honokaa, largest town along the Hamakua Coast, and then down the coast to Hilo is a distance of about 55 miles/88 km. For the first 16 miles/26 km, from Waimea to Honokaa, you'll see truck farms, new subdivisions, pastures punctuated with eucalyptus, misty forest, and finally an expanse of bright green sugarcane.

At Waimea's outer edge, a gravel road (the middle part of which calls for 4-wheel drive) wanders off over the side of Mauna Kea for some 40 miles/64 km to Humuula in the Saddle (see page 170). About 8 miles/13 km up, at Mana, the prim little white house of John Parker and several generations of Parkers is now a family museum.

From Honokaa to Hilo, the wide, smooth highway follows the coast on Mauna Kea's long northeastern slope. Cane fields spread out above and below the road and end in cliffs above the sea.

Honokaa to Waipio Valley Lookout

Though the highway by-passes Honokaa, be sure to detour through this strongly Portuguese settlement perched on the hillside about a mile down a spur road from the highway. Fruit trees adorn the front and back yards of the pastel-colored buildings lining the main street. Note the many restored structures: the 1930s People's Theatre, the popular Hotel Honokaa Club (restaurant), and the United Methodist Church on the main street; another eye-pleasing frame church, the Catholic Our Lady of Lourdes, is uphill on a side street.

Drive downhill to the classic sugar plantation camp at Haina, overlooking the Hamakua Sugar Company mill above the sea. Halfway down the hill is solid evidence—the Hawaiian Holiday Macadamia Nut Company—to support Honokaa's claim as macadamia nut capital of the world. The retail store (open daily from 9 A.M. to 6 P.M.) offers free samples. Self-guided tours of candy making and nut processing take place in the factory next door on weekdays from 9 A.M. to 3:30 P.M.

Honokaa and environs provide a few good places to shop for local crafts. Kamaaina Woods, just off Highway 19, offers a look at craftsmen producing bowls, dishes, and vases from koa, monkeypod, and other island woods. At Waipio Woodworks in Kukuihaele you can buy paintings, sculpture, pottery, and woodwork from local craftspeople. The general store in Kukuihaele also sells regional handicrafts.

Paved road (Highway 240) continues beyond Honokaa for 10 miles/16 km to the lookout park on Waipio Valley's east rim. From here, you gaze down on one of nature's masterpieces. A stream below lazes along the 6-mile/10-km-long valley, checkered with taro patches and bounded by 2,000-foot-high cliffs. Up the coast, a white ribbon of surf unwinds and disappears behind a bold headland. The old horse trail that zigzags up the opposite bluff crosses deeply furrowed tableland to the next big valley, Waimanu.

The lookout park has a pavilion, rest rooms, and drinking water. You can hike the jeep road down into the valley or take the 4-wheel-drive tour (see page 168). A small hotel offers limited accommodations.

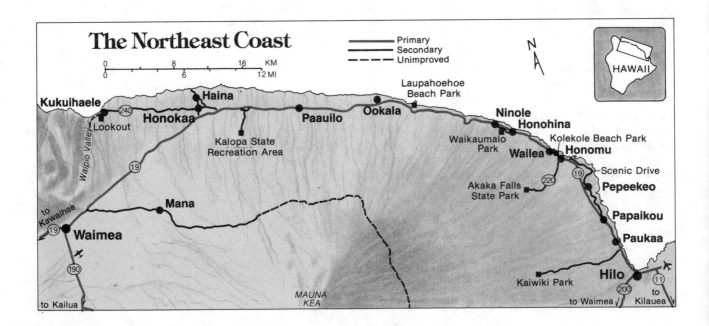

Hidden waterfalls *cascade from jungled slopes, tumble into deep gorges along the Hamakua Coast in northeastern Hawaii.*

Once the birthplace of Kamehameha *and later a sugar-growing region, North Kohala retains a sense of history and a feeling of old Hawaii. Today, the countryside is a pastoral scene of small farms.*

...Along the Northeast Coast

The Hamakua Coast

If you stick to the main highway, you'll pass through mile after mile of cane fields, span jungle-clad gorges on the widened bridges of an old standard-gauge railway, and arrive in Hilo before you know it. Even if you're in a hurry, stop at one of the bridges to see the trestle underneath and the old road winding in and out of the canyon.

Kalopa State Recreation Area, between Honokaa and Paauilo, is reached by a side road that heads inland up the slopes of Mauna Kea. Over 600 acres of mountainside and narrow ravines comprise a native forest reserve of ohia lehua, koa, and other trees.

A detour into Paauilo, a classic plantation town, provides a glimpse of old Hawaii. Graceful gardens surround original old plantation houses. A large sugar mill stands at the end of the road.

A trio of coastal parks lie within 10 miles/16 km of each other: Laupahoehoe (monument lists people lost in a tidal wave), Waikaumalo (uphill along a stream), and Kolekole (under the highway bridge).

Akaka Falls State Park is reached by turning off the highway at tiny Honomu. The charming street displays a Catholic church, two temples, and the balustraded Honomu Plantation Store. Stop here for ice-cold sugarcane, fresh macadamia nuts, and photos showing the Hamakua Coast in the early 1900s.

The 4-mile/6-km road into the park goes through cane fields to this 66-acre arboretum of giant gingers, ferns, ti, azaleas, orchids, and bamboo. An easy trail loops through the lush, thickly canopied gorge past Akaka Falls, which drop 442 feet over a mossy precipice in Kolekole Stream, and Hapuna Falls, which drop from a height of 100 feet.

Hawaii Tropical Botanical Garden lies just 7 miles/ 11 km north of Hilo overlooking Onomea Bay. Near Pepeekeo, take the 4-mile Scenic Route to the coast. There's minibus transportation from the parking area near the Old Yellow Church to the 17-acre nature preserve of tropical forest, flowering plants, waterfalls, streams, lily lake, and rugged ocean coastline. The self-guided tour includes miles of trails. The garden is open daily 9 A.M. to 5 P.M.; the last minibus goes to the garden at 4 P.M.

INTO WAIPIO VALLEY—REALM OF ROYALTY

Honokaa is the gateway to Waipio Valley, the awesome gap that is the most accessible place along the primitive *pali* coast of the mile-high Kohala Mountains. The only road leading in calls for a 4-wheel-drive vehicle or hiking. There are 1½-hour narrated tours of the valley by 4-wheel-drive vehicle. Waipio Valley Shuttle departs from Waipio Woodworks Art Gallery in Kukuihaele (775-7121) and Hawaii Resorts Transportation (885-7484) leaves from Hawaiian Holiday Macadamia Nut Factory; horseback riding in the valley is also an option.

Down In the Valley

It's a steep mile down into the valley; the grade reaches 26 percent. Then you follow dirt roads and wheel tracks, splash through mud and across streams, and plow through thickets of ferns, ginger, guavas, and *noni* apples.

A fork to the beach lands you close to the mouth of the main stream, where you can dip (ocean swimming here is dangerous). Though the road inland turns into a network, you'll probably find your way to the delapidated buildings that were built as examples of native houses (a Borneo longhouse, Nepalese stone house, and Thai, Philippine, and Malaysian huts) when the Peace Corps operated a training camp here.

It's easy to spot the broad road near the camp that goes back into the valley to a pavilion of steel and bronze-colored glass up on the hillside. The building was designed to be a restaurant but never opened.

Hiilawe Falls, behind the pavilion, drops 1,000 feet from the top of a side canyon, but the stream that feeds it is used for irrigation, and the falls are not always running. You'll discover other waterfalls, large and small—some with swimming holes. Nanaue Falls, on the far side of the valley, drops into a series of pools; you can safely climb rocks to two of them.

The small, utilitarian Hotel Waipio has limited rooms for under $10 a night. You must bring your own food and cook it in the community kitchen. Mosquitoes can be a problem.

A Short History

When white men first visited Waipio, in 1823, they found a continuous garden of taro, bananas, and sugarcane. There were fishponds, several *heiau*, and a place of refuge. The visitors learned from the nearly 1,500 inhabitants about sojourns of early kings, one of whom had sacrificed 80 people before the demands of his god were satiated. Here, in 1780, Kamehameha received his symbol of authority from reigning chiefs and was singled out as future ruler.

Chinese immigrants arrived in the late 1800s and grew rice until the 1930s. You'll meet taro growers (a few still live in the valley) and fishermen. Some people have weekend cabins in the valley. There is a poi factory, but most growers stuff their crops into gunny sacks and haul them out by jeep or truck for processing.

ANCIENT TEMPLES
LINK HAWAII'S PAST AND FUTURE

Traditional Hawaiian society was organized according to the *kapu* (taboo) system, strictly enforced codes dictating political, social, and religious activity. The *heiau*, or temples, played a major role in this system (see page 160). As the domain of *alii* (chiefs) and *kahuna* (priests), the link with gods and goddesses, and a sanctuary for refugees, these sites commanded great respect. A visit to a heiau helps visitors understand this important part of ancient Hawaiian life.

Ramparts of Lava Rock

Some heiau date back to A.D. 600; most were completely abandoned early in the 19th century when Kamehameha the Great died. As the kapu system was abandoned, the growing influence of American missionaries filled the void.

With their cluster of lashed wood and thatched grass huts, atop mortarless foundations of black volcanic rock, heiau resembled tiny settlements; the stone bases are usually all that remain today. Once, carved wooden figures and stone altars for offerings to the gods (occasionally human sacrifices) rested on the massive lava rock platforms. Structures on the upper level served as prayer houses and storage for ceremonial materials.

But even the heiau's stark platforms are impressive sights; larger temples measured about 125 by 250 feet within 13-foot walls that rose as high as 30 feet. Their usually desolate coastal locations lend an eerie sense of isolation and displacement. Often, the only nearby sign of human presence is a crushed rock and stone footpath leading to the temple.

A "Hawaiian Renaissance"

Interest in the archeological and social significance of heiau grew rapidly in the 1960s; several heiau were restored and given national park or historic site status. Like Pacific versions of Independence Hall or Jamestown, the rescued heiau provide tangible evidence of Hawaii's history.

Used as settings for cultural awareness festivities, heiau are helping rekindle interest in the islands' heritage. Coupled with the preservation of the physical traces of Hawaii's culture is a growing awareness of the less-enduring legacies—language, arts, crafts, music, and sports.

Heiau To Visit

A brief summary of several of the major heiau follows. For further information, consult the Bishop Museum (see page 48), the University of Hawaii (see page 51) in Honolulu, or major bookstores.

Puuhonua O Honaunau National Historical Park (see page 160) south of Kailua, Hawaii, is one of the best examples of heiau preservation in the state. The *puuhonua* (place of refuge) gave sanctuary to war refugees, vanquished soldiers, children, women, and the elderly or diseased. Persons violating the kapu system could avoid a death sentence by reaching the heiau. Purification rites performed by a kahuna allowed a criminal to return to society in safety.

Sitting at the edge of Honaunau Bay, the site features a 1,000-foot-long wall and three heiau. Construction dates back to 1550.

Mookini Luakini Heiau at Hawaii's Upolu Point (the island's northernmost spot) is another major archeological site (see page 164). The heiau and an ancient fishing village a few miles away make up the Lapakahi Historical State Park. In addition to being one of the state's oldest known sites, this area is also the birthplace of Kamehameha.

Wahaula Heiau, at the Kalapana entrance to Hawaii Volcanoes National Park, is perhaps one of the easiest heiau to visit. It's located adjacent to the park's visitor center (handy for answers to any questions that you may have), contains well-marked ruins, and offers a bonus—beautiful coastside views of surf crashing against black cliffs. It's also one of the oldest heiau in the islands (see page 153).

Kaneaki Heiau in Oahu's Makaha Valley traces its origins to the 17th century. Under the aegis of the Bishop Museum, Makaha Historical Society, and National Park Service, it is one of the islands' most thoroughly renovated temples.

Originally built for Lono, god of agriculture and fertility, the heiau was converted to a war temple by Kamehameha the Great in 1796. Supposedly, after an invasion fleet headed for Kauai was thwarted by fierce storms, the war god Kukailimoku was appeased by human sacrifices.

For information and directions to Puu O Mahuka above Waimea Bay on Oahu's North Shore, see page 59.

Other heiau can be found throughout the islands. The Southeast Molokai Archeological District contains a large concentration of temples. Iliiliopae, near Pukoo, is exceptionally well preserved (see page 127).

Because of long distances *between districts, campers are particularly popular on the Big Island. Many fine beach parks welcome travelers.*

The scenery is entirely different on this alternate route of about 55 miles/88 km between Waimea and Hilo. The Saddle Road (Highway 200) leaves Highway 190 just 4 miles/6 km south of Waimea and crosses the lonely pass between Mauna Loa and Mauna Kea. Though paved, it's rough, narrow, and off-limits to rental cars. It gives access to hunting grounds and to rugged roads that climb the state's two highest mountains. Big Islanders tell of mysterious happenings—such as rattling cars and eerie lights—that are said to occur in the windy, desolate Saddle before eruptions.

For the first 15 miles/24 km, you climb 3,000 feet through fine pheasant country .with views of the lava-scarred mountains. The Pohakuloa Area of Mauna Kea State Park is set in game bird grasslands at 6,500 feet, where the air is dry and crisp—and downright cold at night. Here you'll find picnic tables, rest rooms, drinking water, and cabins. You'll also see Hawaii's state bird, the *nene*, a native Hawaiian goose which had become almost extinct when a breeding project was started here some 30

years ago. Several hundred birds have been released into their preferred habitat: the arid land at 6,000 to 7,000 feet on Mauna Loa, Hualalai, and Haleakala. The nene is about 2½ feet high, gray and white, and has a black head and semiwebbed feet.

Mauna Kea Roads

If you have a 4-wheel-drive vehicle, you can drive to the 13,796-foot summit of Mauna Kea. Even in an ordinary passenger car (not subcompact), you can make it up to a view point at the 9,400-foot level.

You drive a 6½-mile/10-km paved road from Humuula Junction to Hale Pohaku in Mauna Kea State Park. On the way, look for pheasant and quail, grazing cattle, and wild game—particularly the big Mouflon sheep.

Two routes continue to the summit: a 6-mile/10-km foot trail and a cinder road (soon to be paved) controlled by the State Parks office but open to hikers. This road serves one of the most important centers in the world for observational astronomy. The University of Hawaii now operates a giant observatory in cooperation with the U.S. Air Force and NASA. Other major projects include telescopes built by French, Canadian, and British governments.

From Humuula Junction, a gravel road winds northeast along Mauna Kea's slope, through grazing lands interrupted by clumps of trees. At 7,000 feet you are above the Hamakua rain forest and often enveloped in clouds. The route becomes a 4-wheel-drive trail. It passes close to a monument in a grove of Douglas firs—a memorial to botanist-explorer David Douglas, who was found dead in a cattle trap at this spot in 1834 and for whom the Douglas fir tree was named. About 20 miles/32 km farther along, near Mana, the trail turns again into a graveled road and comes out on Highway 190 at the edge of Waimea.

Mauna Loa Road

The next side road off Highway 200 goes south up to Mauna Loa Observatory. This road is unique in two respects: it's the highest in the Pacific open to passenger car travel, and it climbs terrain said to resemble the surface of the moon more closely than any other place on earth. Choose a clear morning—after you've had your car tuned for high altitude.

On a 17-mile/27-km paved road, you wind from the Saddle up to an isolated scientific community at 11,150 feet, site of a geophysical observatory, solar research unit, and Department of Energy facility. Because many of the instruments are so sensitive that automobile pollution would invalidate the data, a locked chain is placed across the road about 9 miles/14 km below the observatory from 10 A.M. Monday until 5 P.M. Friday. It is lowered over the weekend. Hikers are welcome to use the road any time.

Roadside features are hardened lavas—jet black, silvery, brown, reddish—of shapes so fantastic as to stimu-

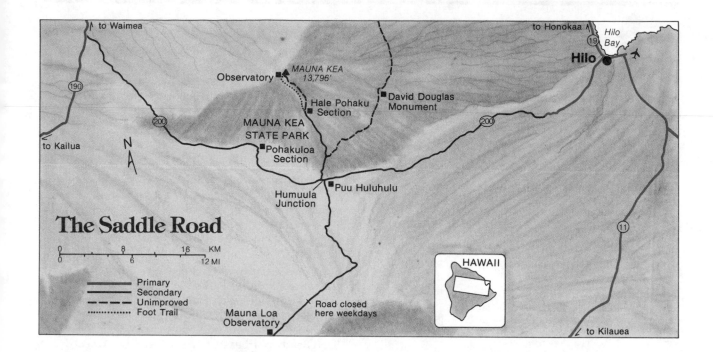

The Saddle Road

0   8   16   KM
0   6   12 MI

Primary
Secondary
Unimproved
Foot Trail

to Waimea

190

200

to Kailua

N

Observatory

MAUNA KEA 13,796'

Hale Pohaku Section

MAUNA KEA STATE PARK

Pohakuloa Section

Humuula Junction

Puu Huluhulu

David Douglas Monument

200

to Honokaa

Hilo Bay

Hilo

19

11

HAWAII

Road closed here weekdays

Mauna Loa Observatory

to Kilauea

late even the most sluggish imagination. About 3½ miles/ 6 km up, you cross a road that ends nowhere—a prisoner-built segment of an abandoned Hilo-Kona route. From 8,300 feet on, you follow Stainback Highway and take in sweeping views of the Saddle and Mauna Kea—unless clouds hang low. In winter, snow banks are not uncommon.

Highway 200 to Hilo

East of the side roads that climb the two mountains, Highway 200 continues toward Hilo across lava flows that have crisscrossed the Saddle over thousands of years.

On the south side of the road, just beyond the Mauna Loa road turnoff, swirly *pahoehoe* surrounds Puu Hulu-hulu, a Mauna Kea cinder cone that looks as if it had been set upon the Saddle floor. Sandalwood grows on its south side.

Farther on, you cross lava from a 1935 outburst that threatened Hilo's water supply until the course of the flow was changed by aerial bombing. You traverse 9 miles/ 14 km of an 1855 flow from a Mauna Loa eruption that lasted 13 months—longer than any other in recorded time. As you near Hilo, the landscape changes from barren plateau into *'ohi'a* and fern forests.

Why Drive the Saddle?

Though Highway 200 is the shortest route across the island, it's not the quickest, but it is used by hunters in search of sheep, goat, boar, and game birds in season; campers; hikers; and 4-wheel-drive enthusiasts. Ski buffs try runs over the fast, wind-packed corn snow that usually covers Mauna Kea's summit cones in winter. There are no ski lifts; a shuttle carries skiers back to the summit.

SOME FASCINATING STATE FACTS

The State of Hawaii Data Book lists some facts that take even local residents by surprise:

A survey conducted in the summer of 1978 among residents and visitors revealed the most popular recreational activity in the islands was not swimming, but walking. However, water-related activities scored high.

Are the islands a tennis player's paradise? Though it's enjoyed by more sports enthusiasts than golf, camping is even more popular.

Where's the highest waterfall? Akaka Falls on the Big Island has a 442-foot straight drop, but several falls drop over 1,000 feet in a series of cascades—Kahiwa Falls, Molokai; Sacred Falls, Oahu; Papalaua Falls, Molokai; and Honokohau Falls, Maui.

Looking for a tunnel? Outside of Oahu's nine subterranean tubes, only Maui has a tunnel (on the road to Lahaina).

If you think people in the islands consume more rice than bread, you're incorrect; bread is eaten by some 70 percent of the population.

What's the noisiest area on Oahu? If you answered Waikiki, you're right. But when you reach Kaneohe, you're in the most quiet neighborhood.

What's the most expensive piece of real estate in the islands? Again, it's Waikiki.

Hawaii, the state's youngest and most geologically diverse island, is a land of snow-capped volcanoes, black sand beaches, verdant grasslands, lava wastelands, dense rain forests, and vividly colored flowers. There is much to do and see—so much, in fact, that we've provided the following guide to help sort through all the activities found on the Big Island.

For further details on any activity listed below, consult your travel agent, hotel activities desk, or the Hawaii Visitors Bureau (Kona Plaza Shopping Arcade, 75-5719W Alii Drive, Kailua-Kona, HI 96740; 180 Kinoole Street, Hilo, HI 96720).

Flightseeing. Hawaii's reputation for landscape variety and geologic wonder can be appreciated in breathtaking detail from the air. Several companies offer excursions. *Plane:* Hawaii Pacific Aviation, Hilo; Big Island Air, Kailua-Kona. *Helicopter:* Alexair, Hilo Bay Air, Orchid Isle Helicopters, Hilo; Kenai Helicopters, Kona Helicopters, Kailua-Kona; Papillon Helicopters, Kamuela; Volcano Heli-Tours, Volcano.

Golf. Hawaii's golf courses come in a variety of locations and terrains, climates and challenges. Choose from a course perched on the rim of an active volcano, one carved from a lava field, mountainside courses, greens sprawled along the sea, or a combination of the above. Courses listed below are open to the public. Yardages are from the regular (white) tees.

Public courses. Hilo Municipal Golf Course, Hilo, 18 holes, 6,228 yards; Volcano Golf and Country Club, Hawaii Volcanoes National Park, 18 holes, 5,965 yards.

Resort/commercial courses. Country Club, Hilo, 9 holes, 2,995 yards; Sea Mountain Golf Course, Punaluu, 18 holes, 6,106 yards; Kona Country Club, Keauhou, Ocean Course, 18 holes, 6,400 yards, Mountain Course, 9 holes, 3,082 yards; Waikoloa Beach Golf Club, Waikoloa, 18 holes, 6,003 yards; Waikoloa Village Golf Course, Waikoloa, 18 holes, 6,142 yards; Francis H. I'i Brown Golf Course, Mauna Lani Resort, Lahuipuaa, 18 holes, 6,259 yards; Mauna Kea Beach Golf Course, Kawaihae, 18 holes, 6,737 yards; Hamakua Country Club, Honokaa, 9 holes, 2,520 yards.

Tennis. Courts, public and private, are scattered across the Big Island in obvious and not so obvious places. The following guide can help you locate them. Condominiums generally have courts for guest use.

Public courts. Hilo: Lincoln Park, 4 courts (with lights); Hoolulu Tennis Stadium, 8 indoor courts (with lights); Waiakea Village Tennis Club, 2 courts. Pahala: Ka'u High School, 2 courts. Naalehu: Naalehu Park, 1 court. Captain Cook: Greenwell Park, 1 court. Kailua-Kona: Old Airport Tennis Courts, 4 courts (with lights); Kailua Playground, 1 court (with lights). Kapaau: Kamehameha Park, 2 courts. Waimea: Waimea Park, 2 courts. Honokaa: Honokaa Playground, 2 courts. Papaaloa: Papaaloa Playground, 2 courts. Hakalau: Hakalau Playground, 2 courts.

Private courts. Hilo: Naniloa Racquet Club, 2 courts. Punaluu: Sea Mountain Tennis Center, 4 courts. Keauhou-Kona; Kona Surf Resort, 3 courts (with lights); Keauhou Surf and Racquet Club, 3 courts (guests only); Kailua-Kona: Kona Hilton, 4 courts (with lights); Hotel King Kamehameha, 4 courts (2 with lights). Waikoloa: Hyatt Regency Waikaloa, 8 courts; Royal Waikoloa, 6 courts; Waikoloa Village, 2 courts (with lights). Anaehoomalu: Mauna Lani Bay Hotel, 10 courts (guests only). Kawaihae: Westin Mauna Kea, 13 courts (guests only).

Swimming. As the youngest of Hawaii's chain of islands, the Big Island has had the least amount of time to develop stretches of white sand. This is not to say that there aren't beaches on Hawaii; there are many, and only here can you choose from black, green, white, or speckled beaches.

Ocean swimming. Onekahakaha Beach Park, Hilo; James Kealoha Beach Park, Hilo; Leleiwi Beach Park, Hilo; Harry K. Brown Beach Park, Kalapana; Punaluu Beach Park (black sand), Punaluu; Whittington Beach Park, northeast of Naalehu (mud-bottomed tide pools); Green Sand Beach, northeast of Ka Lae (need four-wheel drive); Milolii Beach Park, south of Milolii; Hookena Beach Park, south of Puuhonua O Honaunau (City of Refuge) National Historical Park; Napoopoo Beach Park, Napoopoo; White Sands Beach Park, north of Kahaluu; Kailua fishing pier, north side of pier, Kailua-Kona; Anaehoomalu, south of Hapuna; Hapuna Beach, Kawaihae (can be rough); Mauna Kea Beach, Westin Mauna Kea, Kawaihae; Samuel M. Spencer Beach Park, Kawaihae; Waipio Bay, Waipio Valley (black sand).

Freshwater swimming. Reeds Bay, Hilo (salt and freshwater inlets); Harry K. Brown Beach Park, south of Kalapana, has fresh and brackish ponds; streams in Waipio Valley and Waikaumalo and Kolekole parks have dipping spots.

Surfing. The Big Island has a few good surfing beaches, all tending to be rough for beginners. You can rent equipment at Orchidland Surfboard, Hilo.

Board surfing. Honolii, north of Hilo; Harry K. Brown Beach Park, Kalapana; Banyan's and Lyman's Cove, south of Kailua-Kona; Kaloko Point, north of Kailua-Kona.

Body surfing. Hookena Beach Park, south of Puuhonua O Honaunau (City of Refuge) National Historical Park; Hapuna Beach State Park, Kawaihae; Samuel M. Spencer Beach Park, south of Kohala.

Beachcombing, tidepooling, and reef walking. Wear proper foot gear, and remember to leave the reef or rocks as you found them.

Low-tide walking sites. Onekahakaha Beach Park, Hilo; Leleiwi Beach Park, Hilo; Harry K. Brown Beach Park, Kalapana; east coast of Ka Lae (South Point); Puuhonua O Honaunau (City of Refuge) National Historical Park; Kahaluu Beach Park, north of Keauhou.

Skin and scuba diving. Whether it's your first diving experience or one of many, you'll find a trip suited to your abilities. Reefs, lava tubes, caves, and marine preserves offer unusual underwater exploration.

Diving spots. Puuhonua O Honaunau (City of Refuge) National Historical Park; Napoopoo Beach Park and Kealakekua Beach Park, south of Captain Cook; Kahaluu Beach Park, south of Kailua-Kona; coves between Kawaihae and Puako in South Kohala; Samuel M. Spencer Beach Park, south of Kawaihae; Mahukona Beach Park, south of Mahukona.

Diving companies. Fair Wind Sail and Dive, Keauhou-Kona; Dive Makai Charters, Gold Coast Divers, Jack's Diving Locker, Kona Coast Divers, Scuba Schools of Kona, Sea Dreams Hawaii, Sea Paradise, Kailua-Kona; Captain Nemo's Ocean Sports, Kohala Divers Ltd., Kohala area; Mauna Loa Diving Service, Nautilus Dive Center, Hilo.

Boat cruises, charters, rentals.
What better way to experience Hawaii's waters than to skim across them in a trimaran or peer into their depths from a glass-bottom boat? Charter companies: Captain Zodiac, Fair Wind Sail and Dive, Keauhou-Kona; Captain Bean Cruises, Hawaiian Cruises, Kamanu Charters, Pacific Whale Foundation, Kailua-Kona; Captain Nemo's Ocean Sports, Kohala.

Fishing.
Hawaii is renowned for its spectacular sportfishing—the Kona Coast, in particular, has yielded world-record-size marlin, mahimahi, tuna, and wahoo minutes from Kailua's waterfront. There are no seasonal restrictions, no limits, and no license required for ocean fishing. Freshwater fishing, permitted in many of the island's reservoirs, has regulations and requires licensing.

Fishing locations. Surfcasting, spinfishing, and spearfishing. Rocky points, piers, and beaches along the Puna parks, South Point, and west and Hamakua coasts are good for surfcasting and spinfishing. Check local tackle shops for bait and advice about best locations, methods, and tackle. The catch is mostly crevalle, bonefish, and assorted small fish. Spearfishing is good wherever there are reefs, rocky shores, or bottoms of sand and rock. Freshwater fishing: mullet and *aholehole* are plentiful in Waiakea Pond and Wailoa River State Park, Hilo. Five Kohala reservoirs south of Hawi stock catfish, bluegills, and bass.

Charter boats. Make reservations through the following companies: Foxy Lady Sport Fishing, Kona Activities Center, Kona Charter Skippers Association, Kona Coast Activities, Pamela Big Game Fishing (all in Kailua-Kona); Westin Mauna Kea, Kawaihae.

Cycling.
You can get a slower-paced view of the island on a bicycle tour. You'll find bike rental stands throughout the island or listed in the yellow pages under "Bicycles." If you plan on more than a day's outing, bring your own 5 or 10-speed bicycle.

One cross-country trip heads north from Hilo along state highways 19 and 22 to Akaka Falls; the round trip is 32 miles/51 km. The last 4 miles/6½ km are a steep climb; you'll find drinking water at the top.

Another route heads north from Hilo on Highway 19 for about 50 miles/80 km along the beautiful coast to Honokaa and Waipio Valley. Along the way are places to stop for water and restroom facilities. For a traffic-free route that includes spectacular scenery, take sections of old, winding Mamalahoa Highway, which parallels the main route for the first 30 miles/48 km out of Hilo. On the west coast, a nice day trip out of Kailua-Kona is a 6 mile/10 km trek south along the Kona Coast on Alii Drive to Keauhou Bay.

Travel Camp in Hilo conducts one-day rides in Puna or Hawaii Volcanoes National Park with connecting motor transportation from Hilo.

Horseback riding.
Experience another aspect of the Big Island's scenery by traversing the countryside on horseback. Reservations are usually required.

Several of Hawaii's riding organizations are located in Waimea. At the stables of the Westin Mauna Kea, rides are available by the hour. Ironwood Outfitters leads rides across the Kahua Ranch in North Kohala. Waikoloa Countryside Stables offers rides by the hour, including sunset rides. Near Kailua-Kona, Waiono Meadows offers trail rides on Hualalai's slopes.

Hiking, camping, and mountain tours.
If the great outdoors is your playground, the Big Island has plenty to keep you busy. High mountains, volcanoes, beaches, and rain forests provide endless exploration possibilities.

Camping and hiking information. Hawaii Volcanoes National Park extends from sea level to the summit of Mauna Loa (13,677 feet). Cabins and campgrounds are located throughout the park. Trails, ranging in length from a ½-hour to 3 days, are ideal for different levels of hiking. For further information and reservations, write Superintendent, Hawaii Volcanoes National Park, HI 96718.

Waipio Valley's jeep shuttle operates daily, reaching the numerous trails across the valley floor that end at the black sand beach. You'll also see the historical "Z" trail used by ancient Hawaiians. Permits are required for camping. Kalopa State Park's cabins and campgrounds are located on the upslope of Mauna Kea. In the saddle between Mauna Kea and Mauna Loa you'll find fully equipped cabins. Hapuna Beach State Park offers A-frame camping shelters; a number of county parks also have camping facilities.

Reservations for campsites and cabins should be made well in advance. For information on state parks, contact the Department of Land and Natural Resources Division of State Parks, Hilo; for information on county parks, contact the Department of Parks and Recreation, Hilo.

Skiing.
It's hard to imagine skiing right in the middle of the tropics, but you can on Hawaii's Mauna Kea peak. Runs are almost 1 mile/1½ km long and range in difficulty from beginner to expert. There are no lifts, no warming houses, no restaurants, or accommodations. A four-wheel-drive vehicle transports skiers to the top. For more information, contact Ski Guides Hawaii, Waimea.

INDEX

Challenging play and spectacular view at Princeville

Surfer at sunset

Sunset
Proof-of-Purchase
ISBN 0-376-06309-2

Photographers

Ken Bates: 14 all, 30, 103, 105 bottom. **Glenn Christiansen:** 10 bottom left, 13 top right, 37, 43 all, 79, 81. **David E. Clark:** 20. **Ed Cooper:** 36, 71, 154, 167 top. **Chris Fesler:** 8 left, 98 top. **David Franzen:** 10 top right, 12 center left and top right. **Mark Gibson:** 44, 50 left, 58 right, 151, 159 bottom. **Jeff Gnass:** 2, 38, 46 top, 95, 118, 123, 126 top, 159 top. **Hawaii Tourist News:** 27. **Vern Hawkins:** 89. **Cliff Hollenbeck:** 9 top right, 10 bottom right, 11, 15 top right, 19, 22, 28, 46 bottom, 55 bottom, 63 bottom, 87 bottom, 98 bottom, 162 top. **Saxon Holt:** 162 bottom. **Hyatt Regency:** 15 bottom right. **Greg Kaufman:** 106. **Rene Klein:** 111 bottom. **Dorothy Krell:** 105 top, 126 bottom. **Greg Lawson:** 1, 58 left, 96, 131. **Ells Marugg:** 12 bottom right. **David Muench:** 6 right, 146 bottom. **Suzanne Murphy:** 35 left, 104, 111 top. **Don Normark:** 16, 170. **Norman Plate:** 6 left, 7 bottom right, 87 top, 90, 134 top. **Radlauer Productions, Inc.:** 115. **Karen Rantzman:** 134 bottom. **Richard Rowan:** 15 top left, 35 right, 175 all. **William Rubenstein:** 97, 167 bottom. **Ron Sanford:** 8 right. **Elliott Varner Smith:** 9 bottom right. **South Sea Helicopter:** 82. **Ted Streshinsky:** 13 top left and bottom, 45, 74, 88. **Tim Thompson:** 21, 29, 50 right. **Tom Tracy:** 12 top left, 63 top, 146 top. **Darrow Watt:** 12 bottom left. **R. Wenkam:** 3, 7 top right, 55 top, 112, 139, 142. **Walton Wimberly:** 67 all.